Russia's fraught relationship with Ukraine is an essential element of Europe's evolving landscape. Taras Kuzio and Paul D'Anieri offer a refreshing look at the sources of Russian conduct toward Ukraine. They challenge conventional analyses by exploring deeper roots of Russian-Ukrainian conflict and placing Russian tactics against Ukraine in a broader historical context. Their study is a must-read for anyone who wants to understand the future of Russia's relations with Ukraine.

– Daniel S. Hamilton, Austrian Marshall Plan Foundation Professor, School of Advanced International Studies, Johns Hopkins University.

Taras Kuzio and Paul D'Anieri provide an invaluable guide of the complexities of current developments in and Russia's military aggression against Ukraine. The book draws on comprehensive field research, demonstrates deep knowledge and understanding of Ukrainian-Russian relations, and presents an alternative to much of the Western writing on the crisis. The book will be an invaluable source for journalists, policymakers and teaching in academia.

– Andriy Meleshevych, President, National University Kyiv Mohyla Academy.

Two of the West's preeminent Ukraine scholars have written an indispensable book that clearly, concisely and persuasively demonstrates that Vladimir Putin's war against Ukraine is not a response to Western behaviour but the product of longstanding tendencies within Russian policy. Taras Kuzio and Paul D'Anieri' book is a much welcome antidote to the superficiality and ignorance that characterise so much of Western writing on Russia and Ukraine.

– Alexander Motyl, Professor of Political Science, Rutgers University.

The Sources of Russia's Great Power Politics

Ukraine and the Challenge to the European Order

TARAS KUZIO AND PAUL D'ANIERI

E-INTERNATIONAL RELATIONS PUBLISHING

E-International Relations
www.E-IR.info
Bristol, England
2018

ISBN 978-1-910814-39-0 (paperback)
ISBN 978-1-910814-40-6 (e-book)

Production: Michael Tang
Cover Image: Maksymenko Nataliia

A catalogue record for this book is available from the British Library.

E-IR Open Access

Series Editor: Stephen McGlinchey
Copy-editors: Agnieszka Pikulicka-Wilczewska & Cameran Clayton
Editorial Assistants: Gaia Rizzi, Farah H. Saleem, Patricia Salas Sanchez & Shaghayegh Rostampour Vajari

E-IR Open Access is a series of scholarly books presented in a format that preferences brevity and accessibility while retaining academic conventions. Each book is available in print and digital versions, and is published under a Creative Commons license. As E-International Relations is committed to open access in the fullest sense, free electronic versions of all of our books, including this one, are available on the E-International Relations website.

Find out more at: http://www.e-ir.info/publications

About E-International Relations

E-International Relations is the world's leading open access website for students and scholars of international politics, reaching over three million readers per year. E-IR's daily publications feature expert articles, blogs, reviews and interviews – as well as student learning resources. The website is run by a non-profit organisation based in Bristol, England and staffed by an all-volunteer team of students and scholars.

http://www.e-ir.info

Abstract

The 2014 Russia–Ukraine conflict has transformed relations between Russia and the West into what many are calling a new cold war. The West has slowly come to understand that Russia's annexations and interventions, interference in elections, cyber warfare, disinformation, assassinations in Europe and support for anti-EU populists emerge from Vladimir Putin's belief that Russia is at war with the West.

This book shows that the crisis has deep roots in Russia's inability to come to terms with an independent Ukrainian state, Moscow's view of the Orange and Euromaidan revolutions as Western conspiracies and, finally, its inability to understand that most Russian-speaking Ukrainians do not want to rejoin Russia. In Moscow's eyes, Ukraine is central to rebuilding a sphere of influence within the former Soviet space and to re-establishing Russia as a great power. The book shows that the wide range of 'hybrid' tactics that Russia has deployed show continuity with the actions of the Soviet-era security services.

About the Authors

Taras Kuzio is a Non-Resident Fellow at the Centre for Transatlantic Relations at Johns Hopkins School of Advanced International Study and Professor, Department of Political Science, National University Kyiv Mohyla Academy. He is the author and editor of 21 books and think tank monographs, including *Putin's War Against Ukraine. Revolution, Nationalism, and Crime* (2017), *Ukraine. Democratization, Corruption and the New Russian Imperialism* (2015), *The Crimea. Europe's Next Flashpoint?* (2010) and *Ukraine-Crimea-Russia: Triangle of Conflict* (2007).

Paul D'Anieri is Professor of Political Science and Public Policy at the University of California, Riverside. In the fall of 2017, he was Eugene and Daymel Shklar Research Fellow in Ukrainian Studies at Harvard University. He is the author and editor of numerous books and articles on Ukrainian politics and Ukraine's relations with Russia and the West, including *Economic Interdependence in Ukrainian–Russian Relations* (1999) and *Understanding Ukrainian Politics* (2006).

Acknowledgements

Taras Kuzio acknowledges the generous financial support over four years provided by the Ukrainian Studies Fund (USF) of the US and the enthusiastic encouragement of Bohdan Vitvitsky and Roman Procyk. USF funding enabled 15 research visits to cities, villages and military frontlines in Eastern and Southern Ukraine and the ATO (Anti-Terrorist Operation) conflict zone which became the basis for the publication of this book and the earlier published *Putin's War Against Ukraine*.

Paul D'Anieri acknowledges the generous support of the Harvard Ukrainian Research Institute, where he spent the fall semester of 2017 as the Eugene and Daymel Shklar Research Fellow in Ukrainian Studies. The Institute provided exceptional academic resources and a congenial atmosphere for work on this project and on a more in-depth study of Ukraine's relations with Russia since 1991. He is also grateful to the University of California, Riverside for research leave and generous research support.

Contents

List of Abbreviations

ATO   Anti-Terrorist Operation
CIS   Commonwealth of Independent States
DCFTA   Deep and Comprehensive Free Trade Agreement
DNR   Donetsk People's Republic
FARA   Foreign Agents Registration Act
FSB   Federal Security Service of the Russian Federation
GRU   Main Intelligence Directorate (Soviet & Russian military intelligence)
IMF   International Monetary Fund
KGB   Committee for State Security of the Soviet Union
LNR   Luhansk People's Republic
MAP   Membership Action Plan
NKVD   People's Commissariat of Internal Affairs (Soviet secret police)
OSCE   Organisation for Security and Cooperation in Europe
SBU   Security Service of Ukraine
RSFSR   Russian Soviet Federative Socialist Republic
SVR   Foreign Intelligence Service of the Russian Federation

Preface

Russia's seizure of Crimea and prosecution of hybrid war in Eastern Ukraine prompted scholars, analysts, and policy-makers around the world to ask why it happened, what it means for international security in the region and beyond, and how the conflict might be ended or at least managed. Those three questions are inevitably linked.

We have written this book to fill what we see as important gaps in the literature, beginning with the question of why the war happened. We contend that the roots of the crisis go back further than is widely understood and therefore we see the cause of the conflict in long-term factors underlying Russia's policy toward Ukraine. We trace Russia's goals and tactics from the beginning of the post-Soviet era in 1991, and in some cases to the Soviet era. Rather than focusing on historical breaks, we stress the continuity between the Soviet era, the early post-Soviet era, and the crisis since early 2014. The key break was that Russia, in pursuing goals that it held since 1991, chose to use military force in 2014.

Therefore, we contend that Russia's actions in 2014 were not a response to specific events, such as NATO enlargement, EU policy, democracy promotion or revolution in Ukraine because the main drivers of Russian policy were visible *prior* to those events. The events of 2013–2014 in Ukraine certainly spurred resentment, and may have created a sense that a window of opportunity was closing, but they created neither Russia's desire to regain Ukrainian territory nor the tactics that would be used in doing so.

Analysts have sought to define and characterise Russia's tactics as a new kind of 'hybrid warfare'. Except for using the most recent technology, we argue, there is not much new about Russian hybrid warfare. Rather, it shows considerable continuity with both the goals and tactics that the Soviet intelligence services used during the Cold War and that Russia deployed in military interventions from 1991 onwards in Moldova and Georgia. Our focus is not on Putin's personal history in the Committee for State Security (KGB) and its successors, but on the endurance of norms, practices, and institutions from the Soviet to the post-Soviet era to the present.

If the conflict has somewhat different roots than many identify, what are the implications for resolving it? Our conclusions are unfortunately pessimistic. The crisis has exposed a fundamental disagreement over what a European order should look like. The European Union (EU) remains wedded to principles that both stress the sovereign equality of large and small states and reject the use of force. Russia seeks recognition of a Russian 'sphere of influence' beyond its borders and stresses that Russia as a great power is entitled to a veto over what happens in the region.

Whether or not the West should accept Russia's claim has been a main topic of discussion, and here again we believe some important perspectives have been missing. Most importantly, *realism* has been influentially invoked to explain how the war started (the West did not respect Russia's sphere of influence) and to suggest how the conflict might be stabilised (accept a Russian sphere in Ukraine and perhaps elsewhere).

Our critique focuses not on the broad question of when *realpolitik* should and should not trump principle, but on how realism applies to this conflict. Put simply, it is not at all clear that realism would find the causes of the conflict in Western action nor would it find the solution in acquiescing to a Russian sphere of influence in Ukraine. It might just as easily claim the opposite. Some of the most prominent applications of realism to the Ukraine-Russia crisis contradict basic tenets of realist theory. We show that realist theory fits equally well, if not better, with a policy of opposing the expansion of Russian influence. Applying realism to reach specific conclusions about this case relies crucially on additional assumptions, most importantly concerning Russia's aims.

The book proceeds as follows. Chapter one reviews existing literature on the conflict, identifying different schools of thought on why Russia annexed the Crimea and launched military aggression against Ukraine in 2014. We argue that realism has been applied to the case in a way that does not seem realist at all. We also identify the major gaps that we address in the following chapters, particularly the need to look more deeply into the early post-Soviet era and at the role of Ukraine in Russian national identity.

Chapter two traces the evolution of hybrid war from Soviet to post-Soviet Russia. While cyber warfare is based on fundamentally new technology, the tactics of *dezinformatsiya* (disinformation) and *maskirovka* (military deception) have a long history. We point out the similarity in rhetoric used by the Soviet Union and Russia against the goals and policies of the Ukrainian national movement.

Chapter three addresses Ukraine's relations with Russia from 1991 to 2013, highlighting that Russia sought to control Ukraine from the very beginning, that it sought greater control over Crimea in particular, and that these goals were rooted in claims about the very essence of Russian national identity.

Chapter four examines the conflict in Crimea and Donbas, beginning with the

Orange Revolution in 2004. The chapter shows both the medium-term build up to the conflict and the application of specific Russian tactics in 2014.

Chapter five surveys the international repercussions of the crisis and international efforts to resolve it. Like many others, we are pessimistic because we see little common ground between Russia, Ukraine and the West over either principles or territory. Russia's position seems to require that the West acquiesce to a territorial division that establishes a Russian 'sphere of influence'. In the EU, sensitivities about a 'new Yalta' will make that very hard to accept.

A brief conclusion then poses several questions that remain unanswered. Even if the West is willing to accept a territorial concession to Russia, can we assume that Russia will be satisfied and that security would be assured? If the roots of Russian aggression in Ukraine are deep, as we believe, then is it likely that the passing of President Vladimir Putin or a new resurgence of democracy in Russia would change Russian policy? Perhaps not, especially towards Crimea.

Having written this book in the belief that important questions have been overlooked and important perspectives neglected, we make no claim to have addressed all of them. We do hope to have raised issues that will stimulate productive discussion. If this new cold war is anything like the original one, the debates will continue for some time.

1

Causes and Consequences: Assessing the Debate

The crisis in relations between Russia and the West following Russia's annexation of the Crimea and military intervention in Eastern Ukraine has led to a large number of publications written by scholars and commentators from a wide variety of perspectives and specialities, including Russian and Eurasian area studies, international relations and security studies. As one of the most important crises of recent decades, the conflict has attracted the attention of many scholars, regardless of whether they have worked extensively on Ukraine or Ukrainian-Russian relations. Newcomers to this conflict are forced to take at face value some facile characterisations of the situation, rather than recognising the complexity and contestation of many of the key drivers of the conflict.

We identify two gaps in the literature, both of which stem from viewing Russia's actions as a response to recent events. First, few analyses dig into the history of the relationship. As a result, phenomena with deep histories are sometimes seen as recent events. Second, and related, the issue of national identity is often treated superficially leading to an underweighting of national identity concerns as a factor underpinning Russia's actions.

A tradition has persisted from the Soviet era whereby scholars specialising in Russian politics claim expertise on the non-Russian countries which emerged as independent states after 1991. For these reasons, many of the works on the crisis use few primary sources from Ukraine (whether in Ukrainian or Russian) and few show evidence of extensive fieldwork in Ukraine. Ukrainian scholarship on Russian hybrid warfare, such as by the country's leading strategist Volodymyr Horbulin, has been ignored by Western scholars.[1] A

---

[1] Volodymyr Horbulin, ed., *Svitova Hibrydna Viyna: Ukrayinskyy Front* (Kharkiv: Folio, 2017). See also 'Russia's "Hybrid" War – Challenge and Threat for Europe', special issue of the Razumkov Ukrainian Centre for Economic and Political Studies Magazine

dearth of Ukrainian sources and fieldwork in Ukraine naturally leads these works to rely heavily on secondary sources and quotes from official Russian sources. While understandable when the Soviet government restricted travel beyond Moscow to sensitive republics, and when information about the non-Russian republics was difficult to access, there is less reason today to approach countries such as Ukraine via Russia and the Russian media. Not only is travel to Ukraine and other states easy, but Ukrainian sources are widely available via the Internet in both Ukrainian and Russian.[2] The web sites of the Ukrainian government, president and parliament are in both Ukrainian and Russian.

Scholars writing about this conflict face a choice in perspectives that is likely to lead them to being criticised no matter what they do. Those who blame the conflict on Russia's aggression face the accusation that they ignore the actions of the US, NATO, the EU and Ukrainian nationalists, all of which supposedly left Russia little freedom of action to do anything other than intervene militarily. Those who blame the conflict on the West and Ukraine can be accused of defending an attack on a weaker neighbour that clearly violates international law and to many resembles Germany's aggression towards its neighbours in the 1930s. Those who try to take a more 'balanced' perspective risk being seen as naïve or as apologists by both of the previous groups.

While these perspectives compete fundamentally, they tend to share two underlying characteristics. First, they are largely focused on assigning blame, regardless of where they locate it. Second, many, though not all, in their efforts to make their cases, provide clear and simple explanations of the conflict. This leads them to choose and assemble facts and interpretations to support their argument rather than exploring the many areas in which causes are intertwined, interpretations are contested, and 'facts' are interpreted completely differently depending on one's pre-existing perspective.

A good example is the question of the rightful ownership of the Crimean Peninsula. Prior to the crisis, few scholars of international politics paid much attention to it. Those who blame the West for the crisis (both from leftist and realist perspectives) see Russia's annexation of the Crimea as returning the

---

National Security and Defence, nos. 9/10, 2016.

[2]   Ukraine publishes many Russian-language newspapers and Internet web sites while Ukraine's most popular television channel, Inter, broadcasts largely in Russian. Relatively few scholars in the West have a command of Ukrainian, increasing the likelihood of relying on Russian sources. *Zerkalo Nedeli* and *Ukrainska Pravda*, for example, are published in both Russian and Ukrainian. Three of Ukraine's five weekly political magazines are in Russian.

territory to its 'natural' home. This rests on focusing on certain facts – Russian control of the territory from the 1780s to 1954, the notion that the 1954 transfer was a 'gift' or even a whim and the predominance of the Russian language in the peninsula. The viewpoint of the Crimea being more 'Russian' than Ukrainian remains widespread, particularly among Western scholars of Russia and it is commonplace among critics of US foreign policy and realists. Neil Kent's otherwise informative and balanced history of the Crimea writes that the referendum 'was joyfully received by most Crimeans'. He continues: 'There is no doubt that the majority of the population of Crimea supported joining the Russian Federation'.[3] Both assertions are very dubious.

Those who blame the conflict on Russia focus on a different set of facts. The territory was legally part of Ukraine, and thus its seizure violated international law, and to judge Russia's seizure legal on historical or linguistic grounds would set a disruptive precedent. When Crimeans had a chance to vote on their future in a well-prepared referendum, as they did in the 1991 referendum on Ukrainian independence, 54% voted for Ukraine's secession from the Soviet Union. In the 1994 Budapest Memorandum and again in the 1997 Treaty of Friendship, Russia pledged to respect Ukraine's territorial integrity. As Paul R. Magocsi and Andrew Wilson both point out, if length of time within a state is the criterion we use to decide to whom Crimea should belong, then it should be returned to the Tatars who ruled the peninsula from the 13th to the late-18th century.[4] Wilson calculates that the Crimea, although annexed by Russia in 1783, 'was only ever truly Russian from the Crimean War of 1853–56 until 1917' and again from 1945–54; that is, it was under Russian rule for seventy-three years (Crimea was a Soviet republic from 1921 to 1945). The peninsula was Ukrainian for a slightly shorter period of 60 years, but under Tatar rule for four hundred.[5]

Similarly, those who studied Ukraine between 1991 and 2014 find that support for separatism was never backed by a majority of the population in the Crimea or the Donbas. Public backing for secession was a real factor, but in the two decades preceding the crisis, combined support for an independent Crimea and union of the Crimea with Russia varied between 20–40%. The March 2014 referendum claimed an unlikely 'Yes' vote of 97% when Tatars, who make up approximately 15% of the population, boycotted it. A report mistakenly leaked by the Russian Presidential Council on Civil Society and Human Rights showed the real turnout was only 30% (not 83%) and of these

---

[3]   Neil Kent, *Crimea: A History* (London: Hurst, 2016), pp.157 and 160.
[4]   Paul R. Magocsi, *This Blessed Land: Crimea and the Crimean Tatars* (Toronto: University of Toronto Press 2014) and Andrew Wilson, *Ukraine Crisis. What it Means for the West* (New Haven, CT: Yale University Press, 2014).
[5]   A. Wilson, *Ukraine Crisis*, p.100.

only half (i.e. 15%) voted in support of union with Russia.[6]

One can debate at length which of these factors ought to weigh more heavily in assessing who 'should' control Crimea, which has a huge impact on how to allot blame for the larger crisis. Unfortunately, rather than doing so, most analyses choose the version that supports the allotment of blame that has already been predetermined.

Work on the Ukraine-Russia conflict can be divided into five groups. The first emphasises Western expansion as the cause of the conflict, portraying Russia as a passive victim compelled to respond. This includes both those arguing primarily from a leftist position against American influence in the world and those invoking realism to indict Western policy. Works from this perspective tend to stress the nationalist elements in Ukrainian politics and the extremist elements within Ukrainian nationalism.[7]The second and third schools are complementary in that they both see Russia as the driver of the conflict, but they diverge on the drivers of Russian policy. The second school focuses on Russian geopolitical expansion – its desire to undo at least some of the results of 1991. Rather than criticising the West for doing too much, some in this school criticise it for not doing more sooner to help integrate Ukraine in the West.[8] A third school sees the roots of Russian behaviour as driven by the internal needs of the autocratic model built by Putin and the Soviet origins of the *siloviki* (security forces).[9] A fourth perspective, relying largely on geopolitical concepts, sees both sides as being partly to blame.[10] A

[6]   https://www.forbes.com/sites/paulroderickgregory/2014/05/05/putins-human-rights-council-accidentally-posts-real-crimean-election-results-only-15-voted-for-annexation/#5060f511f172

[7]   A leftist perspective can be found in R. Sakwa's *Frontline Ukraine* (London: I.B. Tauris, 2016), and Chris Kaspar De Ploeg, *Ukraine in the Crossfire* (Atlanta, GA: Clarity 2017). A realist perspective is given by John J. Mearsheimer, 'Why the Ukraine crisis is the West's fault: the liberal delusions that provoked Putin', *Foreign Affairs*, vol.93, no.5 (September/October 2014), pp.77-89 and Rajan Menon and Eugene Rumer, *Conflict in Ukraine. The Unwinding of the Post-Cold War Order* (Cambridge, MA: MIT Press, 2015). https://www.foreignaffairs.com/articles/russia-fsu/2014-08-18/why-ukraine-crisis-west-s-fault

[8]   Examples of criticism of Russia's threat to the European security system include Derek Averre, 'The Ukraine Conflict: Russia's Challenge to European Security Governance', *Europe-Asia Studies*, vol. 68, no. 4 (June 2016), pp.699–725 and Elias Götz, 'It's Geopolitics, stupid: explaining Russia's Ukraine policy', *Global Affairs*, vol.1, no.1 (2015), pp.3-10.

[9]   A good example is Mette Skak, 'Russian strategic culture: the role of today's chekisty', *Contemporary Politics*, vol.22, no.3 (July 2016), pp.324–341.

[10]   G. Toal, *Near Abroad* (New York: Oxford University Press, 2017) and Samuel Charap and Timothy J. Colton, *Everyone Loses. The Ukraine Crisis and the Ruinous Contest for Post-Soviet Eurasia* (London: International Institute for Strategic Studies,

final approach sees the conflict as an effort by the Russ-ian government to reassert a particular notion of Russian national identity which sees Russia not as a nation-state but as a 'civilisation', that extends beyond the boundaries of the Russian Federation and is incompatible with an independent Ukraine.[11] This perspective fits with others that blame Russia, but we save it for last because it is relatively underdeveloped and we seek to give it extra attention.

We stress that while in theory these causal factors are distinct, in practice they tend to be combined. Russian leaders, for example, could be motivated by both the geopolitical and domestic payoffs of seizing Crimea. Because almost all of the literature seeks to apportion blame, there is a strong tend-ency to combine different analytical arguments that support the conclusion. This leads to some analytical muddle. For example, the legality of the annexation of Crimea, the role of local Ukrainian versus Russian forces in the Donbas secessionist movements, and the wisdom of NATO enlargement are three entirely distinct questions, and yet there is a strong tendency to join them together. Those who downplay the international legal aspect of the annexation of the Crimea also tend to argue that the Donbas conflict was essentially domestic (and is thus a 'civil war' rather than an 'invasion') and that NATO enlargement was at best foolish and at worst aggressive. The opposite views tend also to cluster. These positions correlate well with views on Western sanctions against Russia.

'The Ukraine Crisis is the West's Fault'

The first group of work portrays Russia as a victim, forced to react to NATO and EU enlargement and democracy promotion into what President Dmitri Medvedev described as Russia's 'privileged zone of interest'. This perspective is advanced by two different groups of scholars from opposing ends of the political spectrum: left-wing critics of US foreign policy and realists. Similarly, the work of Richard Sakwa, Stephen Cohen, Jonathan Steele and John Mearsheimer among others, focuses on NATO, the US and Ukrainian nationalists in explaining the outbreak of conflict.

These works share a basic argument: Russia is a great power, and because of its power and history is entitled to respect and to rights that other states (such as Ukraine) are not. By enlarging NATO into countries that Russia (as the Soviet Union) once controlled, the West (driven by the US) was a threat to Russian national security. Different scholars focus on different policies and events, but the list of misdeeds by the US/NATO/EU includes multiple rounds

---

2017).

[11] Taras Kuzio, *Putin's War Against Ukraine. Revolution, Nationalism, and Crime* (Toronto: Chair of Ukrainian Studies, University of Toronto, 2017).

of NATO enlargement, the discussion of a Membership Action Plan (MAP) for Ukraine (which was not granted) at NATO's 2008 Bucharest Summit, the abrogation by the US of the ABM treaty, the support for colour revolutions in Ukraine, Georgia and elsewhere, the EU's plans for an Association Agreement with Ukraine, and finally support for the Euromaidan protests that ousted Viktor Yanukovych as Ukrainian President. They claim that Yanukovych's ouster was illegitimate, and that the presence of radical nationalists among those on the Maidan created an immediate threat to ethnic Russians or Russian speakers in Ukraine justified Russian intervention. The strength of these perspectives is that they capture many of the same points made by Putin and other defenders of Russia's policies. The primary difference between the 'leftist' and 'realist' versions is that the realist claims to invoke the timeless lessons of realist theory, and to identify Western missteps in those countries' theoretically-misguided adoption of liberal international relations theories. In contrast, the leftists tend to see the root of the problem in US imperialism (as the Cold War-era revisionists blamed the Cold War on US expansionism).

These approaches rely on a selective approach to history, paying little attention to events between Ukraine and Russia during much of the post-Soviet period and particularly during Yanukovych's presidency from 2010 (which is connected to the question of whether his ouster was justified). Issues such as nationalism and regionalism in Ukraine tend to be dealt with superficially. Realists in particular prioritise the immediate external environment and therefore largely ignore domestic factors in Russia and Ukraine. They emphasise the regional fragmentation of Ukraine and view the conflict as a 'civil war' between Ukrainian and Russian speakers, and they criticise the provocative policies of 'Ukrainian nationalists'. Ukrainian citizens have a different view of the crisis, with only 16% of Ukrainians seeing it as a 'civil war' while 72% view it as 'an aggressive war by Russia against Ukraine'.[12]

These perspectives are as notable for what they do not discuss as for what they do. While it is understandable why realist scholars downplay the importance of Ukraine's sovereignty or international law, it is less clear why those claiming to criticise the dominance of the US do so. These approaches resemble Hegelian notions of 'historic' and 'non-historic' peoples (with Ukrainians being in the latter group), but in the literature, the leftists neither defend this position theoretically nor elaborate its implications (who else is deemed non-historic? when are such non-historic nations 'fair game' and when are they not?). In other words, it is one thing to say that the US and NATO were unwise in enlarging eastward, and to believe that this threatened Russia, it is

12   Razumkov Ukrainian Centre for Economic and Political Studies survey, 3 April 2015. http://old.razumkov.org.ua/ukr/poll.php?poll_id=1026

another thing to say that this caused or justified Russia militarily invading a third country, Ukraine. This needs further theoretical elaboration.

Advocates of these two positions have also interpreted data concerning Russian involvement in Eastern Ukraine selectively. This has become more problematic as an increasing volume of evidence from satellites, NATO, Organisation for Security and Cooperation in Europe (OSCE) observers, Western journalists, think tanks (such as Bellingcat), Ukrainian military intelligence and captured Russian soldiers that have all documented Russia's military involvement. Ukrainian military intelligence estimates there are up to 6,000 Russian forces in the Donetsk People's Republic (DNR) and Luhansk People's Republic (LNR) with an additional 35,000–40,000 proxy forces.[13] In June 2017, Russian Foreign Minister Sergei Lavrov undermined the denial that Russian forces are in Eastern Ukraine when he talked of 'our decision to join the fight in Donbas and in Syria'.[14]

Critics of Western policy draw selectively on conspiracy theories that implicate Ukrainian nationalists or the West. De Ploeg cites on thirty occasions Ivan Katchanovski's claims that 'Ukrainian nationalists' were responsible for the sniper killings on the Euromaidan[15]; Katchanovski in turn draws on a highly selective use of sources gleaned from all corners of the Internet and YouTube, to the exclusion of other accounts.[16] There is little dispute among the broad mainstream of scholars, experts and policymakers, based on extensive evidence including eyewitness accounts, court convictions and video footage, that Yanukovych's vigilantes and *Berkut* riot police shot and killed the protestors.[17] In November 2017, on the anniversary of the

---

[13] http://www.pravda.com.ua/news/2017/09/9/7154531/
[14] https://www.unian.info/politics/2006424-lavrov-on-donbas-war-i-heard-criticism-of-our-decision-to-join-the-fight.html
[15] C. K. De Ploeg, *Ukraine in the Crossfire* also frequently cites Sakwa who endorses the book on the cover.
[16] Katchanowski's conspiracy theory of a false flag operation on the Euromaidan where protestors were allegedly murdered by Ukrainian nationalists is cited by many leftist authors on the war. See R. Sakwa, *Frontline Ukraine*, pp.90–93. This explanation is also popular with the Russian government.
[17] For primary sources see '20 Fevralya: Kto dal komandu strelyat po Maidanu?' in Sonya Koshkina, *Maidan. Nerasskazannaya istoriya* (Kyiv: Bright Star Publishing, pp.272–287 and 'Chastyna Tretya: 18 Lyutoho - 20 Lyutoho' in Leonid Finberg and Ulyana Holovach eds., *Maydan. Svidchennya. Kyiv, 2013–2014 roku* (Kyiv: Dukh i Litera, 2016), pp.505–761. On the 'Heavenly Hundred' murdered protestors see O. Trybushna and I. Solomko eds., *Nebesna Sotnya* (Kyiv: Folio, 2014). An extensive bibliography of Western academic studies of the Euromaidan can be found in T. Kuzio, *Putin's War Against Ukraine*, pp.363–367. For secondary sources see Alison Smale, 'Tending Their Wounds, Vowing to Fight On', *New York Times*, 6 April 2014, Andrew Higgins and Andrew E. Kramer, 'Defeated Even Before He Was Ousted', *The New York*

Euromaidan which is officially celebrated as the 'Day of Dignity and Freedom' on 21 November of each year, Russia's information warfare shifted gear and blamed 'Georgian snipers' for the killings.[18] Given Russia's well-documented disinformation efforts (see chapter two), more scepticism might be due.

A similar conspiracy theory blames 'Ukrainian nationalists' for the deaths of 42 pro-Russian protestors in Odesa on 2 May 2014. The Russian Ministry of Foreign Affairs produced a report exaggerating the number of deaths into the hundreds and describing it as a 'massacre' committed by 'Ukrainian nationalists'.[19] What happened that day has been pieced together by local journalists in a blow-by-blow account of the day's tragic events. In Odesa, the first deaths on that day were shootings of pro-Ukrainian protestors and Molotov cocktails were thrown by *both* sides which set fire to the building leading to a total of 48 dying – six from gunshot wounds, 34 from smoke inhalation and burns, and eight from jumping to their deaths.[20]

The 'realist' analysis of the Ukraine-Russia conflict is difficult to assess because many of the ways in which realism has been applied to this conflict by Mearsheimer and others contradicts fundamental tenets of realist theory. Put differently, in many respects the realist analysis of the Ukraine conflict is not realist at all.[21] Thus, Mearsheimer's current views have evolved from the 1990s when he supported Ukraine keeping the nuclear weapons it inherited from the USSR[22], a step which was seen at the time as being highly provocative towards Russia.

Realists focus upon the West's great power relations with Russia[23], and in this view, Ukraine is a side show; indeed, Rajan Menon and Eugene Rumer's conclusions do not once mention Ukraine. The gist of their argument is that the West's movement towards Russia constituted a threat to which Russia

---

Times, 4 January 2015 and Tom Parfitt, 'Families of victims in Ukraine massacre slate investigation into deaths', *The Daily Telegraph*, 19 February 2015.
[18] For an analysis of this new disinformation see the EU's *Disinformation Review*, 30 November 2017 at http://mailchi.mp/euvsdisinfo/dr89-880153?e=16eb39ac8e
[19] R. Sakwa, *Frontline Ukraine*, pp.97–99.
[20] A chronology of the day's events and violence on 2 May 2014 in Odesa can be found in T. Kuzio, *Putin's War Against Ukraine*, p.334.
[21] For another critique of the application of realism to Ukraine, see Dirk Bennett, 'The Realist Case for Arming Ukraine', *The American Interest*, 20 February 2015. https://www.the-american-interest.com/2015/02/20/the-realist-case-for-arming-ukraine/
[22] J. J. Mearsheimer, 'The Case for a Ukrainian Nuclear Deterrent', *Foreign Affairs*, vol.72, no.3 (Summer 1993), pp.50–66. https://www.foreignaffairs.com/articles/ukraine/1993-06-01/case-ukrainian-nuclear-deterrent
[23] J. J. Mearsheimer, 'Why the Ukraine crisis is the West's fault' and R. Menon and E. Rumer, *Conflict in Ukraine*.

was compelled to respond. However, it is not clear the enlargement of NATO and Western policy toward Ukraine actually go against the dictums of realism. Realism finds that states live in an insecure world, and counsels that the smart ones will always try to increase their power. If that is the case, then realism would likely have advised the US and its allies to expand their alliance while they had the possibility to do so. Indeed, the fact that Russia has now sought to move west would likely be seen by realists as further justifying NATO enlargement: it is better for the alliance to be facing Russia in Ukraine rather than in Poland or Germany.

Similarly, it is a contradiction of realism to argue that US policies and NATO enlargement somehow made Russia more aggressive, because in realist theory, states are *always* seeking to expand their power. Thus, realists would expect Russia to take advantage of the opportunities open to it regardless of whether Russian leaders were angry or felt betrayed by the West. Realism holds that interests, not emotions, drive state behaviour. Again, realism just as likely leads to the opposite conclusion: if Russia invaded Ukraine it was not because the West moved too far east, but because it did not move far enough east to prevent Russian territorial expansion. Criticising states for being strong rather than weak cuts against the entire tradition of realist scholarship.

Oddly, the arguments made by self-described realists regarding Ukraine not only contradict realist theory, but they also adopt the position of liberalism, which realists have scorned for generations. A key concept in realism (and liberalism) is the 'security dilemma', the idea that when a state takes steps to make itself more secure, it undermines the security of its neighbour, thus spurring a reaction. Realists regard this as an immutable characteristic of the system, one that is foolhardy to try to overcome. States that refrain from pursuing power are likely to find themselves endangered. Liberalism, anticipating an escalating cycle of response, counsels that both sides can be better off through restraint. Realism sees that restraint as naïve, because states will always seek advantage and can renege or cheat on any deal (as Russia did concerning the Budapest Memorandum and the 1997 Friendship Treaty with Ukraine). Liberals, not realists, advocate that states try to mitigate the security dilemma by either unilaterally or via a formal agreement limiting efforts to increase their power relative to their potential adversaries. Thus, in saying that NATO should have refrained from enlargement, and assuming that this could be counted on to prevent Russia from itself trying to expand, Mearsheimer is adopting a liberal, not a realist, position.

Those invoking realism are applying it more consistently when they criticise the West for adopting policies recommended by liberalism; namely, relying on the spread of democracy and on international institutions to maintain security. Hopes by Western policymakers that the problem of security would be solved in Central Europe have not held up. Again, however, it is not clear that realism would counsel a carve-up of Eastern Europe on Russia's terms rather than an effort to strengthen resistance to potential Russian expansion.

The argument made by Mearsheimer and others retains another important aspect of realism as well; namely, that international politics is about the interests of the 'great powers', and that interests of non-great powers should and inevitably will be secondary to those of great powers. Because great power war is so deadly, avoiding it is a moral imperative that justifies subjecting the needs of lesser powers to those of great power accommodation. Leaving morals aside, because great powers can force the lesser ones to bend to their needs, they will. In this case, the implication is that preserving some kind of great power condominium between the US and Russia requires dividing Europe in a way that leaves Russia satisfied, and hence a 'status quo', rather than a 'revolutionary' state, to use former US Secretary of State Henry Kissinger's terms.

This aspect of the argument, unfortunately, has received relatively little attention, for this is the point on which much of the debate over who is to blame and what should be done next hinges. It is in large part a normative debate, but it also points back to the long-standing disagreements between liberalism and realism. Liberalism (represented in this debate by the position of the EU) believes strongly that respect for international law and state sovereignty is essential to maintaining the security order in Europe, and is the only way to maintain a long-term peace. This is what has brought peace, for example to France and Germany after they fought three wars in 70 years. Liberals find Russia's invasion of Ukraine not only destructive for peace but normatively appalling. Most realists would hold that lasting peace simply is not possible in international affairs.

These two questions prompted by realism deserve more attention. First, do we believe that peace is best preserved by guarding the sovereignty of small states or by sacrificing it to the needs of great powers? Second, is sacrificing the sovereignty of small states a morally acceptable position?[24] As noted above, however, realism does not make it clear whether letting Russia control Ukraine is the height of prudence or a foolish cession of important territory.

---

[24]   W. Wayne Merry, 'The Origins of Russia's War in Ukraine: The Clash of Russian and European "Civilizational Choices" for Ukraine' in Elizabeth A. Wood, William E. Pomerantz, W. W. Merry and Maxim Trudolyubov, *Roots of Russia's War in Ukraine* (Washington DC; Woodrow Wilson Center, 2016), p.30.

'The Russians Went Ape'[25]

The second body of scholarly work focuses upon Russia seeking to expand its influence and gain recognition of its status as a great power. This body of work on the crisis views Russia's hybrid war in Eastern Ukraine as the continuation of its long-standing policy of creating frozen conflicts since the early-1990s in Moldova, Georgia and Azerbaijan. This literature also analyses Russia's revanchist policies within the context of Putin lamenting the disintegration of the USSR and the Russian desire to build new unions, in this case the Eurasian Economic Union. In this respect, those blaming Russia draw on a set of events and policies that those who blame the West largely ignore. Surprisingly, little of this scholarly work drills down deeper to pursue the national identity issues that lead many in Russia to view Ukraine as being an artificial country and failed state.

There may be insight from comparing Russia's view to that seen in previous cases of colonial collapse, such as that of the United Kingdom's colonial relationship with Ireland and France's relationship with Algeria. In both of those cases as well, the colonial power viewed these territories more as an integral 'Near Abroad' rather than as distinct colonies. The British, French and Russians differentiated between peoples closely bound to the metropolis and foreign colonies further afield. Russia appears not to view Ukraine and Belarus in the same manner as Georgia or Uzbekistan and especially the three Baltic States. De-colonisation in the Near Abroad, whether Ireland, Algeria or Ukraine, was more intense and bitter, producing a strong sense of betrayal in London, Paris and Moscow respectively at the independence of regions considered to be part of the metropolis.

The third body of scholarly work agrees that the conflict is largely driven by Russian behaviour, but sees that behaviour rooted in Russia's autocratic domestic politics rather than in its international aspirations.[26] One version of this approach sees Putin's 'militocratic' political system dominated by the intelligence services and military and its 'Chekist' (the name of the first Soviet secret service) operating culture as the root of Russia's military aggression. Alexander Motyl has analysed Putin's Russia as a fascist political system.[27]

---

[25]   A. Wilson, *Ukraine Crisis*, p.vii. Wilson was referencing Norman Stone's explanation of World War II as 'The Germans went ape'.

[26]   During the Cold War, two distinct literatures saw Soviet foreign policy as rooted in domestic politics. One, exemplified by George Kennan's famous 'Sources of Soviet Conduct', focuses on the distinctive nature of the Soviet system. http://www.historyguide.org/europe/kennan.html Another emphasised continuity between Tsarist and Soviet foreign policy, seeing both rooted in autocracy.

[27]   Alexander J. Motyl, 'Putin's Russia as a Fascist Political System', *Communist and Post-Communist Studies*, vol.49, no.1 (March 2016), pp.25–36.

Russian scholar Vladisav Inozemtsev defines Putin's Russia as fascist and imperialist rather than nationalist because it is grounded in language rather than blood, unlike the racist doctrines of Nazism.[28] Although not explicitly racist, collectively defining Russian speakers as 'Russians' has strong ethno-nationalist overtones, especially in Belarus and Ukraine, because it implicitly denies the existence of their national identities. Russia's 'conservative values' messaging is heavily masculine in nature and is linked to a focus on Putin's unique greatness, glorification of the intelligence services, reasserting the myths of the Great Patriotic War and asserting Russia as a great power.[29]

Another variant of this work analyses Russia as a 'mafia state', or 'klepto-cracy', where pursuit of money is as important as nationalism and seeking recognition of Russia as a great power. Mark Galeotti believes there is no inconsistency between widespread corruption and nationalism in Putin's Russia; after all, kleptocrats in many parts of the world are also nationalists. There is often the 'thinnest of lines' between organised crime and paramilitaries in many conflicts. This is also the case in the Crimea and the Russian proxy enclaves in the Donbas – the DNR and LNR.[30] Crimean Prime Minister Sergei Aksyonov, leader of a small Russian nationalist party, is a former organised crime leader with the pseudonym 'Goblin'.

Similarly, Wilson writes that Russia's hybrid war is 'foreign policy as *raiderstvo*' (corporate raiding), extending beyond Russian borders the same techniques that define the mix of business and organised crime that prevails in Russia. Evidence for this is seen in the massive corporate raiding of the Ukrainian state and private assets following Russia's annexation of the Crimea. Nor is this form of politics alien in Ukraine itself, where it was regionally prominent in the Donbas before 2010, and where Yanukovych as president undertook a systematic campaign to gather key business assets among his family and a small circle of allies.

The search for the domestic sources of Russian policy goes all the way down to the individual level and Putin himself. Masha Gessen examines Putin's biography, arguing that his early years and experience as a KGB officer in

---

[28] Vladislav Inozemstev, 'Putin's Russia: A Moderate Fascist State', *The American Interest*, 23 January 2017. https://www.the-american-interest.com/2017/01/23/putins-russia-a-moderate-fascist-state/

[29] Valerie Sperling, 'Putin's macho personality cult', *Communist and Post-Communist Studies*, vol.49, no.1 (March 2016), pp.13–23 and Maryna Romanets, 'Virtual Warfare: Masculinity, Sexuality, and Propaganda in the Russo-Ukrainian War', *East/West: Journal of Ukrainian Studies*, vol. 4, no. 1 (2017), pp.159–177.

[30] Dominic Sandbrook, *State of Emergency. The Way We Were. Britain 1970–1974* (London: Penguin, 2011), p.492.

East Germany (GDR) during the fall of communism tell us a great deal about Putin as a leader.[31] Putin saw first-hand how a popular protest had led to a revolution in the GDR and two decades later he viewed them closer to home on Russia's borders in Georgia and Ukraine. Putin took away from the GDR a uniformly negative view of political instability under Presidents Mikhail Gorbachev and later in the 1990s under President Boris Yeltsin, one reason being because political strife could be used by Western intelligence agencies and governments to foment regime change.[32] In November 2017, the 100th anniversary of the Bolshevik Revolution, a popular revolution whose revolutionaries had received assistance from Germany which led to regime change, was not celebrated by Putin's Russia. Clifford G. Gaddy and Fiona Hill write that Putin's roots in the Soviet secret services go much deeper through his father who was one of only a few who survived as a member of an NKVD (Soviet secret police) unit sent behind enemy lines in Nazi occupied Estonia.[33] Putin appears to be the key player in Russia's foreign policy, so questions about him as an individual seem highly relevant. Can Putin be best understood as an improviser and gambler who is spontaneous and emotional, or as a cold, calculating strategist? Is Putin a nationalist or does he use nationalism instrumentally to win votes in order to maintain popular support and undermine the democratic opposition?

Geopolitics

The fourth perspective sees the conflict as part of a broader geopolitical competition between Russia and the West. This perspective focuses on relations between the West and its institutions (NATO and the EU) on the one hand and Russia on the other, and tends to reduce Ukraine's role to that of a battleground in a competition between Russia and the West. Samuel Charap and Timothy J. Colton discuss the 'dynamic interaction' between geopolitics, geo-ideas and geoeconomics while Toal invokes 'critical geopolitics'. While specific assertions vary, a primary focus is the extension of Western institutions eastward and increasing opposition to this in Russia. This school of thought sees the source of the conflict in the reliance of the West on a post-Cold War security architecture in Europe that excluded Russia. Many of these works fit more comfortably with realist theory than those blaming the conflict

[31] Masha Gessen, *The Man Without a Face: The Unlikely Rise of Vladimir Putin* (New York: Riverhead, 2012).
[32] See https://www.theatlantic.com/international/archive/2013/02/how-the-1980s-explains-vladimir-putin/273135/ For a study of how conspiracy theories frame post-Soviet leaders see T. Kuzio, 'Soviet conspiracy theories and political culture in Ukraine. Understanding Viktor Yanukovych and the Party of Regions', *Communist and Post-Communist Studies*, vol.44, no.3 (September 2011), pp.221–232.
[33] Clifford G. Gaddy and Fiona Hill, *Mr. Putin: Operative in the Kremlin* (Washington DC; Brookings Institution Press, 2015), pp.366–367.

on the US.

While Menon and Rumer see this 'architecture' problem as the fundamental cause of the conflict, Charap and Colton see it as only a permissive cause.[34] For Charap and Colton, the driving force for the conflict was the collision between eastward-moving Western institutions and Russia's defence of its traditional sphere of influence. 'It was the contestation over the lands between Russia and the West that led to the explosion in Ukraine and sent tensions spiralling out of control'.[35] They see overlapping 'geopolitical', 'geoeconomic' and 'geoideational' conflicts.[36] In this view, an immediate cause of the conflict was the EU's inability to foresee Russia's negative response to the Eastern Partnership enlarging into Eurasia. Just as many criticised NATO for assuming its enlargement could not be seen as a threat by Russia much of this literature criticises the EU for ignoring what Charap and Colton call the 'geoeconomic' consequences of its expansion eastward. By 2013, it was the EU, not NATO, that was taking the lead in pushing into territory that Russia considered vital to its security. Moreover, including Ukraine in a Deep and Comprehensive Free Trade Agreement (DCFTA) with the EU would undermine Russia's long-term efforts to build its own Eurasian Union trade bloc that included Ukraine.

Many of these authors, including Menon and Rumer, Charap and Colton, and Toal, strive to be even-handed in criticising both Russia and the West for their roles in the conflict. This is captured in the title of Charap and Colton's book *Everyone Loses*. Toal similarly rejects characterisations of Russia as an imperial power because they 'rest on superficial conceptions of geopolitics'.[37] Toal believes that Putin's reactions were shaped by a broader range of factors than those narrowly looked at by realists or by liberals focusing on Russia as an imperial power. These factors included a Ukrainian 'nationalising state', colour revolutions in Russia's neighbours, NATO and EU enlargement and state dynamics.[38] Although Toal recognises that NATO membership was not on offer to Ukraine, he believes Russia's concern over the future of Sevastopol 'was reasonable'.[39] Similarly, Charap and Colton appear to place greater blame on the West than Russia for the conflict.

National Identity and Nationalism

---

[34]   R. Menon and E. Rumer, *Conflict in Ukraine*, p.162 and S. Charap and T. J. Colton, *Everyone Loses*, pp.26–7.

[35]   S. Charap and T. J. Colton, *Everyone Loses*, p.27.

[36]   S. Charap and T. J. Colton, *Everyone Loses*, pp.29–30.

[37]   G. Toal, *Near Abroad*, pp.20–21 and 26–33.

[38]   G. Toal, *Near Abroad*, p.298.

[39]   G. Toal, *Near Abroad*, p.215.

The final body of scholarly publications, which is also the smallest, analyses national identity in Ukrainian-Russian relations and Russian chauvinism towards Ukrainians. In light of the large literature on Russian nationalism, it is odd that it has been underemphasised as a source of Russian behaviour in Ukraine, while scholars and journalists, especially those defending Russia or criticising the West, put great emphasis on nationalism in Ukraine, where nationalism is much less salient and extreme nationalists much less influential than in Russia.[40] No presidential candidate would win a Ukrainian election espousing an ethnic nationalist programme. Meanwhile, no Ukrainian nationalist party managed to cross the threshold to enter parliament in the 2014 elections – in the same year Russia invaded Ukraine. In Ukraine, civic patriotism rather than ethnic nationalism has greater public support because of the country's regional and linguistic diversity. Polls show that three-quarters of Ukrainians hold negative views of Russian leaders but not the Russian people – which would be expected if ethnic nationalism was dominant in Ukraine. The relative imbalance in attention to nationalism in Russia and Ukraine might stem from two factors. First, because there is so much scholarship on Russia, and most scholars and journalists know much more about Russia, nationalism is only one of many factors likely to work its way into an account of Russian behaviour. In contrast, with much less scholarship on Ukraine, and many scholars and journalists much less familiar with Ukraine, it is easy to focus attention on a familiar and evocative theme, such as nationalism. That is especially true in light of a second factor, the concerted effort by Russian leaders to exaggerate the role and extremism of nationalism in Ukraine. In this section, we review the role of nationalism and national identity in explanations both of Russia's and Ukraine's behaviour.

The role of Russian nationalism underpins, to some extent, the literatures discussed above focusing on Russian great power aspirations and Russian domestic politics as sources of the conflict. Some also see nationalism as the direct cause, Ivan Krastev writes, 'It is Putin the conservative and not Putin the realist who decided to violate Ukraine's sovereignty. His march on Crimea is not realpolitik it is *kulturkampf*'.[41]

Russian nationalism has a long history and it was prominent in Russian foreign policy discussions in the 1990s, as a large literature at that time shows, but President Yeltsin never wholeheartedly embraced it. Similarly,

---

[40]   On Ukraine, see Andrew Wilson, *Ukrainian Nationalism in the 1990s: A Minority Faith* (New York: Cambridge University Press, 1996). On Russia, see Paul Chaisty and Stephen Whitefield, 'Putin's Nationalism Problem' in Agnieszka Pikulicka-Wilczewska and R. Sakwa eds., *Ukraine and Russia: People, Politics, Propaganda and Perspectives* (Bristol: E-International Relations, March 2015), pp.165–172.
[41]   Ivan Krastev, 'What does Russia want and why?' *Prospect*, 6 March 2014. http:// www.prospectmagazine.co.uk/politics/what-does-russia-want-and-why

Russian designs on Crimea surfaced repeatedly throughout the post-Soviet period (see chapter four). Charles Clover writes that after 2000, the 'emergence of a virulent nationalist opposition movement took the mainstream hostage'.[42] In the 1990s, the red-brown coalition opposed to Yeltsin, the regime's controlled 'nationalist opposition' Vladimir Zhirinovsky and Aleksandr Dugin had been on the extremes of Russian politics.

As Toal stresses, Putin's rejection of Western influence in Russia's 'privileged zone of interests' and alienation from the West was 'years in the making'.[43] The traditional theory of Eurasianism, in which Russia is viewed not as a colonising empire but as a positive civilisation that extends beyond Russia's borders, was rejuvenated and popularised. In this view, Russians, Ukrainians and Belarusians are parts of a single *Russkii Mir* (Russian World) civilisation, the division of which into separate states is artificial. In Russia's domestic minorities policy, which recognises a wide array of groups, there is no recognition of Ukrainians, who by numbers are the second largest minority, simply because they are not seen as distinct and do not possess autonomous territorial institutions.[44]

It is this *Russkii Mir* civilisation which Russian nationalists fear is under threat from the West. Galeotti and Andrew Bowen write that Putin does not see himself as an empire builder but as 'defending a civilisation against the 'chaotic darkness' that will ensue if he allows Russia to be politically encircled abroad and culturally colonised by Western values at home'.[45] The works of Eurasianist ideologists such as Dugin, who in 2014 called upon his fellow Russians to 'kill, kill Ukrainians'[46] have provided a new post-Soviet world outlook and identity for Russia's ruling elites and *siloviki*.

Putin embraced nationalism after the colour revolutions, and went further after widespread street protests to his return to the presidency in 2012. Clover writes that the 'Orange fever' in Russia in the mid-2000s helped what was seen as extremist rhetoric at that time 'become the standard jargon of state policy a mere decade and a half later'.[47] Putin publicly articulated this

---

[42]   Charles Clover, *Black Wind, White Snow: The Rise of Russia's New Nationalism* (New Haven, Conn.: Yale University Press, 2016), p.287.

[43]   G. Toal, *Near Abroad*, pp.208.

[44]   A discussion of the Ukrainian minority in Russia is not included in Federica Prina, *National Minorities in Putin's Russia. Diversity and assimilation* (London: Routledge, 2016).

[45]   Mark Galeotti and Andrew Bowen, 'Putin's Empire of the Mind', *Foreign Policy*, 21 April 2014. http://foreignpolicy.com/2014/04/21/putins-empire-of-the-mind/

[46]   'Putin's Advisor Dugin says Ukrainians must be "killed, killed, killed"', 12 June 2014. https://www.youtube.com/watch?v=MQ-uqmnwKF8

[47]   C. Clover, *Black Wind, White Snow*, pp.282 and 315.

view in his February 2007 speech to the Munich security conference.[48] Since his re-election in 2012, Putin's promotion of 'conservative values' has condemned multiculturalism, the welcoming of Muslim immigrants, gay marriage and the decline of the nation-state (all themes which have resonated with populist nationalists in the EU and the US).

When President Petro Poroshenko hailed Ukraine's achievement of a visa-free regime with the EU as his country's final break with Russia, Putin responded by associating Europe with homosexuality: 'By the way, there are many more blue uniforms (gays) there than here, so he shouldn't relax too much, and just in case, he should keep a look out about him'.[49]

While it is not surprising that Russian nationalists are on the same page as Putin, the majority of opposition democratic political leaders, such as Alexei Navalny, also support Russia's annexation of the Crimea. This is significant because it indicates that Russian nationalism, and in particular its views toward Ukraine, are not isolated to Putin and his team, and therefore will not automatically pass when he eventually leaves office.

The role of nationalism in Ukraine has attracted more attention, primarily from those who see Russia's intervention as justified. Three related arguments are made. First, the coalition that came to rule in Ukraine after the Euromaidan was illegitimate and threatening because it contained representatives of extreme nationalist parties. Second, the role of those groups in the protests constituted sufficient danger to ethnic Russians and Russian speakers to justify their desire to secede and Russia's intervention to protect them. Third, the unsuccessful effort by Euromaidan revolutionaries in parliament to annul Yanukovych's 2012 language law was depicted as constituting a further threat to the rights of Russians and Russian speakers (the measure passed but was not signed into law by acting head of state Oleksandr Turchynov).[50]

Among those who study Ukraine, the influence and the extremism of the various nationalist groups are a matter of considerable debate. What has attracted less attention, however, is that the same authors who are blistering in their criticism of US interference seem to advance a standard for military

---

[48]   http://www.washingtonpost.com/wp-dyn/content/article/2007/02/12/AR2007021200555.html

[49]   https://www.rferl.org/a/putin-unwashed-russia-poroshenko-ukraine-gay/28557438.html

[50]   These arguments appear in 'Cultural Contradictions' in Sakwa's *Frontline Ukraine*, p.270–277. Mearsheimer ('Why the Ukraine crisis is the West's fault', p.4) writes that the interim Ukrainian government 'contained four high-ranking members who could legitimately be labeled neofascists'.

intervention in one's neighbours that is enticingly low and surprisingly vague.

A common framework for understanding the crisis is to portray Ukraine as divided between governments pursuing pluralist policies and governments pursuing what Sakwa calls 'monist' (nationalist) policies – by which Sakwa means policies that reject pluralism. In this view, the 'civil war' was caused by pluralism being overthrown by 'monist' nationality policies which are intolerant of Russian-speakers and espouse Russophobia.[51] As scholars of Ukraine have explored for over two decades, however, simple binaries (e.g. between 'monist' and pluralist or between ethnic and linguistic categories) are highly misleading in Ukraine. Moreover, these critics of 'monism' oddly ignore the politics of Yanukovych, who was assiduously trying to eliminate any potential political competitors as well as economic rivals. The desire to stop him before he fully consolidated autocracy in the country was one of the underlying sources of support for the Euromaidan protests, and helps explain why various oligarchs supported his ouster.

In addition, talk of multiculturalism in Russian-controlled regions, whether the Crimea or the DNR and LNR, is a myth. In the Crimea, Tatars have come under sustained repression, its leaders banned from returning to the Crimea and their unofficial parliament *Mejlis* has been banned. The Ukrainian Orthodox Church-Kiev Patriarchate has been banned. In the DNR and LNR, Ukrainian language schools and media have been closed down and Ukrainian Orthodox Church-Kiev Patriarchate and Protestant Churches banned.

Upwards of a quarter of citizens in Eastern Ukraine considered themselves to have mixed Russian-Ukrainian ethnicity, and the majority of Ukrainians speak both Russian and Ukrainian, depending on the circumstances. Moreover, even Russian/Ukrainian is in some cases a false distinction, as people often intermingle the two. Similarly, as Volodymyr Kravchenko points out, the dichotomy of a Ukraine divided between 'monism' and 'pluralism' shows little understanding of modern Ukrainian identity, as in fact 'the two are partially intertwined and interdependent'.[52] Exaggerating these differences, however, has a profound impact, as it prompted observers to predict conflict in Ukraine,

---

[51]   See R. Sakwa, *Frontline Ukraine* and *Bruno De Cordier*, 'Ukraine's Vendee War? A Look at the 'Resistance Identity' of the Donbas Insurgency, *Russian Analytical Digest*, no.198 (14 February 2017). http://www.css.ethz.ch/content/specialinterest/gess/cis/center-for-securities-studies/en/publications/rad/rad-all-issues/details.html?id=/n/o/1/9/no_198_identity_politicsnr_198_identity

[52]   Volodymyr Kravchenko, a historian from Kharkiv and director of the Canadian Institute of Ukrainian Studies at the University of Alberta, writes that, 'In terms of theory, Sakwa's book contains nothing new. In terms of Ukrainian studies, its significance is even smaller'. *East-West: Journal of Ukrainian Studies*, vol.3, no.1 (2016), p.163. https://www.ewjus.com/index.php/ewjus/article/view/173

and therefore to see it as 'normal' when it happened. Predictions of Ukraine disintegrating into a civil war between its eastern and western regions have been published since as long ago as the early 1990s.[53]

The primary question we face in evaluating nationalism as a cause of conflict is whether it is a fundamental source of behaviour or is being used instrumentally by leaders to build support for policies they have chosen on other grounds. Because nationalism can be used by politicians instrumentally, it is compatible with various explanations concerning underlying driving forces. Even if we believe that nationalism is exploited by the Russian leadership to build support for itself, the fact that it appears to work so well means that nationalism must be part of our understanding of the current conflict. Similarly, even if Ukrainian nationalists are adept at gaining attention, they may not be having much influence on policy. A major difference between Russia and Ukraine is that invoking nationalism is a successful strategy to win votes in Russia but not in Ukraine; indeed, no Ukrainian president has ever won an election with a nationalist programme.

Tied to the question of nationalism is that of identity which can be either ethnic or civic or, as is the case in most Western democracies both. The Russian view of identity is based on language and culture (together encompassing the nebulous term 'civilisation') and therefore Russians and Russian speakers irrespective of their citizenship are 'Russians'. Here the term 'Russians' becomes confusing in English as it can have three meanings: (1) ethnic Russians (*Russkii*) in the Russian Federation; (2) Russians citizens (*Rossiyanyn*) in the Russian Federation; and (3) the three eastern Slavs (*Russkii* as pertaining to the members of the *Russkii Mir* who emerged together from Kiev Rus). Although there is a similarity between one and two to the difference between 'English' and 'British', the confusion lies in the use of only word ('Russian') to describe both.

The Russian understanding of identity is coupled with three further factors pertaining to Ukraine and Belarus: (1) Ukrainians, Belarusians and Russians are 'one people'; (2) Belarus and Ukraine are artificial states; (3) the borders of Belarus and especially Ukraine are artificial, referring not only to the Crimea but also to Eastern and Southern Ukraine (so-called *Novorossiya*). Russian views of identity and Ukraine and Ukrainians clash with reality on the ground (as seen in the failure of the *Novorossiya* project) and are diamet-

---

[53] See for example, E. Rumer, 'Eurasia Letter: Will Ukraine Return to Russia?' *Foreign Policy, n*o.96 (Autumn 1994), pp.129–144. For an alternative viewpoint see Paul D'Anieri, 'Ethnic Tensions and State Strategies: Understanding the Survival of the Ukrainian State', *Journal of Communist Studies and Transition Politics*, vol.23, no.1 (March 2007), pp.4–29.

rically opposed to how Ukrainians view their own identity in ethnic, civic or ethnic-civic terms. Ironically, Putin's military aggression has strengthened Ukrainian identity and made Russian understanding of Ukraine and Ukrainians even more obsolete.

Conclusion

As the fragmented nature of this literature review has demonstrated, the field has not yet developed a clear set of analytical debates that define the topic. The dominant debate – over who is to blame – is one that is unresolvable. Analytically, so far, the works on the topic come from a bewildering array of paradigms, levels of analysis, geographical foci, and conceptualisations of the problem. Underlying these, however, is a series of issues that seem to shape much of the discussion even if they are not addressed directly. Here we identify several.

A first basic problem concerns the principal of the sovereign equality of states. Russia's position, and that of many works on the topic, answers the question clearly in the negative, or at least with considerable qualification. For realists, the question itself is naïve. But many others who do not claim to be realists accept, to some degree or another, the idea that Russia has special rights or privileges due to its size and power. For those who do not espouse realism, the question is what are those privileges and where do they end. Charap and Colton are correct to write, 'It should surprise no one that a country of Russia's capabilities and ambitions will seek influence over its periphery; the US or China are no different in that respect'.[54]

The bigger question is how much, and to what extent we consider such ambitions legitimate? Put more pointedly, how legitimate is it to injure the interests of the region's other states in order to serve Russia's? One suspects that the 'legitimacy' claim does us little good, because it runs head on into other legitimate claims. Thomas Graham and Menon, for example lay out a compelling case that Russia's concept of its role as a power has been consistent over time, and has been impinged by the events of the post-Cold War period. But they leave unaddressed the crucial question of how far we should impinge on other states – including Ukraine – to satisfy Russia's conception of its great power status.[55] How does one resolve competition over claims of legitimacy, other than via the naked exercise of power? One important question, therefore, is how to answer the question of what exactly

---

[54]   S. Charap and T. Colton, *Everyone Loses*, p.24.
[55]   Thomas Graham and R. Menon, 'The Putin Problem', *Boston Review*, 12 September 2017. http://bostonreview.net/politics/thomas-graham-rajan-menon-putin-problem

one country's interests are beyond its borders, and how far they extend geographically. Can some mix of *realpolitik* and principle solve the problem? If not, is the diverse group of scholars advocating for recognising Russia's rights beyond its borders ready to endorse the realist position?

Absent any shared agreement between Russia and the West on that question, a second question presses. How do we know when acceding to the demands of a powerful state to extend its influence will solve security problems, and when such concessions will make them worse? There may be too few historical cases to arrive at good empirical generalisations. As a result, analogies will be used, and in this case the comparison to Germany's territorial demands in the 1930s has been made. Russia's behaviour since 2014 is ambiguous enough to be consistent both with the view that it stopped where it did because it was satiated, and the view that it stopped where it did because of pushback, both from within Ukraine and from the international community. In terms of territory, there is a good case to be made that Russia can be satisfied somewhere within the boundaries of the former Soviet Union. Normatively, however, Russia shows signs of being a revolutionary power, hoping to overturn both the prevailing distribution of power and the rules of the game that others in Europe have accepted for some time. Perhaps no task is as urgent as correctly assessing the extent to which concessions will satisfy, or stoke, Russia's ambitions.

If the questions above seem to push the answers into the realist court, we have to acknowledge as we did earlier in this chapter that realism too has its limits. The question of when to appease and when to confront is one that realism can answer only in retrospect (Neville Chamberlain's cutting a deal with Adolf Hitler in 1938 looked highly cynical and realistic in the moment). If there is to be a new carve-up of Europe, such as that reached at Yalta in 1945 or in earlier partitions of Poland, what border should the West seek, and how should it pursue that interest? Mearsheimer's argument points directly to such a 'grand bargain', but he and others are silent on where the new line should be, and how it should be redrawn when constellations of power change in the future.

Another series of important questions relates to the relationship between the domestic and international sources of Russian foreign policy. Those who see Russian behaviour as the main cause of the conflict can draw on both its great power aspirations and several aspects of its domestic politics. In this instance, those arguments are complementary, but that complementarity makes it hard to say which might have more influence in the longer term, or what might happen when those motives conflict rather than reinforce one another. In particular, the notion that a change in government in Russia would lead to a less assertive foreign policy causes fear among some in Russia and hope among many in the West, but it is not clear that the prediction will come true. In the 1990s, Yeltsin was often exhibiting autocratic control, not democracy, when he held back the mix of communist and nationalist revanchists that came to dominate the State Duma. Frozen conflicts in Moldova, Georgia, and Azerbaijan happened on Yeltsin's watch in the 1990s. The assumption that a democratic Russia could be part of a 'Europe whole and free' has yet to be decisively tested. We need to understand the domestic dynamics of Russian foreign policy better than we do.

These are not the only questions one can pose, but these are questions on which we can imagine fruitful debate and in some cases, progress on empirical questions. Moreover, by framing these issues as specific instances of broader problems, these questions would allow us to bring to this case large literatures in international relations, history, and comparative politics.

Further Reading

Allison, Roy, 'Russian 'deniable' intervention in Ukraine: how and why Russia broke the rules', *International Affairs*, vol.90, no.6 (November 2014), pp.1255–1297.

Bateman, Aaron, 'The Political Influence of the Russian Security Services', *Journal of Slavic Military Studies*, vol.27, no.3 (September 2014), pp.380–403.

Bergman, Max and Carolyn Kenney, *War by Other Mean: Russian Active Measures and the Weaponization of Information* (Washington DC: Center for American Progress, 6 June 2017). https://www.americanprogress.org/issues/security/reports/2017/06/06/433345/war-by-other-means/

Darczewska, Jolanta, *The Anatomy of Russian Information Warfare: The Crimean Operation, a Case Study,* no.42 (Warsaw: Centre for Eastern Studies, May 2014). https://www.osw.waw.pl/sites/default/files/the_anatomy_of_russian_information_warfare.pdf

Delcour, Laure and Kataryna Wolczuk, 'Spoiler or facilitator of democratization? Russia's role in Georgia and Ukraine', *Democratization*, vol. 22, no. 3 (April 2015), pp.459–478.

Galeotti, Mark, *Crimintern: How the Kremlin uses Russia's criminal network in Europe* (London: European Council on Foreign Relations, 18 April 2017).

http://www.ecfr.eu/publications/summary/crimintern_how_the_kremlin_uses_russias_criminal_networks_in_europe

Gude, Ken, *Russia's 5th Column* (Washington DC: Center for American Progress, March 2017). https://www.americanprogress.org/issues/security/reports/2017/03/15/428074/russias-5th-column/

Horvath, Robert, *Putin's Preventive Counter-Revolution: Post-Soviet Authoritarianism and the Spectre of Velvet Revolution* (London: Routledge, 2012).

Kryshtanovskaya, Olga. and Stephen. White, 'The Sovietization of Russian Politics', *Post-Soviet Affairs*, vol.25, no.4 (October 2009), pp. 283–309.

Kuzio, Taras, 'Crime, Politics and Business in 1990s Ukraine', *Communist and Post-Communist Politics*, vol.47, no.2 (July 2014), pp. 195–210.

Kuzio, T., 'Competing Nationalisms, Euromaidan and the Russian-Ukrainian Conflict', *Studies in Ethnicity and Nationalism*, vol.15, no.1 (April 2015), pp.158–169.

Laruelle, Marlene, *The 'Russian World': Russia's Soft Power and Geopolitical Imagination* (Washington DC: Center on Global Interests, May 2015). http://globalinterests.org/wp-content/uploads/2015/05/FINAL-CGI_Russian-World_Marlene-Laruelle.pdf

Moshes, Arkady, *The crisis over Ukraine – three years on: Is a 'grand bargain' totally ruled out? FIIA Comment 12, 2017* (Helsinki: Finish Institute of International Affairs, 15 May 2017).

Nimmo, Ben, *Anatomy of an Info-War: How Russia's Propaganda Machine Works, and How to Counter It,* Central European Policy Institute, 15 May 2015. http://www.cepolicy.org/publications/anatomy-info-war-how-russias-propaganda-machine-works-and-how-counter-it

Potapova, Kristina, *How We Have Become an Enemy in the Eyes of Russia: The EU as Portrayed by Kremlin Propaganda, In Focus* (Brussels: Wilfried Martens Centre for European Studies, March 2017). https://www.martenscentre.eu/sites/default/files/publication-files/kremlin-propaganda-european-union-enemy-russia.pdf

Shkandrij, Myroslav, 'Living with Ambiguities: Meanings of Nationalism in the Russian-Ukrainian War' in Olga Bertelsen, ed., *Revolution and War in Contemporary Ukraine: The Challenge of Change* (Stuttgart: Ibidem Verlag, 2016), pp.121–138.

Torbakov, Igor, 'Ukraine and Russia: Entangled Histories, Contested Identities, and a War of Narratives', in O. Bertelsen ed., *Revolution and War in Contemporary Ukraine,* pp.89–120.

2

The Soviet Origins of Russian Hybrid Warfare

This chapter analyses the Soviet origins of Russia's use of hybrid warfare, assassinations, information and cyber warfare. Ukraine and Ukrainian nationalism were – and continue to remain – key targets for Soviet and Russian hybrid and information warfare. The EU's weekly *Disinformation Review* documented nearly 1,000 fake news stories issued in one small period October 2015–July 2016 directed against Ukraine and the three Baltic States.[1]

In the decade before the crisis, Russia's hybrid, information and cyber warfare were first used against Ukraine and its neighbours and later against Europe and North America. Putin actively intervened in the 2004 Ukrainian presidential elections, visiting Kiev during the first and second rounds, lending Russian political technologists (Gleb Pavlovsky, Marat Gelman, Igor Shuvalov, Sergei Markov and others) and providing hundreds of millions of dollars in assistance to the Yanukovych campaign. The most egregious example of Russian interference was the poisoning of Viktor Yushchenko and the less well known foiled terrorist attack on his elections headquarters.[2] Andrew Wilson's study of Russia's political technologists' manipulation of the media and election campaigns was published a decade before the 2014 crisis. As Brian Whitmore writes,

> Estonians were getting hacked by Russia long before it was cool. Ukrainians had to deal with Kremlin interference in their elections before it became trendy. Georgia and Moldova had to live with disinformation, fake news, and active measures before these things

---

[1]   *Disinformation Review* is published by the EU Stratcom Task Force. https://euvsdisinfo.eu/

[2]   T. Kuzio, 'Russian Policy to Ukraine During Elections', *Demokratizatsiya*, vol.13, no.4 (Fall 2005), pp.491–517.

became fashionable catchphrases. It's a good idea to pay very close attention to what Russia does to its neighbours, because it often foreshadows things Moscow will later try out farther to the West.[3]

This chapter is divided into three sections. The first is a comparative study of Soviet and Russian hybrid and information warfare. The second and third sections analyse Soviet and Russian approaches to non-linear warfare through goals, tactics and results.

The Soviet Union and Russia Compared

Very active periods of Soviet and Russian hybrid and information warfare have taken place during periods of conservative and nationalist retrenchment, when the USSR was ruled by Leonid Brezhnev, Yury Andropov and Konstantin Chernenko from the mid-1960s to mid-1980s and under President Putin since 2000. Putin was socialised into the Soviet system during the Brezhnev era when he joined the KGB in 1975. Soviet conservatives and Russian nationalists look with nostalgia to the Brezhnev era and denigrate liberal anti-Stalinist reformers Nikita Khrushchev and Gorbachev who ruled before and after. Gorbachev in particular is loathed because he is associated with the disintegration of the USSR. The myth of the Great Patriotic War was created during the Brezhnev era and such a myth required praise of Joseph Stalin as the Soviet leader who built a modern, industrialised Soviet superpower that won the war and with its mighty nuclear arsenal was feared by the West. Promotion of the Great Patriotic War myth has always therefore gone hand in hand with a cult of Stalin (and a concomitant downplaying of his crimes against humanity). Anti-Western xenophobia and Russian great power nationalism, coupled with Putin's anger at the West's alleged unwillingness to respect Russia as a great power, are driving forces underpinning the information warfare against NATO and EU members.[4]

Putin moved twice to the nationalist right during the decade leading up to the 2014 Ukraine-Russia crisis. The 2003 and 2004 Rose and Orange Revolutions in Georgia and Ukraine respectively influenced Putin's first move to the right. Anton Shekhovtsov believes this also triggered an important change in attitudes among Russian leaders towards working with the extreme right in

[3]   Brian Whitmore, 'We're All Russia's Neighbors Now', *Radio Liberty-Radio Free Europe*, 29 June 2017. https://www.rferl.org/a/were-all-russias-neighbors-power-vertical/28585339.html

[4]   T. Kuzio, 'Why Vladimir Putin is Angry with the West: Understanding the Drivers of Russia's Information, Cyber and Hybrid War', *Security Policy Working Paper* No.7 (Berlin: Federal Academy for Security Policy, February 2017). https://www.baks.bund.de/en/newsletter/archive/view/971

Europe.[5] By 2007, the year Putin gave his inflammatory speech to the Munich Conference on Security Policy,[6] Russian nationalism was the dominant influence among the majority of Russian leaders and public and United Russia, Putin's party of power, had become a 'nationalist party of Russia'.[7] Marlene Laruelle writes that United Russia has 'become one of the major actors of the nationalist narrative'.[8] Putin's second turn even further to the nationalist right came after his re-election in 2012 when he focused on integrating Ukraine into his Eurasian project, began describing Russians and Ukrainians as 'one people', promoted a conservative values agenda and aligned Russia with anti-EU extreme right and left political forces. Putin believed the Rose and Orange Revolutions and large street protests in Moscow in 2011–2012 were Western conspiracies directed against Russia. The protests came during the midst of what Moscow viewed as the Western orchestrated Arab Spring in Libya, Egypt, Yemen, Syria and Bahrain. Shekhovtsov argues the colour revolutions, Moscow protests and Arab Spring generated widespread paranoia in the Russian leadership culminating in the need to find international allies. This in turn led to a predilection to Russian cooperation with populist nationalists and neo-fascist groups in Europe and North America.[9]

The Soviet Union was very active in the field of *dezinformatsiya*. Although much of what Russia undertakes is new, the USSR long practiced 'subversion, disinformation and forgery, combined with the use of special forces'.[10] In the 1930s, the Soviet Union's information warfare was highly successful in covering up knowledge in the West of the artificial famine (*Holodomor* [*to murder by famine or terror famine*]) that killed over four million people in Ukraine. *New York Times* correspondent Walter Duranty[11] won a Pulitzer Prize for his coverage of the USSR and yet was one of many who deliberately

---

[5]   Anton Shekhovtsov, *Russia and the Western Far Right: Tango Noir* (London: Routledge 2018).

[6]   http://www.washingtonpost.com/wp-dyn/content/article/2007/02/12/AR2007021200555.html

[7]   Marcel H. Van Herpen, *Putin's Wars: The Rise of Russia's New Imperialism* (Lanham, ML: Rowman and Littlefield, 2015), p.117.

[8]   Marlene Laruelle, *Inside and Around the Kremlin's Black Box: The New Nationalist Think Tanks in Russia* (Stockholm: Institute for Security and Development Policy, 2009), p.19. http://isdp.eu/content/uploads/images/stories/isdp-main-pdf/2009_laruelle_inside-and-around-the-kremlins-black-box.pdf

[9]   A. Shekhovtsov, *Russia and the Western Far Right*.

[10]   'The Fog of Wars', *The Economist*, 22 October 2016. http://www.economist.com/news/special-report/21708880-adventures-abroad-boost-public-support-home-fog-wars

[11]   S. J. Taylor, *Stalin's Apologist*; Walter Duranty, *The New York Times's Man in Moscow* (New York, Oxford: Oxford University Press, 1990).

or unwittingly became 'useful idiots'[12] in covering up the *Holodomor*.[13]

The Soviet secret police, the KGB 'had a special department responsible for 'active measures', designed to weaken and undermine the West'.[14] Active measures were treated as different to espionage and counter-intelligence and included written and spoken disinformation, efforts to control the media in foreign countries, the use of foreign communist parties and front organisations controlled by the Communist Party's International department, clandestine radio stations, blackmail and political influence through collaborative elites. The means for the USSR to pursue active measures included forgeries (a well-known example was that of a US military manual and 'secret' diplomatic letters)[15], rumours, insinuations and 'altered facts' and lies – all very similar to today's 'fake news'.

The USSR had long undertaken 'wet actions' (assassinations) against opp-onents of the Soviet regime. Ukrainian nationalist leader and social democrat Symon Petlura was assassinated by a Soviet agent in Paris only four years after the USSR was founded. The USSR undertook hybrid warfare in pursuit of regime change in Afghanistan, Africa and Central and Latin America. The USSR long deployed Special Forces in developing countries in advance of invasions or to train local forces and national liberation groups.

Modern technology and social media provide Russia with greater opportunities to use hybrid, informational and cyber wars. British domestic intelligence MI5 chief Andrew Parker warned that Russia is using 'a whole range of powers to push its foreign policy in increasingly aggressive ways – involving propaganda, espionage, subversion and cyber-attacks'.[16]

Russia's post-modern approach to information warfare propaganda is

---

[12]   A term that Soviet leaders used to describe Westerners who could be useful for Soviet propaganda. The term has often been used to describe British socialist George Bernard Shaw and Duranty. See Fintan O'Toole, 'Why George Bernard Shaw Had a Crush on Stalin', *New York Times*, 11 September 2017. https://www.nytimes.com/2017/09/11/opinion/why-george-bernard-shaw-had-a-crush-on-stalin.html

[13]   Chapter 14, 'The Cover-Up' in Anne Applebaum, *Red Famine: Stalin's War on Ukraine* (London: Allen Lane, 2017), pp.302–325.

[14]   'The Fog of Wars', *The Economist*, 22 October 2016.

[15]   Soviet 'Active Measures', Forgery, Disinformation, Political Operations, Special Report no.88 (Washington DC: Bureau of Public Affairs, Department of State, October 1981). http://insidethecoldwar.org/sites/default/files/documents/Soviet%20Active%20Measures%20Forgery,%20Disinformation,%20Political%20Operations%20October%201981.pdf

[16]   https://www.theguardian.com/uk-news/2016/oct/31/andrew-parker-increasingly-aggressive-russia-a-growing-threat-to-uk-says-mi5-head

different to Soviet messaging because many narratives are broadcast on multiple media to undermine the entire concept of a single truthful narrative. Unlike the USSR, contemporary Russia does not just offer an alternative truth but also deconstructs the very idea of objective reporting. Russia's post-modern approach to information warfare propaganda has been undertaken alongside an increasingly effective use of digital media. Russia has invested large resources in its information and cyber warfare capabilities.

The Soviet Union

Goals

Soviet hybrid operations had a range of goals, including: (1) infiltrating and undermining national liberation movements and dissident groups within the USSR and discrediting their Western sponsors; (2) dividing and weakening NATO and the EU; (3) fanning opposition to the US military and nuclear presence in Europe; and (4) competing with the US, UK and France for spheres of influence in Latin America and the developing world.

The first and perhaps most urgent goal was to counter the biggest domestic threat to the USSR which came from nationalist movements seeking the independence of their homeland (rather than from democratic dissidents who sought a democratised USSR). The biggest nationalist threat came from Ukrainians and the three Baltic States. From the 1960s to the 1980s, Soviet propaganda and ideological campaigns had attacked Ukrainian and Baltic dissidents and nationalists and émigré diasporas by portraying them as 'Nazi collaborators', 'bourgeois nationalists' and agents of Western and Israeli intelligence agencies. The Polish communist regime, which had fought a brutal war against Ukrainian nationalists in its Southeast from 1944–1947 and ethnically cleansed 150,000 Ukrainians in *Akcja 'Wisła' (Operation Vistula)*, also attacked Ukrainian nationalism.

The Soviets expended huge expense on these ideological campaigns through the KGB-controlled Society for Cultural Relations Abroad which published the free weekly newspaper *News from Ukraine/Visti z Ukrayiny*. In addition to lauding Soviet achievements and praising Soviet nationalities policies, they published ideological tirades and stories about Ukrainian 'Nazi collaborators' and their ties to Western intelligence services.

The term 'Banderite' (follower of the controversial World War II-era nationalist leader Stepan Bandera), used by the Soviet regime to denote a sadist, murderer and Nazi accomplice, was revived by Putin's regime in its information war against Ukraine. Nearly any supporter of increased Ukrainian autonomy could be denigrated in such a manner: national communists, liberal dissidents, and nationalists in the USSR and Orange and Euromaidan Revolutionaries in Ukraine were and are presented as being in the pay of the West and harbouring 'Nazi' and 'fascist' inclinations. A *Nezavisimaya Gazeta* Russian journalist writes 'The idea of an independent Ukraine is Russophobic by definition. That is, either Russia and Ukraine are one country, or they are enemies'.[17]

Russian nationalists were never attacked by the Soviet regime because they did not seek an independent state; Alexander Motyl therefore believes it is a myth to call them 'nationalists'.[18] Russian democratic dissidents and nationalist opposition were therefore different to national democrats and nationalists in Ukraine, the three Baltic States and other non-Russian republics of the USSR. In August 1991, the Russian SFSR did not declare independence from the USSR and the annual 'Russia Day' holiday is based on the June 1990 Russian Declar-ation of Sovereignty.

Another Soviet goal also resonates today: increasing divisions within Europe and in Trans-Atlantic relations. The Soviet Union promoted 'peace movements' and nuclear disarmament. US intelligence documented Soviet funding of 'peace' groups in Europe[19] to such organisations as CND (Campaign for Nuclear Disarmament) in the UK which included many prominent leaders of the Labour Party then and today.[20] In 1986, the Soviet World Peace Council (WPC), a Soviet front organisation, held its congress in Denmark, the first occasion the WPC had held an event in a NATO member. Contemporary Russian strategies have similar goals of furthering divisions in Europe by supporting separatist groups, and anti-EU populist nationalist Brexit-type referendums.[21] NATO was always viewed as a major threat to Soviet security and therefore an important target for all manner of Soviet active measures.

---

[17]   K. Bennet, 'Russia's Imperial Amnesia', *The American Interest*, 9 May 2017. https:// www.the-american-interest.com/2017/05/09/russias-imperial-amnesia/

[18]   Alexander J. Motyl, 'The Myth of Russian Nationalism' in *Sovietology, Rationality, Nationality: Coming to Grips with Nationalism in the USSR* (New York: Columbia University Press, 1990), pp.161–173.

[19]   https://www.cia.gov/library/readingroom/docs/CIA-RDP85M00364R001001530019-5.pdf

[20]   Clive Rose, 'The Peace Movement in the United Kingdom since 1963' in *Campaigns Against Western Defence: NATO's Adversaries and Critics*, RUSI Defence Studies Series (London: Palgrave Macmillan, 1986), pp.137–155.

[21]   Gustav Gressel, *Fellow Travellers: Russia, Anti-Westernism, and Europe's Political Parties*, (London: European Council on Foreign Relations, 14 July 2017). http://www. ecfr.eu/publications/summary/fellow_travellers_russia_anti_westernism_and_europes_ political_parties_7213

Tactics

The Soviet secret police conducted assassinations since the mid-1920s which came to be known as 'wet operations'. These targeted opponents and what Moscow deemed to be 'traitors'. Russia's use of poisons and other agents predated the attempted assassinations of Yushchenko and Alexander Litvinenko by more than seven decades.

In 1926, the assassination of Petlyura in Paris was followed by three further assassinations of Ukrainian nationalist leaders: Yevhen Konovalets in Rotterdam in 1939 and Lev Rebet and Bandera in Munich in 1957 and 1959 respectively.[22] The assassination of Rebet was viewed as a trial run for Bandera, using a cyanide poison gun that the KGB had developed which left no traces and simulated a heart attack. Despite the embarrassment produced by the defection of KGB assassin Bohdan Stashynskyy in 1961 the USSR continued to undertake 'wet operations' through to the mid-1980s. In 1978, Bulgarian BBC journalist Georgi Markov was murdered in London using ricin poison administered by an umbrella.

In 1981, an attempted assassination of Pope John Paul II, whom the Soviet Union feared was supporting the anti-communist Solidarity movement in Poland, by a far right Turkish nationalist failed. The plot revealed many details of how the USSR used false flag operations to disguise its involvement. The attacker had been unknowingly working on behalf of the Bulgarian secret police and they in turn had been coordinating their actions with the KGB and GRU (Main Intelligence Directorate [Soviet military intelligence]). Soviet archives brought to the West by KGB defector Vasili Mitrokhin showed the extent of the Soviet penetration of Italy and other European countries and how the GRU was behind the attempted assassination of the Pope. GRU 'little green men' Special Forces who invaded the Crimea and mainland Ukraine in February–April 2014 were 'straight from the KGB playbook'.[23]

The USSR supported nationalists, separatists, anarchists and leftist extremists for their political usefulness rather than for ideological reasons. The USSR had forty training bases for such groups with an annual expenditure of $200 million with other training bases in Soviet satellite states Hungary, Czechoslovakia, Bulgaria and the GDR. The USSR and its Eastern European allies, particularly the GDR and Bulgaria, supported terrorist groups in

---

[22]   Serhii Plokhy, *The Man with the Poison Gun: A Cold War Spy Story* (New York: Basic Books, 2016).

[23]   Luke Harding, 'Spies, sleepers and hitmen: how the Soviet Union's KGB never went away', *The Guardian*, 19 January 2014. https://www.theguardian.com/world/2014/nov/19/spies-spooks-hitmen-kgb-never-went-away-russia-putin

Germany (Red Army Faction), Italy (Red Brigades), France (Corsica), Spain (Basques), Greece (Revolutionary Organisation 17 November), Canada (Front de libération du *Québec*) and the UK (The Official IRA, especially their political wing – the Workers Party[24]). The USSR also backed national liberation movements in Africa and Central and Latin America.[25] The KGB developed airplane hijackings as a tactic, and these grew in the 1970s to become a trademark of Palestinian liberation groups.[26]

The Soviet Union employed extensive *dezinformatsiya*, producing false stories and conspiracy theories. There are estimates the USSR conducted 10,000 *dezinformatsiya* operations during the Cold War, the most famous of which was that the CIA invented AIDS.[27] Soviet active measures actively fanned anti-Americanism during the 1980s.

Results

The USSR imprisoned and executed Ukrainian nationalists as late as 1987 and its anti-nationalist propaganda declined in intensity only in the late-1980s. The Soviet Union's decades of anti-(Ukrainian) nationalist propaganda had successes and failures. On the success side, the stereotype of the Western Ukrainian nationalist who collaborated with the Nazis and is a Russophobe was established among many in Russia, some in Eastern Ukraine, and even among many in the West. Putin's government has effectively built on this Soviet legacy. In Eastern Ukraine, old stereotypes were enhanced by Russia's information warfare in 2013–2014 and contributed to transforming protests into an insurgency. Russia's information war against Georgia in 2008 and Ukraine since 2013–2014 inflamed public opinion which incited its proxies to ethnically cleanse Georgians and commit human rights abuses in South Ossetia and the Donbas.[28] The UN and international human rights organisations have raised questions of human rights abuses of civilians and prisoners of war.[29] Amnesty International described the summary executions of Ukrainian prisoners as amounting to war crimes.[30]

---

[24] Kacper Rękawek, *Irish Republican Terrorism and Politics: A Comparative Study of the Official and the Provisional IRA* (London: Routledge, 2011)

[25] Nick Lockwood, 'How the Soviet Union Transformed Terrorism', *The Atlantic*, 23 December 2011. https://www.theatlantic.com/international/archive/2011/12/how-the-soviet-union-transformed-terrorism/250433/

[26] N. Lockwood, 'How the Soviet Union Transformed Terrorism'.

[27] Thoms Boghardt, 'Soviet Bloc Intelligence and Its AIDS Disinformation Campaign', *Studies in Intelligence*, vol.53, no.4 (December 2009), pp.1-24.

[28] M. H. Van Herpen, *Putin's Wars*, p.229.

[29] See Valeriy Makeyev's memoirs as a prisoner of war in his *100 Dniv Polonu* (Kharkiv: Folio, 2016).

[30] https://www.amnesty.org/en/latest/news/2015/04/ukraine-new-evidence-of-

Despite the successes, Soviet suppression of Ukrainian nationalism did not succeed in undermining Ukrainians' desire for independence in 1991, and that independence, as was recognised at the time, was the crucial factor in dismantling the Soviet Union. Today, civic nationalism remains strong, and popular support for the extreme right in Ukraine is comparatively low by European standards. In large part due to Russia's actions, greater numbers of Ukrainian citizens have re-identified as ethnic Ukrainians increasing their share from 72.7% and 77.8% in the 1989 Soviet and 2001 Ukrainian censuses respectively to 92% today. The Ukrainian language has become more popular: 'It used to be cool to speak Russian. Now it's cool to speak Ukrainian'.[31] Ukrainian scholar Volodymr Kulyk has outlined the increase in popularity of Ukrainian over Russian language media, film and books since 2014.[32]

Russia

Goals

The tactics and approaches that Russia carried with it institutionally from the Soviet era were matched with a newfound focus on the importance of what it understands as 'soft power'. Moreover, the role of new technology, beginning with the use of mobile phones and text messaging during the colour revolutions alerted Russian officials to the power of social media. The response has been a concerted effort to develop these weapons for the purposes of the state, and they are now deployed systematically to promote Russia's revival as a great power and to sow dissension within the Western alliance and international organisations. These tools are used by Putin for three goals.

The first goal is to pay the West back for its interference in domestic affairs in Russia and in Russia's 'zone of privileged interests'. If the West can interfere in the 2012 Russian presidential elections and foment regime change during the Euromaidan, Russia believes it can intervene in US and European elections.[33] Because Ukraine is seen as inextricably linked with Russia (see chapter three), Russian leaders do not believe the West has the same right to interfere in Ukraine as Moscow does. The problem is not with regime change

---

summary-killings-of-captured-soldiers-must-spark-urgent-investigations/

[31]   http://policymagazine.ca/pdf/11/PolicyMagazineJanuaryFebruary-2015-Baran.pdf

[32]   Volodymyr Kulyk, 'V usikh typakh mediy spozhyvachi viddayut perevahu produktam ukrayinskoyu movoyu', *Detektor Media*, 9 August 2017. http://detector.media/rinok/article/128765/2017-08-09-v-usikh-tipakh-medii-spozhivachi-viddayut-perevagu-produktam-ukrainskoyu-movoyu

[33]   T. Kuzio, 'Why Vladimir Putin is Angry with the West'.

in principle, as Foreign Minister Lavrov showed in 2008 when he proposed to US Secretary of State Condoleeza Rice that Russia withdraw its forces from Georgia in exchange for the removal of President Mikhail Saakashvili.[34]

Russian efforts to influence the 2016 US presidential election[35] have drawn by far the most attention of Russia's efforts to shape elections in other countries, but there were also prominent efforts to shape the 2017 election in France as well as others. The details of these efforts and of their impact are still being uncovered, so rather than dig into this episode in detail, we simply note that it comprises an important example of Russia's broader strategy.

A second goal is to use information and cyber warfare to undermine the world order which was created after 1991 and which, Putin believes, was meant to keep Russia down and weak. This means challenging the norms on which US hegemony relies, and in particular promoting the idea of a multipolar world guided by traditional norms of non-interference as preferable to a world led by the West and promoting universal values of human rights and liberal democracy. Charap and Colton argue that the EU's belief in the 'inherent superiority of its systems and structures' led it to act 'as if Russia did not exist'.[36] The Commonwealth of Independent States (CIS) Customs Union and Eurasian Union were presented by Putin as a Eurasian alternative to the EU for post-Soviet states. Russia continues a long-standing Soviet objective of seeking to replace NATO with a pan-European security organisation led by the OSCE where it would hold a veto.

Exploiting internal crises in the EU, such as the migration crisis and backing anti-EU populist nationalists, provides Russia with opportunities to weaken the EU. 'Conservative values' messaging on threats to national sovereignty, globalisation, same sex marriage, migration, and Islam has appeal among European and US populist nationalist voters.[37] Russian politicians and media have been enthusiastic about Brexit and British intelligence believes Russia was involved in the collapse of the voter registration website in the run-up to the UK's referendum on EU membership. An extensive investigation found

---

[34]   Condoleeza Rice, *No Higher Honour: A Memoir of My Years in Washington* (New York: Crown Publishers, 2011, p.688.

[35]   Scott Shane and Vindu Goel, 'Fake Russian Facebook Accounts Bought $100,000 in Political Ads' and S. Shane, 'The Fake Americans Russia Created to Influence the Election' *New York Times*, 6 and 7 September 2017.
https://www.nytimes.com/2017/09/06/technology/facebook-russian-political-ads.html?mcubz=1 and https://www.nytimes.com/2017/09/07/us/politics/russia-facebook-twitter-election.html?smid=tw-nytimes&smtyp=cur

[36]   S. Charap and T. J. Colton, *Everyone Loses*, pp.99 and 179.

[37]   'Russia Still Has Many Friends in Europe', *The American Interest*, 6 July 2017.
https://www.the-american-interest.com/2017/07/06/russia-still-many-friends-europe/

suspicious Russian hacking that may have assisted the Brexit vote.[38] Growing evidence of Russian interference in the 2016 US elections and Brexit referendum have led the UK government to open its own investigation.

Russia's efforts to promote separatist movements in the West are in tension with its own determination to prevent Chechen independence and to integrate the post-Soviet region, but so far the contradiction has not appeared to be a problem. Russia has supported a range of separatist movements in the UK and elsewhere who have been invited to congresses in Moscow organised by the government-backed Anti-Globalisation movement in September 2015 and August 2016.[39] Russian social media and media outlets backed Scotland's independence in the September 2014 referendum. Since then former SNP (Scottish National Party) leader and First Minister of Scotland Alex Salmon has launched a chat show (with much controversy) on *Russia Today*.[40] Russian servers stepped in to support the illegal September 2017 Catalan referendum on independence after the Spanish authorities closed local servers counting the votes.[41]

Russia has supported anti-EU political forces in international organisations through manipulation of the media and the provision of financial 'loans'. In March 2015, *Rodina* (Motherland), a nationalist party loyal to Putin, organised a meeting of 150 representatives of European populist nationalist and neo-Nazi parties, such as the British National Party, at the 'International Russian Conservative Forum' who 'railed against Freemasons, LGBT people, and "Zionist puppet filth"'.[42] In the European Parliament, extreme right and left parties routinely support Russia's annexation of the Crimea, oppose Western sanctions and send 'observers' to elections in the Crimea and DNR and LNR.

France and Germany have been key targets of Russia's information and cyber warfare. Marine Le Pen received an $11.7 million 'loan' from Russia at

[38] https://www.opendemocracy.net/uk/brexitinc/adam-ramsay/how-did-arron-banks-afford-brexit
[39] Mansur Mirovalev, 'What's Behind Russian Support for World's Separatist Movements?' *NBC*, 23 July 2016. http://www.nbcnews.com/news/world/what-s-behind-russian-support-world-s-separatist-movements-n614196
[40] https://www.theguardian.com/media/2017/nov/17/be-ashamed-alex-salmond-courts-controversy-rt-russia-today
[41] https://www.politico.eu/article/russia-catalonia-referendum-fake-news-misinformation/ and https://elpais.com/elpais/2017/11/11/inenglish/1510395422_468026.html
[42] These political forces are analysed in https://www.buzzfeed.com/maxseddon/europes-far-right-comes-to-russia-in-search-of-shared-values?utm_term=.qj054zodr#.snOvGZRjb

the end of 2014. In France's 2017 elections, a senior French intelligence official was cited as saying, 'It is clear that Russia is sympathetic to Le Pen in the elections'.[43] The Front National (FN) never hid this and FN strategist Bertrand Dutheil de la Rochère speaking of Putin and Le Pen said, 'We share a similar vision of the world'.[44]

Russia's information and cyber warfare targeted the campaign of Emmanuel Macron because the other three leading candidates (populist nationalist Marine Le Pen, Gaullist François Fillon, and Trotskyist Jean-Luc Melenchon) had issued pro-Russian statements blaming Ukraine and the West for the crisis, called for the recognition of Russia's annexation of the Crimea and supported the dropping of sanctions. Russia undertook a range of 'active measures' against Macron during the election campaign that included the opening of 70,000 Facebook accounts and tens of thousands of 'bots' to spread anti-Macron content through social media. Thousands of emails were hacked from Macron election campaign servers and dumped on the Internet two days before the second round.[45]

Tactics

The continuity between Soviet KGB and Russian FSB (Federal Security Service)/GRU special operations was vividly seen in the first half of the 1990s, two decades before the 2014 crisis.[46] They rely on a wide array of Russian government agencies, sometimes working in close coordination,

---

[43]   Michael Stothard, 'Putin awaits return on Le Pen investment', *The Times*, 24 March 2017.

[44]   M. Stothard, 'Putin awaits return on Le Pen investment'.

[45]   Joseph Menn, 'Russia used Facebook to try and spy on Macron campaign', *Reuters*, 27 July 2017. http://www.reuters.com/article/us-cyber-france-facebook-spies-exclusive-idUSKBN1AC0EI?feedType=RSS&feedName=topNews&utm_source=twitter&utm_medium=Social and Charles Bremner, 'Russia 'used Facebook' to spy in French election', *The Times*, 28 July 2017.

[46]   Following the disintegration of the USSR, Yeltsin chose not to abolish the security services or reform them as independent Russia inherited all the central institutions of the Soviet state. The KGB was divided into parts separating foreign and domestic intelligence into the SVR and FSB respectively, and creating independent structures for government communications and Border Guards. The driving force was distrust in the KGB which had backed the August 1991 putsch and hope the president could control the new institutions better. See J. Michael Waller, 'The KGB Legacy in Russia', *Problems of Post-Communism*, vol.42, no.6 (November/December 1995), pp.3–10, M. Galeotti, *Heirs of the KGB: Russia's Intelligence and Security Services* (Alexandria, VA: Jane's Information Group, 1995); and Yevgenia Albats, *The State Within a State: The KGB and its Hold on Russia – Past, Present, and Future* (New York: Farrar, Straus & Giroux, 1999).

sometimes separately, with the Presidential Administration in central control.[47]

The series of Russian interventions beginning in the early 1990s facilitated tactical continuity from the Soviet era to the post-Soviet era. In Georgia, former Soviet intelligence officers provided support to Abkhaz separatists in Georgia who were on the verge of being defeated. A ceasefire was called, Russian proxies were re-armed by Russia and provided with Russian FSB and GRU advisers. The proxies then re-launched the war, winning territory and forcing Georgia to accept the freezing of separatist control. When Russian proxies prove too weak to win, Russian regular army forces have been used repeatedly, as in Moldova's Trans-Dniestr in 1992, Georgia's Abkhazia and South Ossetia in 1992 and 2008, and Ukraine's Donbas in 2014–2015.[48] In Azerbaijan, Russian proxies were not required because Armenian paramilitary forces supplied with Russian arms defeated the Azeri forces.

Russia's promotion of proxies in contested regions within its neighbours' borders has foreshadowed its tactics in Ukraine, bolstered by the Russian view that Ukraine itself is an artificial construct. Russian proposals to divide Ukrainian territory and for Russia to annex its Russian-speaking regions have been long-term staples of Russian nationalist dissident thought in the USSR and among contemporary nationalist circles in Russia.[49] Alexander Solzhenitsyn's 'Rebuilding Russia' published in 1990 and his appeal issued a year later during Ukraine's referendum on independence both called into question Ukrainian control over Eastern and Southern Ukraine.[50]

In Ukraine's 2004 presidential elections, the strategy of Russian political technologists was to promote 'directed chaos'[51] when a variety of Soviet-style active measures were undertaken by Russian political technologists against Yushchenko. This included registering 'technical' candidates supporting Yushchenko who were Russophobes and extremists, circulation of forged

[47]   Mark Galeotti, *Controlling Chaos: How Russia Manages Its Political War in Europe* (London: European Council on Foreign Relations, 1 September 2017). http://www.ecfr.eu/page/-/ECFR228_-_CONTROLLING_CHAOS1.pdf
[48]   Oscar Jonsson and Robert Seely, 'Russian Full-Spectrum Conflict: An Appraisal After Ukraine', *Journal of Slavic Military Studies*, vol.28, no.1 (March 2015), pp.11.
[49]   Russian analyst Vitaliy Tretyakov wrote during the Orange Revolution, 'The most favourite strategic scenario for Russia is undoubtedly a division of Ukraine, whereby its eastern Russian speaking part will join Russia'. *Ekspert*, 6 December 2004.
[50]   Robert Coalson, 'Is Putin 'Rebuilding Russia According to Solzhenitsyn's Design?' *RFERL*, 1 September 2014. https://www.rferl.org/a/russia-putin-solzhenitsyn-1990-essay/26561244.html
[51]   T. Kuzio, 'State-Led Violence in Ukraine's 2004 Elections and Orange Revolution', *Communist and Post-Communist Studies*, vol.43, no.4 (December 2010), pp.383–395.

leaflets, publication of critical books and pamphlets, propaganda accusing him of being a 'fascist' and an American stooge, conducting terrorist attacks which were blamed on his team, and having fake nationalists dressed in SS-style black uniforms parading up and down Kiev in support of his candidacy.[52] All of these were intended to bolster the notion that Yushchenko was an extreme anti-Russian nationalist, and even a neo-Nazi. In other words, many of the strategies pursued in 2014 were already being pursued a decade earlier in Ukraine at a time when Ukraine was not on the radar of NATO and EU enlargement. 'We've been told that we're safe and we shouldn't make Russia angry (by joining NATO)', Poroshenko told the Ukrainian parliament, 'But Russia attacked Ukraine – which was outside all blocs – and has killed more than 10,000 of our citizens'.[53] Indeed, if 'directed chaos' was Russia's aim in Ukraine in 2004, Galeotti believes that Russia's aim in the Donbas is 'uncontrolled, weaponised chaos'.[54]

In September 2006 and July 2009, four Russian diplomats were expelled from Georgia and two from Ukraine respectively for espionage. Russia's reaction in both cases far surpassed its typical response after the expulsion of Russian spies from Europe and North America. Following the expulsion from Ukraine, President Medvedev sent an open letter to Yushchenko with a long list of demands to change its domestic and foreign policies.[55] Medvedev's open letter not only laid out foreign policy demands, such as Ukraine not seeking NATO membership, but also demands over Ukrainian nationality policies; for example, ending the Ukrainian official view of the *Holodomor* as a famine directed against Ukraine that should be treated as a genocide. Russia's information war continues to disparage Ukraine's official views of the *Holodomor*.[56] Ukrainian and Russian nation-building policies have been diametrically opposite with the former condemning Stalinism and the latter promoting a cult of Stalin.[57]

[52] T. Kuzio, 'Russian Policy to Ukraine During Elections'.
[53] http://www.president.gov.ua/news/poslannya-prezidenta-ukrayini-do-verhovnoyi-radi-ukrayini-pr-43086
[54] M. Galeotti, *Hybrid War or Gibridnaya Voina? Getting Russia's non-linear military change right* (n.p.: Mayak Intelligence, 2016).
[55] M. H. Van Herpen, *Putin's Wars*, p.209 and T. Kuzio, 'Russia-Ukraine Diplomatic War', *Eurasia Daily Monitor*, vol.6, no.147 (31 July 2009) and 'Ukrainian-Russian Diplomatic War Intensifies', *Eurasia Daily Monitor*, vol.6, no.158 (17 August 2009). https://jamestown.org/program/russia-ukraine-diplomatic-war; https://jamestown.org/program/ukrainian-russian-diplomatic-war-intensifies/
[56] See the review of Russian media attacks against the November 2017 anniversary of the *Holodomor* undertaken by the EU's *Disinformation Review* (30 November 2017) at http://mailchi.mp/euvsdisinfo/dr89-880153?e=16eb39ac8e
[57] T. Kuzio, 'Stalinism and Russian and Ukrainian National Identities', *Communist and Post-Communist Studies*, vol.50, no.4 (December 2017), pp.289–302.

'Wet operations' by intelligence agents, Russian proxies and organised crime working on behalf of the Russian government have continued into the present day with the assassinations of Chechen leaders and FSB defectors abroad. Russian intelligence conducts assassinations and terrorist campaigns inside Ukraine[58] and assassinations and attempted coups d'état abroad.

There are close parallels between the attempted poisoning of Yushchenko in 2004 and that of former KGB agent Alexander Litvinenko in London in 2006, with the dioxin and radioactive polonium used in their poisoning produced in Russian laboratories inherited from the USSR and run since 1991 by the Russian secret services. The Ukrainian authorities accused Russia of being behind the poisoning of Yushchenko but it remains unclear exactly who carried out the attack and whether the intention was to murder or incapacitate him. An extensive British government enquiry into the assassination of Litvinenko blamed the murder on Russian authorities, and the investigation concluded that Putin 'probably' approved his murder.[59] Since 2014, Russian intelligence services have conducted a targeted series of assassinations in the West and Ukraine. US intelligence ties fourteen assassinations abroad (outside Ukraine) to Russia.[60]

In 2017, targeted assassinations increased inside Ukraine. In March, Russian exile Denis Voronenkov, who had fled Russia into exile in Ukraine and was a key witness in the criminal case against former President Yanukovych, was murdered in Central Kiev. In March and June, Colonel Maksym Shapoval, commander of Ukraine's military intelligence Special Forces, was murdered in a car bomb in Kiev. Colonel Oleksandr Kharaberyush, also Ukrainian military intelligence, was assassinated in Mariupol and Security Service of Ukraine (SBU) Colonel Yuriy Voznyy was killed and three others wounded in a car bomb in the village of Illinivka, near the anti-terrorist operation (ATO) front line. In June, Chechen exile Adam Osmayev, who had led a battalion fighting Russian forces in Chechnya, was seriously wounded in an attack by a Chechen organised crime leader from St. Petersburg posing as a journalist for *Le Monde*. In October 2017, a second attempt assassinated his wife Amina and wounded him while they were driving a car in Kiev. Four months later, Timur Mahauri, a Chechen with Georgian citizenship and a volunteer fighter in the Chechen battalion of Sheykh Mansur, was killed in a car bomb in Central Kiev.

---

[58]   T. Kuzio, 'Ukraine Reignites. Why Russia Should be Added to the State Sponsors of Terrorism List', *Foreign Affairs*, 25 January 2015. https://www.foreignaffairs.com/articles/russian-federation/2015-01-25/ukraine-reignites

[59]   http://webarchive.nationalarchives.gov.uk/20160613090324/

[60]   https://www.businessinsider.nl/russia-assassination-abroad-2017-6/?international=true&r=US

Hybrid warfare in the Donbas is an 'offshoot of political technology' where 'information warfare' plays a central role.[61] 'Lies are part of the coin of the intelligence operative, and facts are fungible'. Such operations come naturally to Putin who spent 'a great deal of time in his professional life bending the truth, manipulating facts, and playing with fictions'.[62] Propaganda espoused by Russia's media, spin-doctors and political technologists is often believed by Russian leaders and public because, 'In place of politics, there is performance art. Instead of debate, there is spectacle. In lieu of issues, there is *dramaturgia*. And in place of reality, there is fantasy'.[63] Peter Pomerantsev writes, 'For what is Russia's policy in Ukraine if not a war on reality?'. Russian trolls on the Internet, Twitter, Facebook and fake websites promote pre-determined narratives and crowd out legitimate debate.[64]

Central to hybrid warfare are 'denial, disinformation and deception'. Invasions are conducted with stealth, deniability and confusion with the blurring of the truth about the presence of forces, their objectives, combat readiness and numbers. This is not new as the USSR always denied it was behind terrorist groups active in Europe and used a false flag operation to blame Turkish nationalists for the assassination attempt on the Pope.

When asked about 'little green men' in the Crimea, Putin sardonically replied, 'There are many military uniforms. You can find them in any shop'. A month later he admitted the 'little green men' were Russian troops. Putin's repeated denials of Russian troops in the Donbas have been replicated in news stories broadcast and printed by Russian, Crimean and DNR-LNR media, as have reports of clearly staged Ukrainian 'terrorist attacks' that have been supp-osedly foiled.[65] 'Humanitarian convoys' transport much needed goods for the civilian population living in the DNR and LNR but they also conceal military equipment for Russian proxy forces. Fridan Vekouah, a Ukrainian undercover agent working in the depots receiving Russian humanitarian convoys was telephoned and told: 'Ok, you will get humanitarian goods, but it is not all humanitarian' and, 'You will take your part, and the military will take their part'.[66]

61   A. Wilson, *Ukraine Crisis*.

62   C. G. Gaddy and F. Hill, *Mr. Putin*., p.391.

63   B. Whitmore, 'Is the Kremlin Drinking Its Own Kool-Aid?' *Radio Free Europe-Radio Liberty*, 3 July 2015. http://www.rferl.org/content/podcast-is-the-kremlin-drinking-its-own-cool-aid/27108528.html

64   Peter N. Tanchak, 'The Invisible Front: Russia, Trolls, and the Information War against Ukraine' in Olga Bertelsen ed., *Revolution and War in Contemporary Ukraine: The Challenge of Change* (Stuttgart: Ibidem, 2016), p.261.

65   See two analyses by the Kharkiv Human Rights Protection Group: http://khpg.org/en/index.php?id=1500817118 and http://khpg.org/en/index.php?id=1502977651

66   Scott Peterson, 'In Sloviansk, rebels leave a trail of Russian expertise – and

In the Russian military encyclopaedia, *maskirovka* is defined as 'a complexity of measures, directed to mislead the enemy regarding the presence and disposition of forces, military objectives, combat readiness and operations'.[67] Pomerantsev describes this virtual Russian world as one where, 'Life is just one glittering masquerade, where every role and any position or belief is mutable' and where fiction and reality are interchangeable.[68] Russian forces which invaded Ukraine in early 2015 were transported from as far away as the Buryat autonomous republic on the Mongolian border. A wounded tank driver, Dorji Batomunkuev from the Russian fifth tank brigade in Ulan-Ude, sensed they were being sent to Ukraine to fight. He recounted to the independent newspaper *Novaya Gazeta*[69] how before invading Ukraine they had painted over their tanks' markings and plates and took off arm patches and chevrons, leaving their civilian passports, military service cards and mobile telephones at the military base and training range.

Oscar Jonsson and Robert Seely describe Russian hybrid warfare as 'full spectrum conflict' where military and non-military factors are placed under one command and directed to a single strategic goal. These factors include information warfare, Special Forces, intelligence services, economic threats, political influence and 'traditional subversion'.[70] Bret Perry divides Russian hybrid warfare in Ukraine into five stages[71]: (1) *Political subversion* – seizing of state buildings, sabotage, assassinations, terrorism, propaganda and insertion of agents. (2) *Proxy* – consolidation of continuous areas, arrival of volunteers, creation of 'self-defence militias', destruction of government infrastructures and beginning of recruitment of local proxies. (3) *Intervention* – threats and preparations for invasion, destruction of government security forces, provision of logistics and support, and disruption by cyber-attacks. (4) *Coercive Deterrence (Strategic Coercion)* – shows of force by the larger neighbour, nuclear posturing and hints and threats of escalation to pressure the country under attack to capitulate. The massing of Russian troops on the border has been used in Georgia and Eastern Ukraine as a deterrent against an attack on its proxy forces as they represent a security guarantee to Russian proxy-controlled regions. They are also meant to deter the West from

Ukrainian ruin', *Christian Science Monitor*, 30 July 2014.
[67]   Andy Jones, 'Proceedings of the 3rd European Conference on Information Warfare and Security', (ECIW, 1 January 2004) p.166. http://www.academia.edu/2612537/ Proceedings_of_the_3rd_European_Conference_on_Information_Warfare_and_ Security
[68]   Ben Macintyre, 'Putin's bodyguard of lies has taken over Russia', *The Times*, 13 February 2015.
[69]   Elena Kostyuchenko's article in Novaya Gazeta (13 March 2015) was translated by The Guardian, https://www.theguardian.com/world/2015/mar/25/russia-ukraine-soldier
[70]   O. Jonsson and R. Seely, 'Russian Full-Spectrum Conflict'.
[71]   B. Perry, 'Non-Linear Warfare in Ukraine'.

supplying arms to Ukraine by reinforcing the argument that whatever the West sends, Russia can send far more. (5) *Escalation* – from camouflaged hybrid warfare to intervention which is the least preferred outcome as it is easily detected. It is preferable to break the opponent's will to resist without launching a full attack.[72] Outright interventions and invasions, as in Georgia in August 2008 and Ukraine in August 2014 and February 2015, are called upon, 'When more subtle forms of violence – subversion and diplomacy – is insufficient for Russia, to reach its political goal...'[73] The goal of hybrid warfare is to achieve the goals without overt involvement.

Galeotti divides the implementers of hybrid warfare into four groups: (1) *'Polite people'*– *Spetsnaz* (including paratroopers and Marines and therefore closer to US Rangers than Delta Force) and conventional forces provide covert training, mobilise locals, and support and lead Russian proxies. Galeotti points out this tradition goes back as far as the role played by Stalin's secret police, the NKVD, in the Spanish Civil War. Similarly, in the 1940s, the NKVD had created fake UPA (Ukrainian Insurgent Army) units, which committed massacres of villagers and stole food to turn the local population against the Ukrainian nationalist underground. From the 1920s through to the 1980s, the Soviet secret police had created fake underground organisations in the USSR which gave their support to émigré groups in order to gather intelligence on the Russian and Ukrainian diasporas, infiltrate their political groups and lure their agents back to the homeland where they could be arrested and if possible turned. Myron Matviyeko, head of the émigré Organization of Ukrainian Nationalists' (OUN-B) Security Service (SB) was captured in 1951 after parachuting into Ukraine and rather than face execution agreed to work with the Soviet secret police, pretending he was running a nationalist underground through to 1960. In the Donbas, the GRU oversee Russian forces and Russian proxies while the FSB keep everybody in line. (2)*'Impolite people'* – self-defence militias and organised crime gangsters who were used in the early 1990s in the Trans-Dniestr, Abkhazia and South Ossetia are being used in a similar fashion in the Crimea and Donbas, two areas with traditionally high levels of criminality.[74] Local proxies, Galeotti points out, are used as political cover, as cannon fodder in skirmishes and battles, for disruption and as muscle. Russian proxies in the Donbas include a 'mix of regular Russian units, and ad hoc collection of nationalists and adventurers'.

---

[72]   Andras Racz, *Russia's Hybrid War in Ukraine: Breaking the Enemy's Ability to Resist, FIIA 43* (Helsinki: Finnish Institute of International Relations, 2015). http://www.fiia.fi/en/publication/514/russia_s_hybrid_war_in_ukraine/

[73]   O. Jonsson and R. Seely, 'Russian Full-Spectrum Conflict', p.11.

[74]   Chapter nine, 'The Rule of Law and Corruption' in T. Kuzio, *Ukraine. Democratization, Corruption, and the New Russian Imperialism* (Santa Barbara: Praeger, 2015), pp.327–38.

A major group drawn upon by the Russian authorities in the Donbas have been Cossacks who have a tradition going back to the Tsarist Empire of acting as the state's vigilantes. Another group have been Chechens supplied by the autonomous republic's pro-Russian President Ramzan Kadyrov.[75] (3) *Intelligence* – the GRU have been the most assiduous in developing contacts with the international criminal network Galeotti describes as the *Crimintern*, a play on the *Comintern*, the Communist International active in 1919–1943.[76] In September 2014, Estonian security service officer Eston Kohver, who was investigating cigarette smuggling, was kidnapped by Russian intelligence agents in a direct snub to the US, coming only two days after President Obama's visit to that country. The FSB permitted the smuggling to take place in return for the criminals being ready to provide favours in return. Cigarette smuggling is just one of many avenues weaponised by Russia.[77] (4) *Civilians* – information warriors and hackers, pro-Putin oligarchs, and domestic and international bankers infiltrate targets in various ways. Billions of dollars of capital have been exported to Western Europe, Cyprus and offshore tax havens earning the UK's capital city the nickname 'Londongrad'. This huge amount of capital purchases real estate, buys places in private schools for the children of oligarchs and corrupt state officials, and hires legions of investment bankers, lawyers, consultants and accountants. Former KGB officer Alexander Lebedev is the owner of the UK's *The Independent*, *Independent on Sunday* and *London Evening Standard* newspapers. The goal is to gain entry and begin shaping the interests and views of the target country's elite.

As events played out in the Donbas, there were clear stages to the escalation of combat. From 1 March to 24 May 2014, agitation and propaganda (i.e. information warfare) was followed by the seizure of state institutions in what Philip A. Karber describes as the transition from protests to terrorism.[78] This is an important juncture as the crisis could not have escalated from protests into an armed insurgency without external backing from Russian intelligence and

---

[75] M. Galeotti, *Hybrid War or Gibridnaya Voina*, pp.59–60.

[76] M. Galeotti, *Crimintern: How the Kremlin uses Russia's criminal network in Europe* (London: European Council on Foreign Relations, 18 April 2017). http://www.ecfr.eu/publications/summary/crimintern_how_the_kremlin_uses_russias_criminal_networks_in_europe

[77] Holger Roonemaa, 'These Cigarette Smugglers Are on The Frontlines Of Russia's Spy Wars', *Buzzfeed*, 13 September 2017. https://www.buzzfeed.com/holgerroonemaa/these-cigarette-smugglers-are-on-the- frontlines-of-russias?utm_term=.cqzXleGXD#.rtDLAqnLM

[78] Philip A. Karber, 'Russia's Hybrid War Campaign: Implications for Ukraine and Beyond', (Washington DC: The Potomac Foundation and Center for Strategic and International Studies, 10 March 2015). http://www.thepotomacfoundation.org/russias-hybrid-war-campaign-implications-for-ukraine-and-beyond/

Special Forces. Gerard Toal writes that the transition from anti-Maidan protests to armed revolt was only made possible by Russian 'armed provocations' in collaboration with oligarchs, veterans, pro-Russian movements and organised crime.[79] Mass anti-Ukrainian propaganda on Russian TV and social media helped transform public protests in the Donbas against the ousting of Yanukovych into an armed rebellion whose militias were then strengthened by Russian Special Forces. Nationalist volunteers were recruited by Russian intelligence services and by Russian TV propaganda. Russian intelligence officers had also been financing and training anti-Maidan ('anti-fascist') vigilantes in Kharkiv and elsewhere in Eastern Ukraine. Many of these vigilantes moved to join Russian proxies in the Donbas after the failed attempt to create a Kharkiv People's Republic.[80]

Between 25 May and 30 June 2014, the crisis escalated into an armed insurgency. In July, artillery in Russia pounded Ukraine and the following month, with its proxy forces on the verge of defeat, Russian forces invaded Ukraine. What made Ukraine different from the frozen conflicts in Moldova and Georgia was that Kiev could have defeated Russian proxy forces.[81] Since the signing of the Minsk 1 accords in September 2014, Russia is conducting a full-blown proxy war against Ukraine. Russia's 'Chechenisation' of its proxy war required the building of a 'large and better equipped fighting force than many of the countries represented around this table'.[82] In January 2015, the US Mission to the OSCE stated:

> The separatist movement at this point is a de facto extension of the Russian military and an instrument of Russian national power. The Russian military has put in place a robust command structure in Eastern Ukraine, ranging from Russian General Staff officers overseeing operations down to junior officers. Russian personnel conduct communications, intelligence gathering, direct military operations, and help correct artillery fire. Separatist fighters have publicly acknowledged that they are operating under instructions from Moscow.[83]

Russia's 'full spectrum conflict' strategy in the Donbas of funding and

---

[79] G. Toal, *Near Abroad*, p.239.
[80] 'The Battle for Ukraine', *PBS*, 27 May 2014. http://www.pbs.org/wgbh/frontline/film/battle-for-ukraine_ and http://www.pbs.org/wgbh/frontline/film/battle-for-ukraine/transcript/
[81] A. Rácz & A. Moshes, 'Not Another Transnistria: How sustainable is separatism in Eastern Ukraine?' (Helsinki: *Finnish Institute of International Affairs*, 1 December 2014).
[82] https://osce.usmission.gov/feb_26_15_ukraine/
[83] A. Rácz & A. Moshes, *Not Another Transnistria*.

supplying proxy forces is little different to what Moscow had earlier pursued in Moldova and Georgia 'when armed groups were manipulated, armed, and if need be, led by agencies of the Russian state until they achieved their ends'.[84] The end state is partition with the breakaway region controlled by Russia, the outcome frozen in time and the country unable to pursue membership in NATO and the EU.[85] In Moldova and Georgia, Russia's proxy forces defeated the country's armed forces leading to a conflict frozen by Russian 'peacekeepers'. With neither side defeated in the Donbas and the war on-going, it cannot be defined as a frozen conflict. US special envoy to the Ukraine peace talks Kurt Volker said, 'This is not a frozen conflict, this is a hot war…'.[86] Galeotti points out that it is, 'Russian artillery and armour, albeit largely based over the border, that represents the real force keeping the Donbas contested, not mercenaries and militias'.[87]

Russia has returned to the Soviet practice of fomenting terrorism and national liberation struggles abroad. The Russian Imperial Movement, with links to Igor Girkin (aka 'Strelkov') and paramilitaries fighting for Russian proxies in the Donbas,[88] is training neo-Nazi groups from Central and Western Europe.[89] Russia uses its Embassy in the Czech capital of Prague as a centre for information warfare and espionage throughout Central Europe.[90] In the Balkans, Russia has sought to stop Serbia from joining the EU. Russia attempted to halt Montenegro from joining NATO through a coup attempt and assassination plot against Montenegrin Prime Minister Milo Djukanovic. Russia's GRU provided US dollars, sophisticated encrypted mobile telephones, a large arsenal of weapons, and training.[91] The plot brought together nationalist Serbs and Russian Cossacks who had fought for Russian proxies in the Donbas. Cossack General Viktor Zaplatin, a Russian citizen, told a rally in Montenegro, 'The Orthodox world is one world. Here we see Serbs, Montenegrins, Russians, and Belarusians'. Aleksandr Borodai, former editor

---

84   O. Jonsson and R. Seely, 'Russian Full-Spectrum Conflict'.

85   A. Racz, *Russia's Hybrid War in Ukraine*.

86   http://www.reuters.com/article/us-ukraine-crisis-volker-idUSKBN1A80M4?il=0

87   M. Galeotti, *Hybrid War or Gibridnaya Voina?*

88   'Russia's Imperialist Warriors', *BBC*, 1 December 2015. https://www.youtube.com/watch?v=rb4rclMm27M

89   Josephine Huetlin, 'Russian Extremists Are Training Right-Wing Terrorists from Western Europe', *The Daily Beast*, 2 August 2017. http://www.thedailybeast.com/russian-extremists-are-training-right-wing-terrorists-from-western-europe and M. Galeotti, 'Moscow's mercenaries reveal the privatisation of Russian geopolitics', *Open Democracy*, 29 August 2017. 'https://www.opendemocracy.net/od-russia/mark-galeotti/chvk-wagner-and-privatisation-of-russian-geopolitics

90   https://www.radiosvoboda.org/a/28697222.html

91   Ben Farmer, 'Russian Military Intelligence Officers Allegedly Spent Months Overseeing a Plot to Kill Montenegro's Prime Minister', *The Daily Telegraph*, 20 July 2017.

of Russian nationalist newspaper *Zavtra* and 'Prime Minister' of the DNR in 2014, sent greetings. Twenty Serbs and Russians were arrested by Montenegro which issued an international warrant for a further two Russians and three Serbs. One of the Serbs sought by Montenegro, Nemanja Ristic, was photographed next to Russian Minister of Foreign Affairs Sergei Lavrov during his 12 December 2016 visit to Belgrade. Serbia arrested Ristic and another Serbian nationalist Predrag Bogicevic for their involvement in the Russian-backed coup. Montenegro accused GRU officers at large Eduard Shishmakov and Vladimir Popov of being the main instigators of the failed coup d'état.[92]

When social media was born it was portrayed as the means by which ordinary citizens could hold their corrupt and unaccountable leaders to account. Ukraine's 2004 Orange Revolution was billed as the first 'Internet revolution'. Twitter, Facebook and other forms of social media became central to mass protests in Iran, the 'Arab Spring', Russian mass protests and the Euro-maidan Revolution. Authoritarian regimes fought back by imposing controls on the Internet and turning social media around to work towards achieving their strategic objectives by using trolls and unleashing bots to flood social media with false and biased information. LinkedIn, a networking website, has become a recruiting ground and source of intelligence for Russia's hybrid war.[93] Social media that were used to undermine states a decade ago are today being used by states to undermine their critics. In Russia, the long Soviet tradition of 'agitation and propaganda' is being empowered by social media. Simon Jenkins writes, 'The 1990s theses that the Internet would turn the world into one vast lovable, liberal community has never looked less likely than today'.[94]

One element of Russia's information warfare has been the extensive publishing and disseminating of *dezinformatsiya*. The EU's External Action Service began publishing a weekly *Disinformation Review* in 2016 to keep abreast of the large volume of disinformation originating in Russia.[95] *Russia Today*, or RT, Russia's flagship propaganda outlet was originally created as

---

[92]   https://www.rferl.org/a/montenegro-coup-plot-trial-resumes-russia-nato-djukanovic-mandic-knezevic/28719631.html
[93]   Jeff Stein, 'How Russia is Using Linkedin as a Tool of War Against Its US Enemies', *Newsweek*, 3 August 2017. http://www.newsweek.com/russia-putin-bots-linkedin-facebook-trump-clinton-kremlin-critics-poison-war-645696
[94]   https://www.theguardian.com/commentisfree/2017/aug/16/donald-trump-supporters-liberals-sneer?utm_source=esp&utm_medium=Email&utm_campaign=GU+Today+main+NEW+H+categories&utm_term=239675&subid=13203085&CMP=EMCNEWEML6619I2
[95]   https://eeas.europa.eu/headquarters/headquarters-homepage_en/9443/Disinformation%20Review

the Kremlin's soft power tool to promote a positive image of Russia abroad but evolved into an instrument to counter international channels, such as CNN and the BBC. An example is that of a highly realistic counterfeit article apparently from *The Guardian* featuring provocative comments attributed to the head of Britain's MI6 intelligence service about using colour revolutions against Russia. The article was reprinted in the Russian media and elsewhere in the world.[96]

Russia has manipulated European and US public opinion by giving its backing to political forces, civic groups and media outlets that sow discord by promoting right-wing causes. In 2016, the Russian media widely disseminated a false story that a 13-year-old Russian-German girl had been kidnapped and raped by Muslim migrants, triggering protests in Germany. A high-level diplomatic spat broke out between German officials and Russian Minister of Foreign Affairs Lavrov, who publicly fanned the false story. Russia's aim was apparently to increase the popularity of the anti-EU extreme right Alternative for Germany.

As the EU's weekly *Disinformation Review* emphasises, some of Russia's most notorious information war has been directed at Ukraine:

> Ukraine is a frequently occurring target in pro-Kremlin disinformation. Some of the more astonishing allegations were even brought to us by the TV channel owned by Russia's Ministry of Defence. Through the years we have seen some truly outrageous claims about Ukraine, from the ludicrous – for example the claim that the Ukrainian army have zombies fighting within their ranks – to the utterly offensive – most infamously the false claim that Ukrainian forces crucified a three year old boy in Eastern Ukraine.

Similarly, Russia presented the downing of Malaysian Airlines flight 17 as having been carried out by Ukrainian forces attempting to assassinate Putin.

In July 2017, the *Disinformation Review* wrote about a bizarre claim:

> We saw the claim that a group of Ukrainian servicemen of the 57th mechanised infantry brigade celebrated a pagan ritual

---

[96]   Craig Silverman and Jane Lytvynenko, 'How A Hoax Made to Look Like a Guardian Article Made Its Way To Russian Media', *Buzzfeed*, 15 August 2017. https://www.buzzfeed.com/craigsilverman/how-a-hoax-made-to-look-like-a-guardian-article-made-its?utm_term=.peqg93pg7#.hoWj6BgjK

and sacrificed a local resident to a Slavic god. The disinformation was repeated in several outlets, and in one it was illustrated by a photo of a soldier eating a hand. The photo, which has been used in the past by pro-Kremlin disinformation articles, in fact originates from the Russian 2008 science-fiction movie: 'We're from the Future'.[97]

Furthermore, much of the *dezinformatsiya* directed against Ukraine tallies with traditional Soviet ideological tirades about 'Nazi collaborators' and Russian nationalist thought about Ukraine as an 'artificial state': The *Disinformation Review* reported in September 2017:

> We have seen several of the usual narratives: 'Ukraine is not a state', 'Ukraine is abandoned by Europe', and 'There is no Ukrainian independent state'. But, the most repeated piece of disinformation was the old favourite linking Nazis and Ukraine. So, the country was accused of being a neo-Nazi mons- ter created by the West, as well as being occupied by Nazis who follow in the footsteps of Joseph Goebbels. There was no specific mention of the actual occupation of parts of Ukraine. Ukraine was also presented as a victim of the 'Evil West' in some outlets – another recurring disinformation theme.[98]

Soviet-style tirades against Ukrainian nationalism did not begin in 2013–2014 but were revived during Ukraine's 2004 elections in response to the new threat from Yushchenko and Our Ukraine which was dubbed as '*Nashism*' (from Yushchenko's party *Nasha Ukrayina* [Our Ukraine] – a term that resembled 'Nazism'). Similarly, just prior to the invasion of Georgia in 2008, 50 journalists from Russia's leading television channels and newspapers arrived in Tskhinvali, South Ossetia.[99] After the conflict had ended, Russia accused Georgia of committing 'genocide' against South Ossetia, an accusation similar to the many Russia has made against Ukraine since 2014.

Information warfare was a central component of Russian activity during the Euromaidan and throughout the initiation of conflict in 2014 when Russian information warfare produced what Stephen Hutchings and Vera Tolz describe as a 'frenzy of anti-Western Cold War rhetoric'.[100] 'Information

---

[97] https://euvsdisinfo.eu/

[98] http://mailchi.mp/euvsdisinfo/dr78-879777?e=16eb39ac8e

[99] Chapter 15 'The War with Georgia, Part III: The Propaganda War' in M. H. Van Herpen, *Putin's Wars*, pp.227–238.

[100] Stephen Hutchings and Vera Tolz, *Nation, Ethnicity and Race on Russian*

troops' were used to prepare public opinion for the military action that followed. Russian propaganda and information warfare mobilised anti-Ukrainian hysteria in the Donbas and Crimea to fever pitch levels during the Euromaidan and spring 2014. During the height of the crisis, a hacked mobile phone conversation between US Ambassador to Ukraine Geoffrey Pyatt and US Assistant Secretary of State Victoria Nuland was released. Nuland was captured uttering a vulgarity about the EU, complicating US-EU collaboration.

The image presented by Russia's information warfare of Ukraine in spring 2014 is of a mortal threat to Russians and Russian speakers. In Putin's 18 March 2014 address welcoming the Crimea as part of Russia he said the Euromaidan revolutionaries resorted 'to terror, murder and riots. Nationalists, neo-Nazis, Russophobes and anti-Semites executed this coup. They continue to set the tone in Ukraine to this day'.[101] This was the opposite to that reported by the Council of Europe following a visit to Ukraine in the same month when they found no change in the status of minority rights, no growth in anti-Semitism or threats to Russians and the Russian language in Western Ukraine. The gravest concern was the plight of Crimean Tatars.[102]

While Russia has been exploiting social media itself, it has been strengthening control of the Internet in Russia, a practice with deep roots in the Soviet regime. Luke Harding points out how the FSB inherited KGB-style paranoia, xenophobia and conspiratorial worldview and is obsessed with searching for domestic and foreign enemies.[103] The banning of virtual private network (VPN) proxies, Andrei Soldatov writes, 'is time-honoured and can be traced back to Soviet times, before the Internet came to Russia. When the Soviet Union was busy preparing to host the Olympic Games in 1980, it was required to provide automatic international phone connections without an operator – something that was unheard of in the Soviet Union'.[104] Soldatov continues:

> The KGB resisted fiercely. To appease them, the Soviet Ministry of Communications suggested that callers dial not only the number they wanted to call, but also their own, so that no one would go unidentified. This is exactly the same

---

Television. Mediating post-Soviet difference (London and New York: Routledge, 2015), p.258.

[101] http://en.kremlin.ru/events/president/news/20603

[102] Ad hoc Report on the situation of national minorities in Ukraine adopted on 1 April 2014, Council of Europe. https://rm.coe.int/16800c5d6f

[103] L. Harding, 'Spies, sleepers and hitmen'.

[104] Andrei Soldatov, 'The Kremlin's VPN Ban Has KGB Roots', *Moscow Times*, 1 August 2017. https://themoscowtimes.com/articles/ban-on-vpn-has-kgb-roots-58546?utm_source=push&utm_campaign=010817

proposal the Russian government is offering Internet users today. Back then, the KGB got what it wanted. Today, it seems that for the people on Lubyanka Square nothing has changed.

Russia's cyber warfare did not begin in 2014. Seven years earlier Russia had initiated a cyber and information warfare attack on Estonia, ostensibly in retaliation for Estonia's decision to relocate a Soviet memorial to World War II. The cyber-attack affected Estonia's functions for a month, and the information campaign prompted riots against the relocation of the memorial. A year after the attacks, NATO opened a Cooperative Cyber Defence Centre in Tallinn.

Coping with cyber warfare and hacking is a difficult undertaking when countries are as closely intertwined as were Ukraine and Russia until 2014. For a number of years after the 2014 crisis, Ukrainian officials continued to use Russian email addresses (such as .ru), Russian mail servers, and Russian search engines, such as Yandex. Many Ukrainians used VKontakte, a Russian analogue to Facebook which is controlled by the Kremlin, since 2014.[105] As a NATO report asked, why did the Russians need to hack Ukrainian accounts when they had access to their emails?[106] In May 2017, a Ukrainian presidential decree banned VKonakte, Yandex and Russian email servers.[107]

Cybersecurity experts 'believe Russia is using' Ukraine 'as a cyberwar testing ground – a laboratory for perfecting new forms of global online combat'. Since 2014, the country has been subject to 'a digital blitzkrieg' and 'a sustained cyber assault unlike any the world has ever seen'.[108] 'A hacker army has systematically undermined practically every sector of Ukraine: media, finance, transportation, military, politics, energy', Andy Greenberg writes. 'Wave after wave of intrusions have deleted data, destroyed computers, and in some cases paralyzed organizations' most basic functions'. Cyber-attacks cut off electricity to nearly a quarter of a million Ukrainians just before Christmas in 2015, another attack hit Ukraine's power grid in December 2016 and a third was unleashed in June 2017.

---

[105] Nickolay Kononov, 'The Kremlin's Social Media Takeover', *New York Times*, 10 March 2014. https://www.nytimes.com/2014/03/11/opinion/the-kremlins-social-media-takeover.html

[106] Keir Giles, *Handbook of Russian Information Warfare* (Rome: NATO Defence College, November 2016). https://krypt3ia.files.wordpress.com/2016/12/fm_9.pdf

[107] http://www.president.gov.ua/documents/1332017-21850

[108] Andy Greenberg, 'How an Entire Nation Became Russia's Test Lab for Cyberwar', *Wired*, 20 June 2017. https://www.wired.com/story/russian-hackers-attack-ukraine/

Results

Russia's information warfare has an audience in regions such as Latin America and among supporters of the extreme right and left in Europe. In France, Greece and elsewhere in Europe, extreme left anti-Americanism has a long pedigree. Socialist political leaders, such as UK Labour leader Jeremy Corbyn, and extreme right politicians in Europe have been criticised for agreeing to appear on *Russia Today*.[109] UK Labour and Conservative MPs have been also criticised for accepting large fees in exchange for agreeing to appear on *Russia Today*.[110] As a repercussion from the ongoing US investigation into Russia's interference in the 2016 US presidential elections, *Russia Today* and *Sputnik* news agency were ordered to register under FARA (Foreign Agents Registration Act) which is administered by the US Department of Justice.[111] Registering with FARA is usually only a requirement for lobbyists and consultants working on behalf of foreign governments. Registration under FARA automatically led to the removal of *Russia Today* and *Sputnik's* official accreditation to attend press conferences and undertake media activities in the US Congress. To what degree Russian information warfare can be credited for the growth of pro-Putin sentiments is difficult to say as they could be a product of many factors, such as the domestic populist backlash against the liberal establishment. Anti-Americanism and support for Putin have also grown among the extreme right in Europe.

In the US, it is not clear whether Russian information operations or other factors are the cause of a notable flip in attitudes toward Russia and Putin. Fully a third of Republican voters expressed confidence in Putin in 2017, up from 17% in 2015, compared to only 13% of Democratic voters. While nearly two-thirds of Democratic voters see Russia as a threat to national security only 46% of Republican voters do.[112] This reverses a long historical trend in which Republicans have been more hawkish on Russia.

Another success was the use of disinformation to swing a close referendum vote in the Netherlands on approval of the EU-Ukraine Association Agreement.[113] The Association Agreement was temporarily blocked, and the

---

[109]   https://www.opendemocracy.net/od-russia/maxim-edwards-thomas-rowley/corbyn-and-russia-hysteria-and-hindsight
[110]   https://www.thetimes.co.uk/article/mps-are-regular-guests-on-putin-s-pet-tv-channel-rt-kremlin-corbyn-barry-gardiner-richard-burgon-john-mcdonnell-peter-dowd-chris-williamson-sam-delaney-mike-freer-david-davies-nigel-evans-crispin-blunt-david-amess-daniel-kawczynski-philip-davies-sg0dnnnpk
[111]   https://www.fara.gov/
[112]   http://www.npr.org/2017/07/06/535626356/on-russia-republican-and-democratic-lenses-have-a-very-different-tint
[113]   Andrew Higgins, 'Fake News, Fake Ukrainians: How a Group of Russians Tilted a

price raised to include the demand that the EU not offer Ukraine a membership perspective.[114]

Not all of Russia's information war has succeeded. Numerous theories about the shooting down of MH17, the most colourful of which was that the flight was full of shop floor dummies rather than real people, failed to change Western public opinion about who shot down the airliner.

Russia's English-language television station RT has been an increasingly visible tool of Russian information efforts. RT, social media and the proliferation of alternative news web sites has pursued influence for Russia in four areas: (1) fanning anti-Americanism and hostility to pro-Western popular protests, such as the Euromaidan (films depicting the Euromaidan as a Western anti-Russian conspiracy have been made in France and by US film director Oliver Stone);   (2) promoting Islamophobia and hostility toward immigrants, coupled with support for anti-EU populist nationalism; (3) planting of false news stories which are laundered into a more acceptable 'clean' variant by being re-tweeted and 'liked' by large numbers of people – eventually the stories are believed as the truth or become seen as credible alternative perspectives; (4) collection of *kompromat* which is integrated with Russia's other information and cyber warfare policies. RT has sought to build its Western audience by luring Western journalists and public figures to work at its English-language television channel. CNN senior anchor Larry King was paid $250,000 to interview Ukrainian Prime Minister Nikolai Azarov, who is in exile in Moscow and wanted by Interpol, after which he received his own show on Russia Today. Former UKIP (United Kingdom Independence Party) leader Nigel Farage was offered his own show on RT.

Whitmore points out that 'Agitprop has its limits. Active measures have a downside, and often result in blowback'.[115] Some of Russia's operations have been successful but others have been massive failures. The adoption of new tougher US sanctions in summer 2017 was a backlash against Russia's interference in the US 2016 elections. France and Germany, once broadly supportive of Russian interests in Europe, are now opposing Russia's position on Ukraine and supporting sanctions. At a joint press conference during Putin's visit to France, Macron attacked Russia's actions directly: 'When news outlets spread despicable lies', he said, 'they are no longer journalists. They

Dutch Vote', *New York Times*, 16 February 2017. https://www.nytimes.com/2017/02/16/world/europe/russia-ukraine-fake-news-dutch-vote.html

[114]   http://www.politico.eu/article/dutch-block-aspirational-communique-at-eu-ukraine-summit/

[115]   B. Whitmore, 'The Daily Vertical: The Limits of Dark Power', *RFERL*, 27 July 2017. https://www.rferl.org/a/daily-vertical-limits-dark-power/28642894.html

are organs of influence'. '*Russia Today* and *Sputnik* did not behave as media organisations and journalists, but as agencies of influence and propaganda, lying propaganda – no more, no less'.[116] This was the first occasion a Western leader had been so blunt about Russia's information and cyber warfare against Western democracies.

There are two potential difficulties with the pursuit of hybrid warfare. The first is that it needs certain conditions to successfully work. In the Crimea, Russian hybrid warfare found perfect conditions which were far less prevalent in Eastern-Southern Ukraine. Russian policies have increased Putin's popularity at home[117] but at the same time have severely damaged Putin's and Russia's reputation around the world where few people trust Putin and Russian leaders.[118] Critical views of Putin and Russia are especially prominent in the US and Europe.[119] RT has been unable to capture large audiences in key Western states such as Britain, Germany, the US and Canada. In the UK, RT has 0.04% of viewers, according to the Broadcast Audience Research Board.

The second problem is a backlash from the country that is the object of Russia's hybrid warfare. Russia's unprecedented intervention in the 2016 US presidential elections mobilised support in both houses of Congress for far tougher sanctions against Russia, numerous ongoing investigations of President Trump's ties to Russia and suggestions the US may be considering sending military equipment to Ukraine. In Ukraine, Russia's annexation of the Crimea and military aggression have permanently severed the bonds of what many in Eastern Ukraine had viewed as that of Russian and Ukrainian 'brotherly peoples'. Peacefully integrating Ukraine with Russia is less likely now than ever before.

The different outcomes of Russian hybrid warfare in the Crimea and the Donbas shows how local conditions matter. In the Crimea, there was a near complete Russian penetration of the security forces that were locally recruited, a large Black Sea Fleet base and a receptive Russian-speaking population with a history of supporting separatism in the 1990s. Additionally the peninsula was self-enclosed and connected to the Ukrainian mainland

---

[116] https://www.vox.com/world/2017/5/30/15712296/macron-putin-standing-up-to-russia-rt-propaganda

[117] http://www.pewglobal.org/2017/06/20/russians-remain-confident-in-putins-global-leadership/

[118] http://www.pewglobal.org/2015/08/05/russia-putin-held-in-low-regard-around-the-world/ See Maria Snegovaya, 'Kremlin Is Losing the Information War', *Moscow Times*, 17 September 2017. https://themoscowtimes.com/articles/kremlin-is-losing-the-information-war-op-ed-49642

[119] http://www.pewglobal.org/2017/08/16/publics-worldwide-unfavorable-toward-putin-russia

only by a thin strip of land and there was popular domestic support in Russia itself for annexation from pro-Putin *and* opposition sectors of society. None of these six factors existed in the Donbas and South-East Ukraine. Kent believes that Kiev looked upon the Crimea as 'a region apart' and the 'Cinderella of the Ukrainian state'.[120] Added to this important difference with Eastern Ukraine is that the country's military *and* Ukrainian nationalists (in the latter case, contrary to Russian propaganda) were not willing to fight for the Crimea.[121]

Rather than saying that 'Ukraine constituted a near-ideal target'[122] for Russian hybrid warfare, it would be more accurate to say that the Crimea was the near-ideal target. In Eastern-Southern Ukraine, Russia appears to have achieved only limited success, failing to spur a more decisive rebellion in Donbas or a broader rebellion into *Novorossiya*. Russia's need to maintain a permanent military commitment to the Donbas will be a continuous drain on resources and a continuous sore spot in its relations with the West.

Moreover, while the effect should not be exaggerated, the invasion has strengthened the Ukrainian state and civil society. Ukrainians volunteered in a wide range of areas to support the war effort and to fight Russia on the battlefield, in the information sphere and collecting for and delivering supplies to Ukrainian forces. StopFake,[123] established by academics and students at Kiev Mohyla Academy, began exposing Russian disinformation three years before the EU set up its own unit. By the 2016 US elections, StopFake had gone from 'provincial do-gooders to international media stars' offering advice to European countries.[124] StopFake says it warned Facebook in 2015 – a year ahead of the US elections – about Russian fake news and its misuse of this social media platform.[125] Other civil society and semi-official groups have also emerged, such as *Kibersotnia* ([Cyber Company] a group of Ukrainian hackers), Information Resistance (led by former military and intelligence officers), Euromaidan Press and the Ukraine Crisis Media Centre.[126] Many

---

[120] N. Kent, *Crimea*, p.150.

[121] T. Kuzio, 'Farewell, Crimea. Why Ukrainians Don't Mind Losing the Territory to Russia', *Foreign Affairs*, 13 March 2014. https://www.foreignaffairs.com/articles/russia-fsu/2014-03-13/farewell-crimea

[122] A. Racz, *Russia's Hybrid War in Ukraine*, p.88.

[123] https://www.stopfake.org/en/news/

[124] Vijai Maheshwari, 'Ukraine's fight against Fake news goes global', *Politico.eu*, 12 March 2017. http://www.politico.eu/article/on-the-fake-news-frontline/. See also Andrew E. Kramer, 'To Battle Fake News, Ukrainian Show Features Nothing but Lies', *New York Times*, 26 February 2017. https://www.nytimes.com/2017/02/26/world/europe/ukraine-kiev-fake-news.html

[125] https://www.ft.com/content/c63d76d4-bd1e-11e7-b8a3-38a6e068f464

[126] Olena Goncharova and Veronika Melkozerova, 'War for Minds', *Kyiv Post*, 18

other initiatives run by civil society, national governments and international organisations (EU, NATO) have emerged.[127]

The Ukrainian authorities have also undertaken a wide range of policies to reduce ties with Russia. Even as sanctions were being imposed in 2014–2017, polls showed that Ukrainians had become more sceptical towards Russian media sources. Sanctions against Russian media outlets, journalists, artists, books, films, social media and numerous Russian television channels have reduced Moscow's ability to pursue information warfare against Ukraine, while also raising concerns about freedom of speech. A February 2017 presidential decree on a new Information Security Doctrine for Ukraine explained why these steps were undertaken:

> Russia is using the newest information technology for influencing people's minds in Ukraine, aiming to inflame national and religious tensions, spread propaganda, advocating aggressive war, to violently change the constitutional order or violate the sovereignty and territorial integrity of the Ukrainian state.

The most contentious areas where Russia's actions have led to Ukraine pushing back has been in the sphere of national identity. As chapter three and chapter four show, Ukraine's relations with Russia will no longer be 'fraternal' and 'brotherly' – at the very least while Putin is in power. An important area for Ukrainian national identity has been the establishment of a distinct Ukrainian mythology of World War II to replace the Soviet/Russian version. While the Russian/Soviet version refers to the Great Patriotic War beginning with Germany's invasion of Russia in 1941, Ukraine's version focuses on World War II, beginning with the Nazi and Soviet invasion of Poland/Eastern Ukraine in 1939, which fits with the broader European narrative of the war. Since 2015, Ukraine has celebrated the end of the war on the 8th of May – as in Europe, rather than on the 9th of May – as in Russia. This symbolically refutes Soviet history, replaces the notion of a common wartime experience with Russia to that of a distinct Ukrainian experience and links Ukraine's suffering in World War II to the current war in Eastern Ukraine. Ukrainian TV advertisements have brought together veterans from both wars with fathers sending their sons off to fight the latest invader of Ukraine. The older generation were among the six million Ukrainians in the ranks of the Soviet army who had fought the Nazis and the younger generation are continuing

---

August 2017. https://www.kyivpost.com/ukraine-politics/war-for-minds.html
[127] 'Initiatives to counter disinformation spring up in the Russian language', *EU Disinformation Review*, 5 September 2017. https://euvsdisinfo.eu/initiatives-to-counter-disinformation-spring-up-in-the-russian-language/

the fight in the ranks of Ukraine's army and National Guard – this time against Russia. The core message is, 'We won then and we will win now'.[128] Four controversial de-communisation laws adopted in 2015 point to a separation between a de-communising Ukraine and a Russia that is re-Sovietising and promoting a cult of Stalin.

Conclusion

In contrast to the view that Russia's use of hybrid warfare in Ukraine was novel, this chapter has sought to show that Russia's behaviour in 2014 and since in Ukraine had deep roots in the practices both of the Soviet Union and in Russia before 2014. During the Cold War, *dezinformatsiya*, and *maskirovka* were constantly employed to undermine the regime's challengers, especially national independence movements such as those in Ukraine and the Baltic States. While employed more sporadically, imprisonment and assassination of Ukrainian opponents of Soviet rule was also part of the Soviet repertoire, even after the death of Stalin in 1953. In addition to undermining internal threats to Soviet rule, these tactics were aimed westward, providing finance and disinformation to support the groups that most undermined Western unity.

When the Soviet Union disintegrated in 1991, the Russian government took over its institutions, including the KGB and GRU, essentially intact. And while the KGB was renamed and reorganised into the Federal Security Service (FSB) and Foreign Intelligence Service (SVR), it was not fundamentally reformed. The continuity we see should therefore not be surprising. This is especially true since Russia under Putin is increasingly run by people whose roots were in the Soviet security apparatus.

The tactics we see in Ukraine since 2014 bear strong resemblance to those employed from the beginning of the post-Soviet era, in Trans-Dniestr and Georgia. They include sponsoring and arming proxies to pursue separatism, supporting them when needed with regular Russian army forces, denying the involvement of Russian forces, and seeking to insert Russia as a peacekeeper or mediator.

The focus on hybrid operations, while its roots are deep, took on new life due to three factors. The first was the increasing Russian focus on the concept of its understanding of 'soft power', and the mutation of the concept from one of passive influence to promoting active control. Second was the Russian

---

[128] Yuliya Yurchuk, 'Meanings: The "Day of Victory" after the Euromaidan' in Tom Beichelt and Susann Worschech eds., *Transnational Ukraine? Networks and Ties that Influence(d) Contemporary Ukraine* (Stuttgart: Ibidem, 2017), pp.89–114.

interpretation of the colour revolutions as 'hybrid' operations driven by external actors that both justified and demanded hybrid responses. The third factor has been the explosion of new media, including social media that have opened up considerable new opportunities for disinformation while also creating the potential for cyberwarfare.

Understanding the long-term continuity underlying Russian hybrid operations is important because it shows that what happened in 2014 was not an improvised response to a temporary challenge. Rather, it was a way of doing business that has long-standing precedent and will likely continue until something very substantial happens to disrupt it. If we perceived a lull in activity after 1991, that period now appears much more likely than the current one to appear anomalous in the long term.

Further Reading

Ambrosio, Thomas, *Authoritarian backlash: Russian resistance to democratization in the former Soviet Union* (Farnham and Burlington, VT: Ashgate Publishers, 2009).

Blake, Heidi, Tom Warren, Richard Holmes, Jason Leopold, Jane Bradley and Alex Campbell, 'From Russia With Blood', *Buzzfeed*, 15, 19, 20 June and 28 July 2017:

https://www.buzzfeed.com/heidiblake/poison-in-the-system?utm_term=. yxkkyY02W#.kmJ9NbrDE;

https://www.buzzfeed.com/janebradley/scientist-who-helped-connect-litvinenkos-murder-to-the?utm_term=.asdmQD43d#.sbLJ5WBxP;

https://www.buzzfeed.com/tomwarren/secrets-of-the-spy-in-the-bag?utm_ term=.aaX16ErbO#.tkergGwlz;

https://www.buzzfeed.com/jasonleopold/putins-media-czar-was-murdered-just-before-meeting-feds?utm_term=.cyPXAxlZ6#.jnKo5DkKV

Bergmann, Max and Carolyn Kenney, *Russian Active Measures and the Weaponization of Information* (Washington DC: Center for American Progress, June 2017). https://www.americanprogress.org/issues/security/reports/2017/06/06/433345/war-by-other-means/

Bonch-Osmolovskaya, Tatiana, 'Combating the Russian State Propaganda Machine: Strategies of Information Resistance', *Journal of Soviet and Post-Soviet Politics and Society*, vol.1, no.1 (2015), pp.175–218.

Darczewska, J., *Russia's Armed Forces on the Information War Front: Strategic Documents*, no.57 (Warsaw: Centre for Eastern Studies, June 2016). http://www.osw.waw.pl/en/publikacje/osw-studies/2016-06-27/russias-armed-forces-information-war-front-strategic-documents

Feinberg, Andrew, 'My Life at a Russian Propaganda Network', *Politico*, 21 August 2017. http://www.politico.com/magazine/story/2017/08/21/russian-propaganda-sputnik-reporter-215511

Galeotti, M. *Hybrid War or Gibridnaya Voyna? Getting Russia's Non-Linear Military Challenge Right* (Lulu and Mayak Intelligence, 2016). http://www.lulu.com/spotlight/Mayak_Intelligence

Gaufman, Elizveta, 'Memory, Media, and Securitization: Russian Media Framing of the Ukrainian Crisis', *Journal of Soviet and Post-Soviet Politics and Society*, vol.1, no.1 (2015), pp.141–174.

Goren, Roberta, *The Soviet Union and Terrorism* (London: George Allen and Unwin, 1984).

Graff, Garrett, M., 'A Guide to Russia's HighTech Tool Box for Subverting US Democracy', *Wired*, 13 August 2017. https://www.wired.com/story/a-guide-to-russias-high-tech-tool-box-for-subverting-us-democracy/

Green, Joshua, *Devil's Bargain: Steve Bannon, Donald Trump, and the Storming of the Presidency* (New York: Penguin Press, 2017).

Henze, Paul, B. *The plot to kill the Pope* (London: Croom Helm, 1984).

Holland, Max, 'The Propagation and Power of Communist Security Services *Dezinformatsiya*', *International Journal of Intelligence and CounterIntelligence*, vol.19, no.1 (January 2006), pp.1–31.

Kuzio, T., 'Soviet Nationality Policies in Soviet Ukraine' (chapter six) and 'Nationality Policies, Regionalism, and the Crimea in Ukraine' (chapter seven) in *Ukraine. Democratisation, Corruption and the New Russian Imperialism* (Santa Barbara, CA: Praeger, 2015), pp.213–290.

Kuzio, T., 'Soviet and Russian Anti(Ukrainian) Nationalism and Restalinization', *Communist and Post-Communist Studies*, vol.49, no. 1 (March 2016), pp.75–99.

Lucas, Edward and Ben Nimmo, *Information Warfare: What Is It and How to Win It? CEPA Infowar Paper No.1* (Washington DC: Center for European Policy Analysis, November 2015). http://www.cepa.org/sites/default/files/Infowar%20Report.pdf

Lucas, E. and Peter Pomerantzev, *Winning the Information War. Techniques and Counter-strategies to Russian Propaganda in Central and Eastern Europe* (London: Legatum Institute, August 2016). https://cepa.ecms.pl/files/?id_plik=2706

Paul, Christopher and Miriam Mathews, *The Russian 'Firehose of Falsehood' Propaganda Model: Why It Might Work and Options to Counter It* (Santa Monica, CA: Rand Corporation, 2016). http://www.rand.org/pubs/perspectives/PE198.html

Pesenti, Marina and P. Pomerantsev, *Beyond Propaganda. How to Stop Disinformation: Lessons from Ukraine for the Wider World* (London: Legatum Institute, August 2016). http://www.li.com/activities/publications/how-to-stop-disinformation-lessons-from-ukraine-for-the-wider-world

Pomerantsev, P., *Nothing Is True and Everything Is Possible: The Surreal Heart of the New Russia* (London: Faver and Faver, 2015).

Pynnöniemi, Katri and András Rácz eds., *Fog of Falsehood: Russian Strategy of Deception and the Conflict in Ukraine* (Helsinki: Finnish Institute of International Affairs, 10 May 2016). http://www.fiia.fi/en/publication/588/fog_of_falsehood/

Ratsiborynska, Vira, *When Hybrid Warfare Supports Ideology: Russia Today, Research Report no.133* (Rome: Research Division, NATO Defence College, November 2016). http://www.ndc.nato.int/news/news.php?icode=994

Riabchuk, Mykola, 'Ukrainians as Russia's Negative "Other": History Comes Full Circle', *Communist and Post-Communist Studies*, vol.49, no.1 (March 2016).

Rushchenko, Ihor, *Rosiysko-Ukrayinska Hibrydna Viyna: Pohlyad Sotsioloha* (Kharkiv: Tim Pablish Hrup, 2015).

Shultz, Richard H. and Roy Godson, *Dezinformatsia. Active Measures in Soviet Strategy* (Washington: Pegammmon, 1984).

Tumarkin, Nina, *The living and the dead: the rise and fall of the cult of World War II in Russia* (New York: Basic Books, 1994).

Wawrzonek, Michał, 'Ukraine in the 'Gray Zone': Between the 'Russkiy Mir' and Europe', *East European Politics and Society*, vol.28, no.4 (November 2014), pp.758–780.

Wilson, Andrew, *Virtual Politics: Faking Democracy in the Post-Soviet World* (New Haven, CT and London: Yale University Press, 2005).

Wilson, A., 'The Donbas in 2014: Explaining Civil Conflict Perhaps, but not Civil War', *Europe-Asia Studies*, vol. 68, no. 4 (June 2016), pp. 631–652.

3

Russia-West-Ukraine: Triangle of Competition, 1991–2013

Perhaps the most misunderstood aspect of the origins of the Russia-Ukraine conflict is the idea that there was a clear post-Soviet order in the region that subsequently collapsed. Many see the roots of this collapse in the rise of autocracy in Russia; others see it in Western policy (notably the enlargement of NATO). The fundamental problem with these perspectives is that these putative causes emerged well *after* the initial signs that Russia did not accept the political independence of Ukraine and the territorial loss of Crimea and the Donbas.

In this chapter, we examine Ukraine's relations with Russia from the Soviet collapse in 1991 to the 2013–2014 crisis. This analysis shows that Russia never voluntarily accepted Ukraine's independence, made several attempts in the 1990s to assert control over part or all of Crimea, and showed elsewhere (notably Trans-Dniestr) tactics very similar to those employed in Crimea and in the Donbas in 2014 and beyond.

President Putin, justifying the seizure of Crimea in a 2014 speech, referred back to the adoption of Christianity by the Kievan Rus Grand Prince Volodymyr the Great in 988.[1] While there is considerable historical mythology in Putin's claim, it builds on a long literature in Russia and the Soviet Union, asserting that parts of Ukraine are crucial to the foundation of modern Russia.[2] Putin's invocation of this theme exemplifies how Russia's claim to parts of Ukraine is seen as timeless and rooted deeply in history, rather than being contingent upon NATO's perceived expansionism.

---

[1]   http://en.kremlin.ru/events/president/news/20603
[2]   Peter J. Potichnyj, Marc Raeff, Jaroslaw Pelenski and Gleb N. Zekulin, eds., *Ukraine and Russia in Their Historical Encounter* (Edmonton: Canadian Institute of Ukrainian Studies, 1992).

History, National Identity, and Russia's Claims on Ukraine

In understanding Russia's claims on Ukraine, there are at least four strands of thinking. One strand concerns geopolitics – about threats and opportunities now and in the future. A second concerns international law, which on this case is unambiguously in favour of Ukraine. We leave these two issues aside for the moment to consider arguments about *history* and about *people*, because these profoundly affect claims about what state *should* control a particular territory and the people who live on it. The literature on the topic is immense, and here we simply identify themes that are relevant to Russia's claims. The overarching point is that history helps explain both why Russians (and some Western observers) take at face value claims about Russia's rights in Ukraine and why Ukrainians find those claims so threatening. Similarly, today's 'facts' about demographics and language use are based on histories which lead to conflicting interpretations.

The territory that became independent Ukraine in 1991 had spent various lengths of time under rule from Moscow. The Western region of Galicia had been ruled from Moscow only since 1939, when the Soviet Union, under the Molotov-Ribbentrop Pact, invaded what was at that time Eastern Poland. Crimea had been part of Ukraine since 1954, when control was transferred from the Russian SFSR to Ukraine. This transfer is often referred to as a 'gift' but appears to have been a matter of administrative convenience for the Soviets, as Crimea was connected to and supplied from Ukraine, not Russia. Crimea (along with much of Southern Ukraine, including Odesa and the region that Putin has referred to as *Novorossiya*) was seized in the late 18th century from the Ottoman Empire and Crimean Tatar Khanate. Kiev and most of the territory to the east of it had been part of Russia since 1667. The region west of the Dnipro River was mostly acquired as a result of the partitions of Poland in the late 18th century. While the history is complex, it is not hard to see why many in Russia regard much of Ukraine as 'naturally' part of Russia. However, there are (at least) two problems. First, nearly all this territory was gathered by Russia by the use of force, so the legitimacy of Russian control was never uncontested. What some see as Russian territory, others see as Russian empire. For example, despite the fact that the Baltic States were controlled by Russia for many years before their post-World War I period of independence, their 'Russianness' was never accepted uncritically. Second, and related, many of the people on this territory did not identify as Russians, a matter that became complicated over time.

Therefore, the national identity of the residents of different parts of Ukraine has become an important part of discussions over who the territory should belong to. A variety of claims have been made about different regions of

Ukraine, what language people speak, and whether they are 'really' Russians or a separate Ukrainian people. This is not that unusual as it may sound, for Polish nationalists led by Roman Dmowski through to the 1940s believed that Ukrainians were not a nation. Russian and Polish nationalists both saw evidence of foreign conspiracies lurking behind Ukrainian attempts to claim a separate national identity and build an independent state.

National identity, language, ethnicity and regionalism have been the most thoroughly researched topics concerning Ukraine. The results of this research show a complicated and nuanced mixture of identity factors. Most citizens of Ukraine speak both Ukrainian and Russian, sometimes mixing them, and sometimes switching depending on the circumstances (e.g. speaking one with family and another at work). The connection between language and national identity is murky: many people who speak primarily Russian identify as Ukrainians. The language question becomes politicised when a choice must be forced, an issue that comes up primarily in schools and in government business.

Ukraine's tumultuous history has made it harder to address these issues today. The question of whether the Ukrainian language should be promoted either for its own sake or for the interest of the country's unity is made much more fraught by the legacy of Russian and Soviet policy in Ukraine. The Tsarist Russian government in 1876 passed the *Ems Ukaz* (decree), banning publications in Ukrainian, in order to block a rise in Ukrainian national sentiment. After the Soviets took control and briefly allowed a flourishing of Ukrainian (and other non-Russian) cultures, Stalin cracked down, imprisoning Ukrainian nationalists and national communists and promoting Russian. The *Holodomor* fell heavily on the Ukrainian-speaking peasants of Central and Eastern Ukraine and the Kuban region of Northern Caucasus. The result – and this is a history everyone in Ukraine knows, even if it is rarely discussed in Russia or among newcomers to Ukrainian politics in the West – is that the current high level of Russian-speaking in Eastern Ukraine is a direct result of the suppression of the Ukrainian language and the starvation of millions of Ukrainian speakers under Soviet rule, which many Ukrainians regard as *Russian* rule. The Russian government disclaims responsibility for Stalin's repression and points out that many Russians suffered as well, even as Putin increasingly praises Stalin's legacy.

The result is that simply ratifying the status quo seems to some to acquiesce in and perpetuate the results of Tsarist and Stalinist repression. Those seeking to promote the Ukrainian language see it as undoing that oppression, while others see oppression in efforts to change the language in which people are schooled or interact with the government. At the time of independence, leaders sought to defuse the issue by devising a civic (rather than ethnic) definition of citizenship (anyone on Ukrainian territory was a citizen, regardless of one's 'nationality' or language).

One might simply hold a plebiscite, as Russia did in Crimea under very questionable conditions. Ukraine itself held a vote on independence from the Soviet Union in 1991, and in every region (including Crimea) a majority voted for independence (though the margin was lower in the Donbas than in the West, and much lower in Crimea, where 54% supported independence).[3] The regions that have been occupied by Russia are among those with the highest percentage of those who speak primarily Russian. Language policy is a very complicated question in Ukraine, and it has been made more complicated by politicians using it to try to instil fear and mobilise voters in elections.

The broader point, however, and it is essential, is that the Russian Empire and then the Soviet Union controlled vast swaths of Ukraine for many years before 1991. Leading Soviet politicians came from the region, key battles of World War II were fought on the territory, major economic assets were there, and some Russian literature was set there.[4] It is not hard to see why many in Russia regard the idea that Ukraine – and especially Eastern Ukraine and Crimea – is not part of Russia as hard to comprehend. Some in the West have the same reaction.

It is precisely these attitudes that convince many in Ukraine that there is something to fear from Russia. The same history that shows some that Ukraine is part of Russia shows others that Russia is a threat to the language, culture and lives of Ukrainians. Ukrainian distinctiveness persisted despite the concerted efforts of two very autocratic regimes to eradicate it. In this view, Ukraine is a distinct place and a distinct people, but was always ruled by foreigners, and will be again if it does not guard its independence jealously. Put differently, much disagreement about the appropriate relationship between Russia and Ukraine, both within the region and outside it, comes down to one's prior beliefs about the relationship between Ukraine and Russia. Does Russia's historical role in Ukraine justify involvement today? Or does it show why Ukraine must be completely independent? Or does 1991

---

[3]   Voting in Crimea also presents a problem of ratifying historical injustice: Stalin deported the entire Tatar population from Crimea in 1944, increasing the Russian ethnic majority now observed in the peninsula.

[4]   As Timothy Snyder has shown, Ukraine and Belarus bore the brunt of World War II, both in the proportion of soldiers and civilians killed. Of 13 'Hero Cities' identified by the Soviet government after World War II, four (Odesa, Kyiv, Sevastopol and Kerch) were in Ukraine. Two of these, Sevastopol and Kerch, are in Crimea and are now controlled by Russia. See his *Bloodlands* (New York: Basic Books, 2010).

represent a break, such that what came before is irrelevant? Supporters of Russia and critics of the West tend to fall back on the first view. Supporters of Ukraine, and of Western support for Ukraine, tend to fall back on one of the latter two views.

Ukraine and Russia Since 1991

With this brief review of history and national identity issues, we turn to the period since 1991. Russia objected to Ukrainian sovereignty from the very beginning of this period, and repeatedly contested it in the following years. Russian objections to full Ukrainian sovereignty predated NATO enlargement and the rise of Putin, and were shared across almost the entire Russian political spectrum, with only a very narrow group of pro-Western reformers advocating that Russia write-off Ukraine for the sake of concentrating on domestic reform. This wide consensus was obscured by the fact that one of those who sought to put the Ukraine issue behind Russia was Boris Yeltsin, President of Russia from 1990 to 1999. Yeltsin sought to prevent Ukraine from becoming fully independent, but once it seemed beyond his control, he sought to move forward, even as many in his government continued to seek revision of 1991 arrangements.

This chapter reviews several key periods and incidents between Russia and Ukraine since 1991. It is too short to provide a detailed or comprehensive treatment. Rather, it highlights several key episodes that provide insight into the historical depth of contention over the proper relationship between Ukraine and Russia.

These episodes include: (1) The 1991 agreement that formally dissolved the Soviet Union and founded the Commonwealth of Independent States (CIS). (2) The long contentious struggle over ownership of the Black Sea Fleet and its base at Sevastopol, in Crimea. (3) The 1994 trilateral nuclear deal and the accompanying Budapest Memorandum, through which Russia, the UK and the US provided security assurances for Ukraine's territorial integrity and sovereignty in return for Ukraine's agreement to surrender its nuclear weapons. (4) The 1997 Friendship Treaty between Russia and Ukraine, which appeared to signal Russia's acceptance of Ukraine's independence. The treaty was ratified by the state Duma and Federation Council in 1998–1999 with Russian deputies linking the question to the Black Sea Fleet, Crimea and Sevastopol. Moscow Mayor Yuri Luzhkov voiced territorial claims against Ukraine and intervened in Crimean affairs throughout the two decades leading up to the crisis in 2013–2014. (5) The 2004 Orange Revolution, in which Russia backed the fraudulent election of Yanukovych and initiated its tactic of equating pro-Western Ukrainian politicians with 'fascists'. Combined with 'colour revolutions' in Serbia, Georgia and Kyrgyzstan, this episode increased Russian sensitivity to the threat of transnational diffusion of pro-democracy movements to Putin's rule.

1991: The Collapse of the Soviet Union and Formation of the CIS

Both Soviet leaders (represented by Gorbachev) and Russian leaders (led by Yeltsin) opposed Ukraine's independence in 1991. But the battle between Gorbachev and Yeltsin for control in Moscow provided Ukraine with the leverage to insist on complete independence.

When Ukraine's parliament declared independence on 24 August 1991, it scheduled a referendum on independence for 1 December, to be accompanied by elections for President. That autumn, two contests proceeded in parallel. In one of these, Yeltsin sought to seize control of the levers of power from President Gorbachev in Moscow. Essentially, this meant that the government of the Russian SFSR (controlled by Yeltsin) won the loyalty and took over the functions of the much more extensive government of the Soviet Union, (controlled nominally, but increasingly tenuously, by Gorbachev). As a result, the Soviet foreign, defence, finance and other ministries became Russian ministries. In the second contest, Moscow tried to retain some form of devolved control over Ukraine, while Leonid Kravchuk rejected any new agreements until after the 1 December 1991 election and referendum. On this issue, Yeltsin and Gorbachev were united.

On 1 December 1991, Ukraine's citizens voted decisively for independence and for Kravchuk as president. Two things are notable. First, of the leading candidates, Ukrainians chose the less nationalist one (Kravchuk) over the former dissident and nationalist leader Vyacheslav Chornovil. Second, while the independence vote was regionally skewed, with higher support for independence in the West than in the East and South, every *oblast* of Ukraine, including Crimea, Donetsk and Luhansk, voted in favour of independence. These results left Kravchuk in a powerful bargaining position when he met with Yeltsin and Belarusian leader Stanislav Shushkevych on 7–8 December to agree on a new formal relationship between the three states.[5]

Yeltsin faced a dilemma. Gorbachev was still legally the president of the USSR, and there was only one legal way to remove him: dissolving the 1922 Union Treaty that had originally formed the Soviet Union in legal terms. But

---

[5]   See chapter one 'The Demise of the Soviet Union and the Emergence of Independent Ukraine' in P. D'Anieri, Robert Kravchuk and T. Kuzio, *Politics and Society in Ukraine* (Boulder, CO: Westview, 1999), pp.10–44.

dissolving the Union Treaty, legally, meant total independence for Ukraine and Belarus. The only way to square the circle for Yeltsin was to simultaneously negotiate a new agreement to create a looser union. Kravchuk refused, insisting that the new 'Commonwealth of Independent States' take the form of an agreement among states, with each state retaining a veto over any future action, rather than a federation or confederation with some prerogatives reserved for a new 'centre'. Yeltsin faced the choice between finding another way to defeat Gorbachev or accepting Ukraine's independence for the time being and trying to reach a new agreement later. He chose to sign the agreement, which led directly to the cessation of the USSR as a subject of international law and prompted Gorbachev's ignominious resignation on 25 December, accompanied by the replacement of the Soviet hammer and sickle by the Russian tricolour over the Kremlin.

The deal that cemented Ukraine's independence and the collapse of the Soviet Union was not welcomed by Russian leaders, Yeltsin included. Rather it was accepted because there was no other clear way to complete Yeltsin's takeover of the government in Moscow. In the subsequent months, Russia sought with growing frustration to reel this concession back in, insisting that certain prerogatives belonged to the CIS or to Russia, rather than Ukraine. Of particular concern were the armed forces, which Russia sought to maintain as a single military, while Ukraine, seeing a separate army as a defining attribute of an independent state, insisted on dividing. The same was true of nuclear weapons and monetary policy, among other issues. There were very good reasons to maintain a single currency and monetary policy, but Ukraine, again citing sovereignty (and due also to a lack of enthusiasm for macroeconomic stabilisation), refused, leading to hyperinflation in 1993. In the years after 1991, Russia continued to contest Ukraine's sovereignty along two different axes, the CIS and the ownership of the Black Sea Fleet and its base at Sevastopol.

The CIS

Throughout the early post-Soviet years, Russia promoted a federal role for the CIS, which would have legitimised a hegemonic role for Russia in the region. Russia sought central control in three broad issue areas: trade and monetary policy, peacekeeping and nuclear weapons. In the first and third of these, Russia's goals were at least in part supported by the international community. But there was a fundamental conflict of goals on how any cooperation would be organised. Russia was unwilling to create an organisation which limited its power (akin to Germany being 'bound' by the EU), while several others, including Ukraine, refused to be part of an organisation which limited their newly established sovereignty.

On trade and monetary policy, the international community, notably the International Monetary Fund (IMF) – which was a major vehicle for aid to the post-Soviet states – also supported some kind of unified structure. While the Soviet economy was badly in need of structural reform, fragmenting it into 15 separate economies created a separate economic shock, as the gains from trade were lost. Just as Western Europe was implementing the Single European Act in order to gain the advantages of a larger single market, the post-Soviet states were moving in the opposite direction.

The collapse of the single currency, as the Soviet ruble became the Russian ruble, caused further economic harm. Each of the new governments was capable of emitting currency and credit, creating a massive collective action problem. As each paid its salaries in newly created credit, the effects were spread (in the form of increasing inflation) across the entire region. On the currency question, Russia and Ukraine oddly ended up supporting the same policy. Russia was trying to implement structural adjustment, or 'shock therapy', which meant controlling the money supply to limit inflation. Ukraine continued to create currency and credit to keep enterprises afloat, causing inflation in Russia as well as Ukraine. When Ukraine created its own currency, and Russia introduced a new ruble, essentially kicking the other states out of the ruble zone, they both gained monetary autonomy. The downside was that volatility of these two currencies considerably undermined trade in what was still a highly integrated economic space.

The problem was how any integrated space would be governed. As the European Union had concluded, a functioning economic union required delegating some sovereignty to an international or supranational organisation. Ukraine and some others were unwilling to do this, given their historical record of briefly lived independent statehood, their recent experience with Russian dominance of the Soviet Union, and their ongoing experience with Russian questioning of their sovereignty and independence. On top of that problem, there was a fundamental conflict of interest involving voting rules for any supranational decision making.[6]

Given Russia's size within the region (in terms of population and GDP), there was no voting system that did not either give Russia a dominant position (which Ukraine and others rejected) or leave Russia at risk of being outvoted by others (which Russia rejected). Ultimately therefore, Ukraine did not participate extensively in much of what the CIS did, and this caused great frustration in Russia. For Russia, Ukraine was pettily holding up progress,

---

[6]   This dilemma is discussed in depth in P. D'Anieri, 'International Cooperation among Unequal Partners: The Emergence of Bilateralism in the Former Soviet Union', *International Politics*, vol.34, no.4 (December 1997), pp.417–448.

and rejecting Russia's natural leadership in the region. For Ukraine, Russia was trying to reassert the control that Ukraine had only recently escaped.

A more challenging problem was that of peacekeeping in the region. Conflict had broken out between Armenia and Azerbaijan even prior to the Soviet collapse, and in late 1991, Russian speakers (as in the Donbas, mobilised by their Soviet rather than ethno-cultural identity) in the Trans-Dniestr region of Moldova had declared their independence, supported by the Russian 14th Army, which continued to be located there after Moldovan independence. Further unrest was taking place in Georgia, where separatists in Abkhazia, supported by Russian forces, were fighting Georgian government forces.

Russia requested permission to be identified as a peacekeeper for these conflicts, based on the argument that only it had the capability and interest to provide the needed peacekeeping forces. However, both the Georgian and Moldovan governments resisted Russia being identified as a peacekeeper, as Russia had also been involved in supporting one side in the conflict. Ukraine also opposed Russian peacekeeping, as it feared what Russia might do either in Crimea or Eastern Ukraine. In sum, already by 1993, the basic pattern that was exhibited in 2014 was already in place, and was already a source of tension between Russia and Ukraine. In both Moldova and Georgia, Russia fomented separatism, supported it militarily (while denying doing so), and then proposed that more of its troops enter the conflict zone as peace-keepers. Hybrid warfare, it would seem, long pre-dates the Donbas.

Nuclear Weapons

More important for many in the West was the question of control over nuclear weapons. Ukraine's inheritance of the weapons on its territory gave it the third largest nuclear arsenal in the world (after Russia and the US), and the same principle, applied to Belarus and Kazakhstan, meant that the number of nuclear powers suddenly grew from seven to ten. This was seen as threatening by both Russia and the US. The US government, under both George H. W. Bush and Bill Clinton, viewed Ukraine primarily through the lens of nuclear weapons. The US was concerned not only about nuclear proliferation and about the fear that Ukraine could not responsibly handle the weapons, but about the entire framework of arms control between the US and Russia being undermined by this proliferation.[7]

---

[7]   On the nuclear negotiations, see Steven Pifer, *The Trilateral Process, The United States, Ukraine, Russia and Nuclear Weapons* (Washington, DC: Brookings Institution, 2011) and chapter 3 'Controlling the Nukes' in James Goldgeier and Michael McFaul, *Power and Purpose: U.S. Policy Toward Russia after the Cold War* (Washington: Brookings, 2003), pp.41–58.

From 1991 until the resolution of the issue in January 1994, this was the primary focus of US foreign policy regarding Ukraine, and the US and Russia joined forces to compel Ukraine to surrender the weapons. From the US and Russian perspective, Ukraine's July 1990 Declaration of Sovereignty, which stated Ukraine's desire to become an independent and non-nuclear state, was a binding commitment to denuclearise. By 1993, Russia's assertiveness in the region had already convinced many in Ukraine that it should either keep the weapons or at least insist on 'binding' security guarantees in return for surrendering them. A related issue was who would benefit financially from the reprocessing of the uranium, and Ukraine's insistence that it be comp-ensated for the material in weapons that had already been transferred to Russia led to the impression in the US that the Kravchuk government was seeking to extract as much money as possible.

With the Ukrainian economy in freefall, partly due to the Soviet legacy, partly to the breakup of the Soviet economy, and partly due to the absence of reform, Ukraine was in an increasingly desperate position, and found that the nuclear weapons issue kept it isolated. The final issues holding up an agreement were the amount of compensation and the nature of security guarantees Ukraine would receive. Ukraine sought something akin to the NATO Article V guarantee, a commitment that an attack on Ukraine would be regarded as an attack on all NATO members. The US and others were unwilling to make such a commitment, and Ukraine had to settle for security assurances by Russia, the UK and the US that they supported Ukraine's territorial integrity.

To codify these commitments, the US, UK and Russia signed the Budapest Memorandum in December 1994, in which they committed to 'refrain from the threat or use of force against the territorial integrity or political independence of Ukraine, and that none of their weapons will ever be used against Ukraine except in self-defence or otherwise in accordance with the Charter of the United Nations'.[8] The fact that these commitments were a crucial issue in 1994 shows the deep roots of Ukraine's security fears. Ultimately, however, the absence of a mechanism for enforcing the commitments left Russia free to violate them in 2014 and the US and Britain uncommitted to doing anything about it. This was as they wanted it, and Ukraine had few options to change the deal, which prevented Ukraine's ostracism and reduced economic pressure, but left it militarily vulnerable.

The Black Sea Fleet, Crimea and Sevastopol

Ukrainian sovereignty over Crimea and Sevastopol was questioned almost

---

8   http://www.pircenter.org/media/content/files/12/13943175580.pdf

from the beginning of the post-Soviet era, with Russian officials making it clear that they believed even less in Crimea's separation from Russia than in the rest of Ukraine's. Thus, in January 1992, having just signed the deal that dissolved the Soviet Union, President Yeltsin stated 'The Black Sea Fleet was, is and will be Russia's. No one, not even Kravchuk will take it away from Russia'.[9] The issue was not just the fleet (the ships of which were mostly obsolescent), but rather Crimea, where it was based. Russia's claims on Crimea were based partly on history (the territory had only been formally part of Ukraine since 1954), partly on ethnicity and language, and partly on strategic military importance. It is hard to know what was driving what: did Russia seek control of Crimea as a means of controlling a crucial naval base, or did it insist on maintaining a presence on the naval base as a means of maintaining a long-term claim on Crimea and a toehold for a future move?

Regardless of the exact motives (and different Russians likely emphasised different reasons), Russian demands concerning Crimea persisted throughout the entire post-Soviet era. Thus, in keeping with Yeltsin's position, the Russian Congress of People's Deputies passed a resolution in January 1992 questioning the 1954 deal that gave Ukraine sovereignty over Crimea. In June 1992, the two sides agreed to split the assets of the fleet, but the details of the split and of basing rights continued to prevent a deal from being finalised. In September 1993, Russia cut off the gas supply to Ukraine and offered to restore it on the basis of receiving a favourable division of the fleet and rights over the Sevastopol base. These events all predated serious discussion of NATO enlargement.

The problem was complicated during this period by a move among some Crimean leaders to secede from Ukraine. In May 1992, the Crimean parliament declared Crimea's sovereignty (it already had been upgraded in 1990 from *oblast* to autonomous republic within Soviet Ukraine), but a compromise was reached in which Crimea's autonomy was increased and the Crimean parliament rescinded the sovereignty declaration. In 1995, President Kuchma, an Eastern Ukrainian who had been elected on a moderate pro-Russian platform the year before, dissolved the institution of the Crimean presidency and, combined with in-fighting among Russian nationalists, this took the wind out of the sails of Crimean separatism. That essentially resolved the question of secession from within Ukraine, but the conflict over Sevastopol continued. Russia insisted on its right to continue basing its part of the fleet there, and Ukraine resisted.

In 1997, the two sides finally reached a compromise which gave Russia

---

[9]   Sobchak and Yeltsin were quoted in John Rettie and James Meek, 'Battle for Soviet Navy', *The Guardian*, 10 January 1992.

roughly 80% of the fleet's ships, a 20-year (until 2017) lease on part of the base, and the right to keep a force of up to 25,000 personnel at the base. The agreement committed Russia to 'respect the sovereignty of Ukraine, honour its legislation and preclude interference in the internal affairs of Ukraine'.[10] Ukrainian President Yushchenko later announced Ukraine's intention to let the lease lapse in 2017, but in 2010 President Yanukovych lobbied the Ukrainian parliament to vote for the Kharkiv Accords that extended the fleet base to 2042 in return for a cut in gas prices (though Russia continued to charge Ukraine the highest gas price in Europe throughout Yanukovych's presidency).

The Russia-Ukraine Friendship Treaty

With the issue of the Black Sea Fleet and Sevastopol apparently resolved, Russia and Ukraine were able to sign a Friendship Treaty later in 1997. This treaty was seen as putting the two states' relations on a clear basis in international law, addressing many issues that had been left hanging. Among other things, Article II of the treaty states that, 'In accord with provisions of the UN Charter and the obligations of the Final Act on Security and Cooperation in Europe, the High Contracting Parties shall respect each other's territorial integrity and reaffirm the inviolability of the borders existing between them'.

In many respects, this was the high point in post-Soviet Russian-Ukrainian relations, as it appeared to signal Russia's recognition that the disintegration of the USSR in 1991 would not be reversed. However, while Yeltsin said at the signing that, 'My friend President Kuchma and I vow at this sacred place, at the Tomb of the Unknown Soldier, that the treaty that we sign today will be fulfilled'[11], other Russian leaders asserted a revisionist policy. Boris Nemstov, widely regarded as a moderate and pro-Western politician, sought to have Russian firms buy property in Sevastopol, saying, 'Historical justice should be restored by capitalist methods'. Moscow Mayor Luzhkov introduced a measure in the Federation Council to declare Russian sovereignty over Sevastopol,[12] and called the Friendship Treaty the 'surrender of Crimea'.[13] In

---

[10] 'Bound by treaty: Russia, Ukraine and Crimea', *Deutsche Welle*, 3 March 2014. http://www.dw.com/en/bound-by-treaty-russia-ukraine-and-crimea/a-17487632 This article denotes four separate legal documents committing Russia to Ukraine's territorial integrity: the Helsinki Final Act, the Budapest Memorandum, the Black Sea Fleet Agreement, and the 1997 Russia-Ukraine Friendship Treaty.

[11] Michael Specter, 'Setting Past Aside, Russia and Ukraine Sign Friendship Treaty', *New York Times*, 1 June 1997. http://www.nytimes.com/1997/06/01/world/setting-past-aside-russia-and-ukraine-sign-friendship-treaty.html

[12] These examples are from P. D'Anieri, *Economic Interdependence in Ukrainian-Russian Relations* (Albany: State University of New York Press, 1999).

[13] Clifford J. Levy, 'Moscow's Mayor Exports Russia's New Nationalism', *New York*

the coming years, Luzhkov would spend considerable resources from the Moscow city budget to build a branch of Moscow State University in Sevastopol, along with housing for Russian service members and various other buildings.

In 1999, when the Friendship Treaty finally came to the Federation Council for ratification, Luzhkov and others opposed it, fearing that it would reduce Russia's leverage over the region. In 2010, after Yanukovych extended Russia's lease on the base, Luzhkov continued to assert that Sevastopol is a 'Russian city'.[14] In sum, the issue was never really settled for many Russian elites, including moderates as well as radical nationalists. Writing in 1998, Russian historian Alexander Yanov lamented that, 'Three out of the five possible candidates to succeed Yeltsin – Luzhkov, [Gennadiy] Zyuganov, and [Aleksandr] Lebed – advocate the transfer of Sevastopol to Russia, which amounts to open confrontation with Ukraine; the fourth candidate – [Viktor] Chernomyrdin – states publicly: 'Russia is not a country but a continent'.[15]

The idea that the 1997 Friendship Treaty would be a turning point was a recognition that up until that point, Russia had not accepted Ukraine's independence or its full sovereignty over Crimea, especially Sevastopol. The hope was that the treaty would put that contestation to rest, but it did not. From our post-2014 perspective, it demonstrates nearly the opposite of conventional narratives that see the Ukraine-Russia conflict as something that arose after a period of relative comity. In actuality, the relationship was fraught from the beginning due to Ukraine's insecurity and Russia's dissatisfaction with the status quo of an independent Ukraine. The events related so far predated NATO enlargement (agreed in 1997 and implemented in 1999) and the rise of Putin (who was elected President in 2000). There can be little doubt that NATO expansion irritated Russia and that Putin's approach to democracy, to Ukraine and to the West did not help, but they cannot have been the root causes of the tension that was present from the moment of Ukraine's independence. This was rooted more fundamentally in Russia's conception of its national identity, its borders, and its role in the region.

The Orange Revolution

From the Friendship Treaty in 1997 until the Orange Revolution in 2004,

---

Times, 25 October 2008. http://www.nytimes.com/2008/10/26/world/europe/26mayor.html

[14]   T. Kuzio, 'Luzhkov Again Raises Russian Right to Sevastopol', *Eurasia Daily Monitor*, vol. 7, no. 153 (9 August 2010). https://jamestown.org/program/luzhkov-again-raises-russian-right-to-sevastopol/

[15]   Alexander Yanov, 'The Rape of Russia', *Moscow News*, 18 June 1998.

several important developments paved the way for the disruption that was to follow. First, NATO added three new members (Czech Republic, Hungary and Poland) in 1999, over Russia's objections. Second, at almost the exact same time, NATO engaged in a bombing campaign to force the government of Serbia to stop ethnic cleansing in Kosovo. This intervention, which was repeatedly cited later by Putin, caused anger within the Russian leadership and nearly spurred a military confrontation between NATO and Russian forces in Kosovo. Third, Putin replaced Yeltsin as president, and initially had very constructive relations with the West, even as he methodically reduced pluralism in Russia by gaining control over the press, the oligarchs and the regions. This put democracy on the agenda in the region. Fourth, in Ukraine, Kuchma won election to a second term. In doing so, he sought to emulate Russia in reducing competing sources of power, and he sought to do this while maintaining good relations with both NATO and Russia. In both Ukraine and Russia, politics in the years before 2004 were increasingly about whether democracy would survive.

In Ukraine, President Kuchma's efforts to consolidate power encountered considerable opposition, but he seemed to have won a decisive victory when a constitutional referendum in 2000 appeared to have strengthened his power over the parliament and the prime minister. Before the results could be implemented, the release of recordings made in Kuchma's office implying his involvement in the murder of journalist Georgiy Gongadze, as well as various other misdeeds, turned the focus of Ukrainian politics to Kuchma and his growing autocracy. Kuchma decided not to seek to circumvent a constitutional ban on a third term as elections approached in 2004. Instead, he supported as his successor Yanukovych, a former Prime Minister, leader of the Party of Regions, and one of the leaders of the Donetsk Clan. His opponent was Yushchenko, another former Prime Minister under Kuchma, who supported a much more pro-Western policy and had very late in the game joined the broader anti-Kuchma opposition, together with Yuliya Tymoshenko. There was wide consensus that Yanukovych would align Ukraine with Russia, and that Yushchenko would align it with the West, and so the country appeared to be at a tipping point.

The Russian government threw its support behind Yanukovych. Yanukovych's campaign team was largely composed of Russian political technologists. Russian media, which were widely watched in Ukraine, gave extensive favourable support to Yanukovych, and Putin personally travelled to Kiev to support him in both rounds of the elections. Shortly before the first round of the election, Putin appeared at a military parade in Kiev, standing shoulder to shoulder with Kuchma and Yanukovych. This campaign marked the emergence of Russian media and leaders accusing the Ukrainian opposition of being 'fascists', linking them with the World War II era Ukrainian nationalist leader Bandera, whose legacy was highly contested. Russian media also helped present Yushchenko as a pawn of the United States (his wife is an American-Ukrainian), which after the invasion of Iraq was unpopular in Ukraine. These were themes to be used in Russia's information warfare again in 2014, and they resonated in Russia.

After the exposure of fraud in the second round of the 2004 election, Russia continued, along with Yanukovych, to insist that the election was valid and should stand. When a compromise to end the crisis led to the second round of the election being re-run, a Commonwealth of Independent States election monitoring team deemed it illegitimate.

The Orange Revolution was a turning point in Russia's relations with Ukraine and the West, but not for the reasons people expected at the time. In 2004, the hope or fear, depending on one's preferences, was that the Orange coalition was going to reform Ukrainian government, reduce corruption, build a more 'European' state, and align itself with the West. Instead, it engaged in intense infighting, did little to limit corruption, and managed to resuscitate Yanukovych (who by this time was being advised by the American political consultant Paul Manafort[16]) when Yushchenko appointed him Prime Minister.

While the immediate danger to Russia posed by Yushchenko's election receded, the example it set worried Putin and other Russian leaders. The lesson from the ouster of Slobodan Milosevic in Serbia in 2000, of Eduard Shevardnadze in Georgia in 2003, and then of the blocking of Yanukovych coming to power in the Orange Revolution, was that colour revolutions were camouflage for the real purpose of regime change of authoritarian leaders in the post-communist world. This appeared to be a direct threat to Putin's rule in Russia. Putin and many others saw an even more sinister danger: that the revolutions were not really about democracy, but rather were about geopolitics.

The fact that many in the US exaggerated the role of international support in driving these revolutions, and that they openly hoped for something similar in Belarus in 2005, solidified the idea that democracy promotion was not about promoting democracy but about removing governments that did not support the US. In response, Russia began a series of domestic and international initiatives aimed at preventing such protests in Russia. Domestically, these measures included forming the group *Nashi* (Ours) as a pro-Putin youth group to challenge any other youth movements, and limiting the activities of

---

[16]   T. Kuzio, 'Ukrainian Kleptocrats and America's Real-Life House of Cards: Corruption, Lobbyism and the Rule of Law', *Communist and Post-Communist Studies*, vol.50, no.1 (March 2017), pp.29–40.

NGOs, especially those with funding from abroad. Internationally, Russia collaborated with China to form the Shanghai Treaty Organisation, among the missions of which was to promote the value of a pluralist international order in opposition to the West's universalist claims about liberal democracy.[17]

Ukraine between Russia and the West

The role of the West in the background to the conflict between Russia and Ukraine is complicated by the fact that the 'West' encompasses several states and groups of states: the US, Germany, NATO, the EU and various combinations of these. But the overall story is fairly straightforward. From the 'prehistory' of Ukraine's independence, it was clear that Ukraine was important to the West in terms of the West's relationship with Russia, and not as an important factor in its own right. This frustrated Ukrainian leaders, and took them some time to come to terms with, as Ukrainian leaders (including Yanukovych) have tended to exaggerate Ukraine's importance to the West. Ukraine's relations with Russia have always interacted with Russia's relations with the West, and while Ukraine has sometimes used this linkage to its advantage, the eroding relations between Russia and the West increasingly made Ukraine a battlefield, rather than the bridge that it hoped to be.

In the early post-Soviet years, the United States was the primary external actor in the Ukraine-Russia relationship because Europe was focused on its own transformations. These included implementing the Single European Act and single currency, managing the reunification of Germany, and making the transition from state planning and communism to a market economy and democracy in Central Europe.

Ukraine struggled to find an important place in US foreign policy for three reasons. First, the US was focused on Russia, the success or failure of which was seen as much more important than that of Ukraine. Second, US interests in the international politics of the region were essentially conservative – both the Bush and Clinton administrations were focused as much on preserving the status quo in arms control and political stability than in transforming the region. The threats the US feared – breakdown of Soviet-era arms control agreements, nuclear proliferation and ethnic unrest – seemed better prevented by preserving Russia's dominance than by undermining it. Ukraine's reconsideration of its nuclear status played into this conservatism. Third, in contrast to Russia under Yeltsin, Ukraine under Kravchuk and then Kuchma was unwilling to embrace the kind of reform that the 'Washington consensus'

---

[17]   P. D'Anieri, 'Autocratic Diffusion and the Pluralization of Democracy', in Bruce Jentleson and Louis Pauly, eds., *Power in a Complex Global System* (London: Routledge, 2014), pp. 80–96.

insisted was necessary. The notion that Ukraine might provide a necessary check on Russia was not widely shared, though Zbigniew Brzezinski articulated this argument cogently in early 1994.[18]

Several things happened to change this. First, the signing of the Trilateral Agreement on nuclear weapons removed the primary obstacle to a closer US relationship with Ukraine. Second, a series of events in 1993 and 1994 undermined US confidence both in Russian economic and democratic reform, and in Russia's willingness to join the Western community in foreign policy. If there had been a tension before between doing what was right by Ukraine and pursuing US interests vis-à-vis Russia, those two concerns increasingly aligned in favour of supporting Ukraine, both because of its intrinsic importance and because it provided a hedge against Russian reassertion.

Domestically within Russia, events called into question both whether Russia could reform economically and whether it could adopt democracy in some form. The two issues were joined in the violent conflict between Yeltsin and the Congress of People's Deputies in 1993. A sizable majority in Russia's parliament steadfastly opposed Yeltsin's reform plans, and criticised the role of the West in promoting them. If democratic norms were followed, economic reform would likely cease, and hardliners might return to power. Keeping Yeltsin in power and reform moving forward meant taking undemocratic steps: the unconstitutional dismissal of the parliament, the violent emptying of the building, and the unilateral writing of a new constitution. Western leaders were torn between their desire to see Yeltsin triumph and their distaste at the means needed to do so. Ultimately, however, believing that there could be no Russian democracy and reform without Yeltsin, most strongly supported the measures he undertook. At the same time, however, the need to think about other contingencies was clear. That message was reinforced in the 1993 parliamentary elections, in which Vladimir Zhirinovsky's neo-fascist party and the Communist Party outpolled Yeltsin's party. It was reinforced even more beginning in late 1994, when Russia sent its armed forces into the republic of Chechnya, beginning a brutal campaign to prevent its secession.

Internationally, the situation was only slightly better. The arrest of Aldrich Ames for spying for Russia was substantively a minor matter, but received huge attention in the US because it appeared to show that Russia still considered the US an adversary, and was spying on it even as the US was propping up Russia's economy. Other elements of US domestic politics further undermined the relationship: at the very time that many were saying

---

[18] Zbigniew Brzezinski, 'The Premature Partnership', *Foreign Affairs*, vol.73, no.2 (March/April 1994), pp.67–82. https://www.foreignaffairs.com/articles/russian-federation/1994-03-01/premature-partnership

the US should put together a 'new Marshall plan' for Russia, a domestic recession and the 1992 presidential election combined to make a sizable investment in foreign aid impossible. As a candidate, Bill Clinton blasted George H.W. Bush for focusing on international affairs at the expense of the US economy, and as President he chose to focus on energising the US economy rather than Russia's.

All those events pale in long-term importance next to the outbreak of war in the former Yugoslavia. This conflict was central to the worsening of relations between the US and Russia, with far-reaching consequences for Ukraine. In December 1994, Russia vetoed a UN Security Council Resolution intended to limit Serbian economic support for forces fighting in Bosnia. Over the next few years, as efforts to limit the conflict continued, two things became apparent. First, Russia and the US supported very different outcomes in the conflict, undermining the notion that they had become partners rather than adversaries. Second, Russia's use of its UN Security Council veto, and its independent position more broadly, made it clear how problematic it would be to have Russia inside key Western institutions such as NATO.

As a result of the Yugoslav wars, the notion of including Russia within an expanded NATO appeared increasingly problematic. This toxified the discussion of NATO enlargement, because the discussion was increasingly about expanding NATO but not including Russia. That inevitably but inadvertently raised the question of where NATO enlargement would end, and as disagreement over Yugoslavia peaked in 1999 with NATO's intervention over Kosovo, the stakes seemed ever more important.

This erosion of the US-Russia relationship did not directly involve Ukraine, but indirectly it completely changed the context of Ukraine's relations with both Russia and the US. Along with Yeltsin's struggles to consolidate domestic reform, the Russian position on the Yugoslav conflict convinced many US policy makers that they needed to hedge against the possibility that reform would fail or that Russia would become an adversary in Europe. Russia's second war in Chechnya, beginning in 1999, fed that perception. For Russia, these episodes gave weight to the view that events since 1991 were undermining Russia's international role, and that Russia was becoming sidelined in a Europe increasingly dominated by the United States. This made both the US and Russia more interested in Ukraine, which throughout the 1990s maintained pluralist politics and a 'multi-vector' foreign policy.

Throughout the period prior to 2013, there was an imbalance of interest in Ukraine. While Russia was pressuring Ukraine to move more closely toward it, and Ukraine was generally resisting, the situation was the opposite regarding the European Union and the West more broadly, where Ukraine was seeking closer integration with Europe and the West but was being held at arm's length due to the absence of reform. Especially during Kuchma's first term (1994–1999), the IMF struggled with the dilemma of whether to continue aiding Ukraine even though it had not met the conditions of previous loans, or to cut off aid and risk an economic crisis that might drive the country into Russia's arms. Similarly, in the realm of military reform, NATO found that programmes for transformation of the military were consistently unimplemented, but hesitated to cut off aid and the accompanying military contacts.

These dilemmas became sharper during Kuchma's second term (1999–2004). Kuchma had used various tactics to limit the competitiveness of the 1999 election, but as with Yeltsin, the fact that his second-round opponent was a communist led the US to support him anyway. But as he threatened civil liberties and political competition, the West's concern grew more intense. Two events were especially influential. The first was the murder of the journalist Georgiy Gongadze and the crackdown on the opposition of which it was a part. The second was the revelation that Ukraine had made a deal to supply Kolchuga air defence radar systems to Iraq in the run-up to the US-led invasion in 2003. This infuriated the Bush administration, which responded by dramatically reducing interaction with Kuchma's government.[19]

These events strengthened the perception in the West that for Ukraine to succeed, and for the West to support it, its leadership would have to change. Increasing suppression of Kuchma's rivals, including the incarceration of Tymoshenko (to be repeated in 2011), deepened the sense that Kuchma could no longer be a partner. Both US and European leaders transparently preferred Yushchenko in the 2004 presidential elections, but their role both in the election and subsequent protests has been exaggerated.[20]

Following the Orange Revolution, the US and EU both dramatically increased their aid to Ukraine, believing that Ukraine had a unique opportunity to embrace domestic reform and to integrate into Europe. The opportunity for European integration only became possible after the EU launched its Eastern Partnership (a brainchild of Polish Foreign Minister Radosław Sikorski) in 2009 which was implemented after the Euromaidan. Those hopes were

---

[19] It is not clear whether the Kolchugas were ever delivered to Saddam Hussein's regime. From the US perspective, it did not matter.

[20] Ironically, both US democracy supporters (including government employees) and the Russian government had an interest in attributing a large role to the US. For democracy promotion advocates, the Orange Revolution justified further investment in their programs. For Russia, the US role bolstered the notion that the revolution was sponsored from outside rather than being internal and hence more legitimate.

rapidly dashed, as Tymoshenko and Yushchenko attacked one another and as reports of corruption among Yushchenko's administration made it clear that not much had changed. Western governments were disappointed and mystified when Yushchenko appointed Yanukovych, who had been responsible for attempting to steal the 2004 election, to the position of Prime Minister in 2006. At this point, the West in general and the US in particular lost interest, amid what was often known as 'Ukraine fatigue' and preoccupation in the US with wars in Iraq and Afghanistan. The 2008 global financial crisis further distracted the US and Europe from Ukrainian affairs.

In April 2008, NATO leaders met at Bucharest. On the agenda was the question of whether to extend Membership Action Plans (MAPs), which would pave the way to membership (without making a final decision) to Georgia and Ukraine. The US supported this step and Russia opposed it. Both German Chancellor Angela Merkel and French President Nicholas Sarkozy advocated deferring a decision in order to placate Russia. That policy prevailed. While Putin appeared pleased to have avoided something Russia was strongly opposed to, many viewed this as a deferment of a decision, not as a decision against extending MAPs, and eventually offers of membership, to Georgia and Ukraine. The communique issued at the summit stated the intention of offering membership to Ukraine and Georgia in the future. Charap and Colton described this result as 'the worst of all worlds: while providing no increased security to Ukraine and Georgia, the Bucharest Declaration reinforced the view in Moscow that NATO was determined to incorporate them at any cost'.[21] Russia invaded Georgia five months later.

Speaking to the NATO-Russia Council in Bucharest, Putin strongly opposed bringing Ukraine into NATO. In doing so, he drew attention to what he saw as the artificiality of Ukraine's borders and on the presence of Russian speakers in Eastern and Southern Ukraine, an area he would describe as *Novorossiya* six years later.[22] Putin told NATO:

> But in Ukraine, one third [sic[23]] are ethnic Russians. Out of forty-five million people, in line with the official census, seventeen million are Russians. There are regions, where only

---

[21]   Samuel Charap and Timothy J. Colton. *Everyone Loses*, p.88.

[22]   https://www.unian.info/world/111033-text-of-putins-speech-at-nato-summit-bucharest-april-2-2008.html

[23]   Putin dramatically overstated the number of ethnic Russian in Ukraine. According to the most recent (2001) census, 8.3 of Ukraine's roughly 48 million citizens identified as ethnic Russian, comprising 17% of the population, down from 22% in the 1989 census. Similarly, he overstated the portion of Russians in Crimea in the next sentence. It was actually 58%. See State Statistics Committee of Ukraine, 'All-Ukrainian Population Census 2001'. http://2001.ukrcensus.gov.ua/eng/results/general/nationality/

the Russian population lives, for instance, in the Crimea. Ninety percent are Russians. Generally speaking, Ukraine is a very complicated state. Ukraine, in the form it currently exists, was created in the Soviet times, it received its territories from Poland – after the Second World War, from Czechoslovakia, from Romania – and at present not all the problems have been solved as yet in the border region with Romania in the Black Sea. Then, it received huge territories from Russia in the East and South of the country.

Putin warned:

> If we introduce into it NATO problems, other problems, it may put the state on the verge of its existence. Complicated internal political problems are taking place there. We should act also very, very carefully. We do not have any right to veto, and, probably, we do not pretend to have. But I want that all of us, when deciding such issues, realise that we have there our interests as well. Well, seventeen million Russians currently live in Ukraine. Who may state that we do not have any interests there? South, the South of Ukraine, completely, there are only Russians. The Crimea was merely received by Ukraine with the decision of the CPSU (Communist Party of the Soviet Union) Politburo. There were not even any state procedures on transferring this territory.

Following the election of Yanukovych in 2010, the EU supplanted the US as the main Western interlocutor with the Ukrainian government, and the topic shifted from NATO membership, which was clearly a distant prospect at best, and one that Yanukovych did not support, to deeper integration with the EU, which was more popular and less divisive in Ukraine, and which would have a much more significant economic impact. Until then Russia had only opposed NATO enlargement, but from 2010, Russia strongly objected to the EU Association Agreement and to the Deep and Comprehensive Free Trade Agreement (DCFTA) that it envisioned, because such an agreement would preclude Ukraine from joining the CIS Customs Union, as one country cannot be a member of two customs unions.[24] The CIS Customs Union had been established in January 2010, only nine months after the Eastern Partnership, with which it was meant to compete.

---

[24] If one country were a member of both customs unions, goods could flow freely from all the countries in one union through the joint member to all the countries in the other, effectively creating a single large customs union.

Crucially, Putin viewed Ukraine as an important member of Putin's future Eurasian Union and Russia worked towards achieving this goal. Russia clearly viewed the Eastern Partnership as a 'geoeconomic' threat,[25] and many have seen this as another instance where the West forced Russia into a corner. The EU was adamant, however, that no third party could effectively veto an agreement between the EU and another country. This norm was extremely important, as it underpinned the notion of a Europe governed by norms and rules rather than by great powers. Russia believed the exact opposite, namely that Russia as a great power should wield an acknowledged veto over arrangements, especially in its sphere of interest. This combination of incompatible economic plans and contradictory norms set the international stage for the events that took place in the fall of 2013.

Conclusion

This chapter has sought to emphasise two key points. First, Russia's desire to limit Ukraine's independence and to retake control of at least some part of Crimea did not emerge during the Putin era. Rather they were there from the very beginning. Second, the example set by the Orange Revolution was seen as threatening to Russia because such a revolution might be replicated in Russia. Democracy in Ukraine would undermine the claim that democracy could not work in Russia and would undermine Russia's geopolitical position.

The first point is significant because it undermines two arguments about the source of the 2014 conflict that are made both by critics of the West and by critics of Putin. Critics of the West assert that Russia's annexation of Crimea was the West's fault. The central support for this is that NATO enlargement (beginning in 1997) and NATO support for Ukrainian membership (enunciated in the 2008 Bucharest Summit) left Russia little choice but to respond.[26] There is room for considerable debate concerning the wisdom of US, European and NATO policy after 1991, but it cannot be the source of Russia's designs on Ukraine, which very clearly predated any of the policies that critics point to.

The second point is significant because it recasts the feeling of insecurity that Russia felt in the years after the Orange Revolution. While Russian concern about NATO enlargement was real, this was not an existential threat.

---

[25] See S. Charap and T. J. Colton, *Everyone Loses*, p.29. They use Edward Luttwak's definition of geoeconomics as 'the logic of war in the grammar of commerce'. See Edward N. Luttwak, 'From Geopolitics to Geoeconomics: Logic of Conflict, Grammar of Commerce', *The National Interest*, no. 20 (Summer 1990), pp.17–23.

[26] See, for example, J. J. Mearsheimer, 'Why the Ukraine Crisis is the West's Fault'. S. Charap and T. J. Colton, *Everyone Loses*, devote particular attention to the role of the 2008 NATO Bucharest Summit.

Increasingly, democracy was seen as a threat to the Putin regime and by extent to Russia. The more the Putin and the Russian elites based their rule on autocracy rather than democracy, the more dangerous democracy in Ukraine became, for if Ukraine could build a European democracy, why not Russia? This could undermine the legitimacy of Putin's authoritarian model, and the Orange Revolution showed how street protests could turn dissatisfaction into regime change. That some American officials openly hoped for such an outcome was not reassuring.

For Putin and for many Russian great power nationalists, a threat to Putin's regime was tantamount to a threat to Russia's national security. The view that only Putin had been able to stop the decay in Russia, and that the West sought to weaken and surround Russia, meant that democracy was not only a political threat but an existential one. The West can be faulted for not being more sensitive to Russian fears, but the alternative – accepting Russia's right to rule its neighbours – was not without danger. The deeper underlying problem was that as Russia receded from democracy, the assumption that common interests outweighed conflicting interests was reversed. Thus, the disagreement over Ukraine's status increased in salience just at the time that Yanukovych was indirectly forcing his own citizens to take a stand one way or the other.

Because it is not tenable to assert that Russia's designs on Ukraine were caused by Western actions, the real question is whether the West should have acquiesced in Russian claims about a 'sphere of influence' that were present from the very beginning (and indeed go back at least to the end of World War II). That is a much harder question, and one can see arguments on both sides. But, in terms of getting the historical and causal arguments right, instead of saying the West caused the crisis, it is much more accurate to say that Russia had claims on Ukraine, that the West and Ukraine resisted those claims, and that Russia used force to get its way.

Further Reading

Bacon, Edwin, 'Putin's Crimea Speech, 18 March 2014: Russia's Changing Public Political Narrative', *Journal of Soviet and Post-Soviet Politics and Society*, vol.1, no.1 (2015), pp.13–36.

Bukkvoll, Tor, 'Off the Cuff Politics – Explaining Russia's Lack of a Ukraine Strategy', *Europe-Asia Studies*. Vol.53, no.8 (December 2001), pp.1141–57.

Connolly, Richard, 'The Empire Strikes Back: Economic Statecraft and the Securitisation of Political Economy in Russia', *Europe-Asia Studies*, vol. 68, no. 4 (June 2016), pp.750–773.

Grigas, Agnia, *Beyond Crimea: The New Russian Empire* (New Haven, CT: Yale University Press, 2016).

Grigas, A. *Frozen Conflicts: A Tool Kit for US Policymakers* (Washington DC: Atlantic Council of the US, July 2016). http://www.atlanticcouncil.org/images/ publications/Frozen_Conflicts_web_0715.pdf

Flemming Splidsboel, Hansen, 'Framing yourself into a corner: Russia, Crimea, and the minimal action space', *European Security*, vol.24, no.1 (January 2015), pp.141–158.

Karagiannis, Emmanuel, 'The Russian Interventions in South Ossetia and Crimea Compared: Military Performance, Legitimacy and Goals', *Contemporary Security Policy*, vol.35, no.3 (September 2014), pp.400–420.

Krastev, I. and Mark Leonard, 'Europe's Shattered Dream of Order: How Putin is Disrupting the Atlantic Alliance', *Foreign Affairs*, vol.94, no.3, (May-June 2015), pp. 48–58.

Kuzio, T., *Ukraine-Crimea-Russia: Triangle of Conflict, Soviet and Post-Soviet Politics and Society series* (Hannover: Ibidem-Verlag, 2007).

Malinova, Olga, 'Obsession with status and resentment: Historical backgrounds of the Russian discursive identity construction', *Communist and Post-Communist Studies*, vol.47, nos. 3/4, (September 2014), pp.291–303.

Perepylytsya, Hryhoriy, M., *Ukrayina i Rosiya v umovakh spivisnuvannya* (Kiev: Stylos, 2015).

Rácz, András and Arkady Moshes, *Not Another Transnistria: How sustainable is separatism in Eastern Ukraine? FIIA Analysis 4* (1 December 2014). http://www.fiia.fi/en/publication/456/not_another_transnistria/

Sasse, Gwendolyn, *The Crimea Question: Identity, Transition, and Conflict* (Cambridge, MA: Harvard University Press, 2007).

Smirnov, Mikhail, 'Like a Sack of Potatoes: Who Transferred the Crimean Oblast to the Ukrainian SSR in 1952– 54 and How it was Done', *Russian Politics and Law*, vol. 53, no. 2 (2015), pp. 32–46.

Teper, Yuri, 'Official Russian identity discourse in the light of the annexation of the Crimea: national or imperial?' *Post-Soviet Affairs*, vol. 32, no.4 (July 2016), pp. 378–396.

Tsygankov, Andrei, 'Assessing Cultural and Regime-Based Explanations of Russian Foreign Policy: Authoritarian at Heart and Expansionist by Nature?' *Europe-Asia Studies*, vol.64, no.4 (June 2012), pp.695–713.

Tsygankov, A. 'Vladimir Putin's last stand: the sources of Russia's Ukraine Policy, *Post-Soviet Affairs*, vol.31, no.4 (July 2015), pp. 279–303.

Urnov, Mark, '"Greatpowerness" as the key element of Russian self-consciousness under erosion', *Communist and Post-Communist Studies*, vol.47, nos.3/4 (September 2014), pp.305–322.

4

Annexation and Hybrid Warfare in Crimea and Eastern Ukraine

In chapter two we pointed out the need to look more deeply into the origins of Russia's information warfare in the USSR and specifically to locate its roots in campaigns against Ukrainian and Baltic independence movements. In chapter three we emphasised how all shades of Russian political opinion have supported territorial claims against Crimea and Sevastopol since the disintegration of the USSR. Russia's problem with an independent Ukraine was not invented by Putin or brought on by NATO and EU enlargement and democracy promotion. In this chapter, we analyse the annexation of Crimea and hybrid war against the Donbas in a longer historical context going back to the 2003–2004 Rose and Orange Revolutions.

We first address the question of whether the conflict in the Donbas is best defined as a civil or interstate war. The chapter then analyses the Crimea and Donbas over five phases with the key drivers listed in each phase. The phases are important for arriving at an understanding of the dynamics of the triangular relationship between Russia, the West and Ukraine. This chapter shows that Russia's actions in 2014 were consistent with long-term trends in its foreign policy aims and actions. Similarly, as chapter two highlighted, Russian intelligence, political technologists, information operations and local proxies were as active in the decade prior to the crisis as were Western democracy promotion efforts.

Civil or Interstate War – or Both?

Scholars have differed on whether to characterise events in Eastern Ukraine as a civil war or interstate conflict. The question is not merely academic. If the conflict there is a civil war, then its roots are within Ukraine. If so, Russia might play an important role in resolving it. If the conflict is seen as an interstate war, the involvement of Russian regular army forces becomes a natural focus. In this case, while Russia must still be part of the solution, it must also be regarded fundamentally as part of the problem. Its role in resolving the conflict will be as a belligerent, not as a mediator.

Equally important, whether the war is a civil war or interstate war changes our view of what is at stake. If the war is an international war, then the question in large part is where the border will be drawn between Russia and Ukraine, though Russia's ability to determine certain aspects of Ukraine's policies is also at stake. If the conflict is a civil war, then it is more fundamentally about who will run the government of Ukraine and under what political system. This was made clear again in 2017, when DNR Prime Minister Aleksandr Zakharchenko proposed a new territorial entity of *Malorossiya* (Little Russia) to replace Ukraine. Zakharchenko was not proposing secession from Ukraine, but the takeover of Ukraine by a new, fundamentally different regime. The proposal reinforced the framing of the conflict as one among Ukrainians over the government of Ukraine. While the proposal was met with bewilderment, it 'is in line with the Kremlin's longstanding strategic goal to take back all of Ukraine under Russian domination as part of the so-called *Russkii Mir*'.[1] Little Russia would be a weak federalised state with Donetsk as its capital city that would join the Eurasian Union and no longer seek NATO and EU membership.

Not surprisingly, those who tend to blame the conflict on the West see it is a civil war, and those who blame it on Russia as an interstate war. Empirically, debate has centred around two questions. The first is the chronology of events from the Euromaidan through to the invasion of Russian *spetsnaz* led by Alexander Girkin in the second week of April 2014. The second is to what extent the evolution of the protests into an armed movement was a home-grown rebellion or was from the outset a Russian proxy war.

While many conflicts include both civil and interstate components, the ambiguity about this conflict is not accidental, as Russian strategy from the outset has been to obscure who is doing the fighting. This was most visible with the 'little green men' deployed in Crimea, whose unit markings had been removed to obscure their origins, but has been the case in Eastern Ukraine as well, where both fighters and supplies from Russia have been hidden or disguised as coming from Ukraine. These actions were coordinated with Russian information operations portraying both Crimea and the Donbas as internal Ukrainian secessionist movements.

---

[1]   Pavel Felgenhauer, 'The Russian-Ukrainian Conflict Could Be Escalating', *Eurasian Daily Monitor*, vol.14, no.96 (20 July 2017). https://jamestown.org/program/the-russian-ukrainian-conflict-could-be-escalating/

A civil war challenges the sovereignty of an internationally recognised state, and takes place in theory within the boundaries of a recognised state, though in practice most civil wars have international components to them. While definitions of civil war vary, they generally refer to conflict between groups *within* a single state and with a high level of casualties (generally 1,000; some specify within a single year).[2] Most also add the notion that one combatant in a civil war is the state, and another combatant aims to take power at the centre or in a region, or to change government policies.[3]

The key definitional difference between 'civil' or 'intrastate' wars and interstate wars is who the combatants are. In a civil war, only one of the sides is a state. In an interstate war, two or more combatants are states. Thus, the definitional question in the case of Ukraine is whether Ukraine is fighting domestic rebels or Russia. In practice, it is fighting both, and judgments differ on whether Russia's involvement is central or peripheral. Our judgment is that, as was the case in Crimea, the conflict in Donbas is more fundamentally driven by Russia than by internal Ukrainian forces, and has lasted as long as it has, and has produced the level of casualties it has, largely because of the forces and supplies contributed by Russia.

Focusing on chronology, there is disagreement over *when* exactly Russian involvement in Eastern Ukraine became a driving force in the conflict in Donbas. From summer 2014 onward, there is relatively little dispute, as there was extensive evidence of Russian involvement following artillery attacks from Russia, entry of Russian army forces into Eastern Ukraine, and supplying, training and leading of Russian proxy militias in the region. Prior to that, however, there is less agreement, leaving some to argue that Russia intervened in what was already a civil war in Ukraine, rather than actually fomenting the conflict. Scholars downplaying Russian intervention have tended to frame Ukraine's conflict as a civil war between Russian and Ukrainian speakers brought about by Ukrainian nationalism.[4] Such analyses emphasise the volunteer origins of Russian fighters in Ukraine. A 2014 analysis by Laruelle differentiated between nationalist volunteers and mercenaries travelling to the Donbas, leaving out entirely the question of those sent by the Russian government.[5]

---

[2]   Nicholas Sambanis, 'A Review of Recent Advances and Future Directions in the Quantitative Literature on Civil War', *Defence and Peace Economics*, vol.13, no.3 (January 2002), p.218.

[3]   N. Sambanis, 'A Review of Recent Advances.'

[4]   R. Sakwa, *Frontline Ukraine*. For an alternative view see A. Wilson, 'The Donbas in 2014'.

[5] | Pal Kolstø, 'Crimea vs Donbas', in P. Kolstø and Helge Blakkisrud eds., *The New Russian Nationalism. Imperialism, Ethnicity and Authoritarianism 2000–2015* (Edinburgh: Edinburgh University Press, 2016), p.703.and M. Laruelle, 'Is anyone in

Scholars who have instead emphasised Russia's role in the conflict have pointed to the importance of Russia's security guarantee to the DNR and LNR. Galeotti writes that, 'The DNR and LNR are, of course, Russian proxy actors, armed, shielded and above all funded by Moscow'. But, he adds the caveat, 'However, they are also loose coalitions of self-interested adventurers, from the leaderships down to local militia commanders'.[6] For those emphasising the Russian origins of the conflict, the central point is that without Russian financial subsidies and a security guarantee, the two separatist enclaves would not survive.[7]

The Ukrainian government has defined fighters loyal to the DNR and LNR as 'terrorists' and is fighting the war as an ATO under a 2003 law 'On Terrorism'. This framing of the conflict was intended to avoid defining the conflict as a war, as international organisations do not lend to countries at 'war'. A secondary reason was defining the conflict as a 'war' would require full scale mobilisation of military resources and mass conscription and a state of emergency which would limit democratic freedoms, and there was opposition to this within Ukraine.

This is not to say that there was not serious and organised opposition in Eastern Ukraine to the events taking place in Kiev in early 2014. A central question is how these grievances were transformed into mass violence. Whereas the violence in Kiev occurred when the state unleashed violence against protestors, in Eastern Ukraine the state had no ability to do so. When Yanukovych fled from Kiev and Euromaidan revolutionaries took power, the Ukrainian state was too weak and fragmented to use its security forces to crush protests. Ukraine launched its ATO on 13 April only *after* proxies from Russia and protestors stormed and took control of state buildings in Donetsk (6 April) and Russian *spetsnaz* invaded Ukraine (11–12 April).

The vast literature on civil conflict focuses both on grievances – why people rebel – and on capacity – factors that sustain or undermine rebellion.[8] Grievances can arise from contestation over economic, identity, religious and/

---

charge of Russian nationalists fighting in Ukraine?' *The Washington Post*, 26 June 2014. https://www.washingtonpost.com/news/monkey-cage/wp/2014/06/26/is-anyone-in-charge-of-russian-nationalists-fighting-in-ukraine/?utm_term=.2949f0b544f8

[6]   M. Laruelle, 'Is anyone in charge of Russian nationalists fighting in Ukraine?'

[7]   Julian Ropcke, 'How Russia Finances the Ukrainian rebel territories' and 'Putin's shadow government for Donbass exposed', *Bild*, 16 and 29 March 2016. http://www.bild.de/politik/ausland/ukraine-konflikt/russia-finances-donbass-44151166.bild.html and http://www.bild.de/politik/ausland/ukraine-konflikt/donbass-shadow-government-45102202.bild.html

[8]   See James D. Fearon and David D. Laitin, 'Ethnicity, Insurgency, and Civil War', *American Political Science Review*, vol.97, no.1 (2003), pp.75–90.

or ethnic factors. Ted Gurr has stressed the salience of ethno-cultural identities and their capacity to mobilise, levels of grievance, and availability of opposition political activities.[9] The World Bank's Collier-Hoeffler model investigates the availability of finances, opportunity costs of rebellion, military advantage and terrain, ethnic and regional grievances of minorities dominated by majorities, the size of the population and the period of time since the last conflict.[10]

Residents of the Donbas have a strong affinity with their region that in many cases was stronger than their affinity with the Ukrainian state. At the same time, the Donbas has been relatively passive and, as seen in the Orange and Euromaidan Revolutions, unable to mobilise on the same level as that of Western and Central Ukraine. Weaker mobilisation might be explained by the fact that elites from the Donbas were always heavily influential in national level policy. In terms of Albert O. Hirschman's traditional choice of exit, voice or loyalty, the Donbas never needed exit because its voice was so powerful. That changed in early 2014 when Yanukovych was ejected and the Party of Regions surrendered control of parliament.

Mobilisation would be assisted by relative levels of hostility, intensification of political cleavages, disintegration of institutions, and loss of government legitimacy. All of these four factors increased in the Donbas in early 2014. The Party of Regions and its allies had mobilised against the nationalist 'Other' and 'fascists' during every election since 2004 and had drawn upon this inflammatory rhetoric in parliament and the media. High levels of tension during the Euromaidan and Russia's barrage of propaganda and information war widened political cleavages further. The political crisis and blocking of government buildings during the four-month long Euromaidan led to the partial disintegration of the Ukrainian state which deteriorated further after the ousting of Yanukovych.[11]

Constructivist approaches to conflict find that mobilisation of protestors is the work of elites (ethnic entrepreneurs) who fashion beliefs, preferences and identities and socially construct and reinforce existing cleavages.[12] A constructivist approach has particular resonance in the Donbas where oligarchs

---

[9]   Ted Gurr, *Peoples Versus States: Minorities at Risk in the New Century* (Washington DC: US Institute of Peace, 2000).

[10]   Edward Wong, 'A Matter of Definition: What Makes a Civil War and Who Declares It So?' *New York Times*, 28 November 2006.

[11]   See P. D'Anieri. 'Anarchy, the State, and Ukraine', in John Heathershaw and Ed Schatz, eds., *Paradox of Power: The Logics of State Weakness in Eurasia* (Pittsburgh, University of Pittsburgh Press, 2017), pp.200–215.

[12]   J. Fearon and David Laitin, 'Violence and social construction of ethnic identity', *International Organization*, vol.54, no.4 (October 2000), pp.845–877.

and the Party of Regions political machine dominated the region in a way resembling Russia's managed democracy. The influence of elites was shown by the ability of Rinat Akhmetov, Ukraine's most powerful oligarch, to halt an attack on the city of Mariupol in the summer of 2014. Akhmetov had chosen not to intervene when the conflict first emerged in the spring. Donbas oligarchs were either working in collusion with radical protestors (e.g. Luhansk oligarch and head of the Party of Regions parliamentary faction Oleksandr Yefremov) or adopted a wait and see position to apply pressure on Kiev, as they had done during the Orange Revolution, when there was a brief abortive movement toward secession at the November 2004 Severedonetsk Congress. Donbas regional elites have been instrumental in mobilising protests in coalminers' strikes in 1989, the transportation of 'political tourists' to Kiev to protest against the disbanding of parliament in 2007 and anti-Maidan protests during the Orange and Euromaidan Revolutions.

Foreign powers have intervened in the majority of civil wars and the longer the civil war continues the more likelihood there will be outside intervention. Nicholas Sambanis writes that 'expected intervention has a robustly positive and highly significant association with civil war'.[13] Foreign powers should be reasonably confident of success; the projected time horizon of the intervention is short and domestic opposition is minimal. All three factors highlighted by Sambanis exist in the Russia-Ukraine crisis. In August 2014 and January/February 2015, Russia's intervention was decisive, defeating Ukrainian forces at Ilovaysk and Debaltseve respectively. Pro-Putin *and* opposition supporters have supported the annexation of the Crimea although Russians have mixed views of military intervention in the Donbas which has less symbolic value in Russian history and identity.[14] In spring 2014, for Putin and Russian nationalists the two historically symbolic and strategic cities in *Novorossiya* were Kharkiv and Odesa (although the former was never part of this Tsarist region) – not Donetsk or Luhansk.

In terms of aiding mobilisation, Russian support was crucial in three distinct respects. First, Russia provided extensive 'information' support, using mass media to paint the new government in Kiev as illegitimate and as determined to oppress Russian-speaking Eastern Ukrainians. Second, Russia provided organisational and material support, using its state capacity to infiltrate organisers and equipment to help coordinate opposition. Third, Russia

---

[13]   N. Sambanis, 'A Review of Recent Advances and Future Directions in the Quantitative Literature on Civil War', p.235.
[14]   See two joint surveys on Russian-Ukrainian relations conducted by the (Russian) Levada Centre and Kyiv International Institute of Sociology at https://www.levada.ru/en/2014/11/05/levada-center-and-kiis-about-crisis-in-ukraine/ and https://michaelcolborne.com/2016/10/27/comparing-ukrainian-russian-attitudes-toward-each-other-kiislevada-centre-data/

provided the actual people being mobilised, both informally, via the volunteers and mercenaries Laruelle analyses, and formally, through the introduction of regular army forces. One cannot definitively answer the counterfactual question of what would have happened to the anti-Maidan protestors in Eastern Ukraine without Russia's support, but there is a strong case to be made that they would have lost out either to local elites or to Ukrainian government forces. That is what nearly happened before increased Russian intervention in the summer of 2014. The view that protests were internally self-sustaining raises the question of why Russia intervened at such high political cost if it were not necessary to sustain the conflict. Similarly, it is hard to imagine the rapid takeover of Crimea succeeding without Russian forces taking a direct role, and it is hard to see how the annexation could have taken place so quickly without the Russian government coordinating processes as disconnected as the referendum in Crimea and the legislation of the State Duma.

From Orange Revolution to Annexation and Hybrid War

The conflict over Crimea and Eastern Ukraine did not begin with the Euromaidan revolution and the ousting of Yanukovych. Chapters two and three emphasised that the longer-term sources of the conflict reach back to the Soviet era and earlier. The discussion in this chapter begins with the Orange Revolution and its impact on Russian views of Ukraine. We analyse the process leading to violent conflict in five phases, with the discussion of each phase beginning with a list of key developments.

Countering the Orange Threat: 2004–2009

- The 2004 Orange revolution brings a pro-Western government to power in Ukraine.
- Expressions of nationalism and anti-Western xenophobia increase in Russia.
- In 2005, the Party of Regions signs a cooperation agreement with United Russia and the following year Russia brokers a coalition between the Party of Regions and Crimean Russian nationalists-separatists.
- Ukrainian radicals receive paramilitary training in Russia in preparation for the 2010 elections.
- Putin's speeches at the 2007 Munich security conference and 2008 NATO summit extend claims about Russia's role in the region.
- The *Russkii Mir* project is launched.
- Russia invades Georgia.
- The Russian government, Party of Regions, Communist Party of Ukraine and Crimean Russian nationalists-separatists recognise the independence of South Ossetia and Abkhazia.

- Russia's deteriorating relations with Ukraine in 2008–2009 lead to the expulsion of two Russian diplomats and President's Medvedev's open letter to Yushchenko.
- EU launches the Eastern Partnership in 2009.

The Orange Revolution was the third colour revolution in four years and the most excruciating for Russia's leaders; indeed, political technologist Pavlovsky described it as 'our 9/11'. [15] Russian nationalism was evident in the 1990s – especially in the 1993 parliamentary elections – but it increased dramatically in response to NATO's bombing of Yugoslavia in 1999 and the West's subsequent support for the Bulldozer Revolution, that ejected Slobodan Milosevic from power, and Kosovo's independence. Ukraine's Orange Revolution was another powerful accelerant. Russia's turn away from the West was clearly spelt out in Putin's 2007 speech to the Munich security conference which was unexpected and shocking to Western audiences, but ultimately ignored as not representing a harbinger of the future direction of Russian policies. Russia's turn away from the West has not been linear and has included two (failed) attempts at US-Russia resets after the 9/11 terrorist attacks and after Obama's election.

Following the end of Leonid Kuchma's second term in office in 2004, the moderate centre ground which had dominated Eastern Ukrainian centrist political forces evaporated and gave way to the more overtly pro-Russian, neo-Soviet and criminal Donetsk clan in the Party of Regions which came to monopolise elections and local councils in Eastern-Southern Ukraine. The Party of Regions won a plurality in three subsequent parliamentary elections (2006, 2007, 2012) and elected its leader, Yanukovych president (2010). In 2014, a political vacuum emerged in Donbas and Eastern Ukraine following the disintegration of the Party of Regions and the Communist Party, which was filled by radical Russian nationalists, pan-Slavists and separatists. Many of these radicals, such as the Donetsk Republic founded in 2005 and banned from 2008–2010, successor to Inter-Movement of Donbas established in 1989, had undertaken paramilitary training in Ukraine and in Russian summer camps. [16]

These camps were run by the International Eurasian Movement led by Dugin, and Putin's senior adviser Surkov, author of the slogan 'sovereign democracy'

---

[15] Quoted in Ben Judah, *Fragile Empire: How Russia Fell In and Out of Love with Vladimir Putin* (New Haven: Yale University Press, 2013).

[16] Tim Judah, *In Wartime. Stories from Ukraine* (New York: Tim Duggan Books, 2015), pp.152–153. Photographs of members of the Donetsk Republic undergoing paramilitary training in 2009 were published by *Novosti Donbassa*, 20 July 2014. http://novosti.dn.ua/details/230206/

and the president's *'kurator'* (overseer on behalf of the Russian president) of the DNR and LNR, was a frequent speaker. The Donetsk Republic is one of two parties of power in the DNR. The founder of the Inter-Movement of Donbas, Sergei Baryshnikov, who was appointed Dean of Donetsk University, believes Ukrainians 'are Russians who refuse to admit their Russianness'.[17] He called for the destruction of Ukrainian identity, which he compared to a 'disease' and 'cancer', by 'war and repression'.[18]

The Party of Regions was different from Eastern Ukrainian centrist parties in three ways. The first was its more pronounced pro-Russian orientation which was seen in 2005 when the Party of Regions signed a cooperation agreement with United Russia and the following year when Russian political technologists brokered an election alliance with Crimean Russian nationalists-separatists. The latter had been marginalised in the second half of the 1990s by President Kuchma, who would have never countenanced cooperation with them. The Party of Regions alliance with Crimean Russian nationalists-separatists paved the way for Russia's annexation of the Crimea, after which most Crimean Party of Regions deputies in the Crimean parliament were elected to Russia's State Duma as United Russia candidates.

In the aftermath of Russia's invasion of Georgia in August 2008, the Party of Regions, Communist Party of Ukraine and Crimean Russian nationalists-separatists supported Russia's recognition of the independence of South Ossetia and Abkhazia, signalling their close relationship with Moscow. A resolution to that effect was adopted in the Crimean Supreme Soviet but a similar resolution failed in the Ukrainian parliament. They were alone in the CIS in following Russia's support for infringing Georgia's territorial integrity. Even Belarus and Kazakhstan, who have backed every integration project in the CIS, refused to recognise the breakaway regions' independence. The action of these three Ukrainian political forces foreshadowed Yanukovych's support for Russia's seizure of Crimea.

Russian propaganda against 'Ukrainian nationalists' did not begin during the Euromaidan; it was already underway during Ukraine's 2004 presidential campaign. In 2005, the transformation of the Walking Alone pro-Putin fan club into the Democratic Anti-Fascist Movement *Nashi* was a reaction to the widespread fear that Russia was next in line for a colour revolution. The 'anti-fascist' label was revived as a means to link the fight against colour revolutions to the myth of the Great Patriotic War and to again denigrate 'Ukrainian nationalists'. The specific goal was to link Ukraine's 'orange' revolutionaries with the anti-Soviet partisans from the World War II-era who

---

[17]   T. Judah, *In Wartime*, p.150.
[18]   T. Judah, *In Wartime*, p.150.

had long been demonised as Nazi collaborators. The launch of the *Russkii Mir* was compared to that of the British Council but this was misleading as it always had close ties with Russian intelligence and pursued more overtly political goals towards neighbouring countries. The CIS Customs Union/ Eurasian Union was directed at all CIS members while the *Russkii Mir* aimed to maintain the unity of Eastern Slavic Orthodox civilisation of the three 'brotherly peoples' who had descended from the medieval state of Kiev Rus.

Ukrainian-Russian relations became increasingly strained in the latter years of Yushchenko's presidency. President Yushchenko had infuriated Moscow when he had travelled with Polish and Baltic leaders to Georgia to voice their support in the face of Russia's invasion. The EU and US, in contrast, imposed no sanctions against Russia and continued with business as usual. The EU's September 2009 Independent International Fact-Finding Mission on the Conflict in Georgia headed by Heidi Tagliavini blamed Georgia for the outbreak of hostilities. The report failed to understand the dynamics of Russia issuing passports to inhabitants of separatist enclaves, its use of proxy forces, armed provocations, and Moscow's desire for regime change. Russian leaders may have believed they had been sent a signal by the West that invading neighbours would not lead to sanctions. In any event, the West's mild reaction to the invasion of Georgia apparently did not sufficiently reassure Russia.

Increased counter-intelligence work by the SBU led to the expulsion of two Russian diplomats for espionage (i.e. supporting separatist groups in the Crimea and Odesa). This infuriated the supposedly more liberal-minded President Medvedev who penned an open letter to Yushchenko listing a whole raft of changes that Russia sought in Ukraine's domestic and foreign policies.[19] A careful reading of these demands shows that Russia's leaders were adamantly opposed to the Ukrainian nation building project and the revival of a Ukrainian historiography independent of Russia and outside the Eastern Slavic *Russkii Mir* civilisation.[20]

Although NATO had balked at providing MAPs for Ukraine and Georgia at the 2008 Bucharest summit, Russia's concerns remained acute because of the EU's unveiling of the Eastern Partnership in May 2009. Geared exclusively for post-Soviet countries such as Ukraine, the Eastern Partnership only offered integration *without* membership. Nevertheless, the EU's interest in enlarging for the first time into Eurasia brought about competition from a Russian counter-proposal that the EU never took seriously. After Yanukovych was elected Ukrainian President, Russia entered the second phase full of

---

[19]   Michael Schwirts, 'Moscow Signals Widening Rift with Ukraine', *New York Times*, 11 August 2009.

[20]   An English translation of Medvedev's letter is in T. Kuzio, *Ukraine*, pp.438–439.

optimism that Ukraine could be re-integrated.

Putin Turns Further to the Right, 2010–2013

- Yanukovych's election brings domestic and foreign policy changes in Ukraine.
- Russia's lease of Sevastopol as a Black Sea Fleet base is extended to 2042–2047.
- Ukraine adopts a non-bloc foreign policy and drops the goal of NATO membership.
- Russian intelligence gradually takes control of and recruits spies within the SBU and Ukrainian military intelligence.
- Russia launches the CIS Customs Union in 2010 as a stepping-stone to a Eurasian Union.
- Widespread anti-Putin Russian protests take place in 2011–2012, fuelling fears that Russia is the next Western target for a colour revolution and regime change.
- Putin wins re-election and turns even further to the nationalist right.
- In 2013, Putin begins to promote the idea of Ukrainian-Russian unity.
- In summer 2013, Russian trade boycotts and *kompromat* are used to pressure Yanukovych to drop European integration.

In Moscow's eyes, the election of Yanukovych had the potential to return Ukrainian-Russian relations to 'normality' and that of 'brotherly peoples'. But the reassurance offered by the election of Ukraine's most pro-Russian president led not to an easing of Russian activity, but to an increase. Although Yanukovych fulfilled all of the domestic and foreign policy demands laid out by Medvedev, Russia remained unsatisfied. In Yanukovych's first year in office he became the first Ukrainian president to eschew characterising the *Holodomor* as a famine directed by Stalin at Ukraine and avoided using the term 'genocide', which was particularly infuriating to Russia. The Party of Regions-controlled Parliament adopted a 'non-bloc' foreign policy (sometimes mischaracterised as 'neutrality'), and dropped the objective of seeking NATO membership. In sum, Yanukovych gave Russia much of what it had long wanted.

Although Ukrainian politics have been routinely presented as one of East-West rivalry, presidential elections have generally been competitions between Eastern Ukrainian elites; only one of Ukraine's five presidents (Kravchuk) has been from Western Ukraine. Moreover, not all Eastern Ukrainians hold similar political views; it was Kuchma who organised a worldwide campaign in support of defining the *Holodomor* as a genocide on its 70th anniversary and who first enunciated EU and NATO membership as Ukraine's goals.

In 2012, the Party of Regions adopted a law on languages that *de facto* upgraded Russian to a second state language, circumventing the process of amending the constitution, for which it had insufficient votes. The Council of Europe's Venice Commission had criticised the law as not meeting the requirements of the European Charter for Regional or Minority Languages which was drawn up to protect endangered languages.[21]

In addition to the language law, Yanukovych also forced through parliament (against the advice of three parliamentary committees) the Kharkiv Accords extending Russia's lease of Sevastopol. The 1997 Black Sea Fleet agreement had provided for a 'temporary' lease of the Sevastopol naval base until 2017. The Kharkiv Accords extended the lease to 2042 (with the option of a five-year extension), in effect making this a permanent Russian naval base. This was a major strategic achievement for Russia, where re-establishing Russian ownership of Sevastopol and Crimea had long been popular across the political spectrum. In addition to pressuring Yanukovych to drop EU integration, Russia made further demands. These included the creation of joint ventures in practically every area of Ukraine's economy, especially the military industrial complex and energy. Russia sought the same control over Ukraine's gas pipelines that it had acquired in Belarus, Armenia and elsewhere. Russia's proposal for a consortium over Ukraine's pipelines would have given Moscow a majority shareholding.

By the 2012 elections, Russia and Russian leaders had become even more nationalistic and anti-Western xenophobia had become a staple in the Russian media. The US-Russian reset had again failed and Hillary Clinton's support for protestors in Moscow made Putin suspicious that the West was fomenting another colour revolution with regime change in mind. Putin's re-election pushed him even further to the nationalist right and he increasingly added social conservatism to nationalism, espousing 'conservative values' and anti-Western xenophobia, aligning with anti-EU populist nationalists, neo-Nazi (such as Greece's Golden Dawn party) and fascist (such as France's Front National) political forces in Europe. Additionally, US White nationalists and Alt-Right, who have become more assertive and prominent in the US in the wake of the Charlottesville riots, have become fans of Putin.[22] US Alt-Right leader Richard Spencer describes Putin's Russia as the 'sole white

---

[21]   http://www.venice.coe.int/webforms/documents/default.aspx?pdffile=CDL-AD(2011)008-e In Spring 2014, when the new parliamentary majority overturned the law, Russian information warfare mobilised protestors, and the claim that Russian-speakers were losing long-held rights was widely disseminated. In fact, acting head of state Oleksandr Turchynov never signed this into law and the 2012 law remains in force.

[22]   https://www.theatlantic.com/magazine/archive/2017/03/its-putins-world/513848/

power in the world'.[23]

Russia's integration strategy relied on the participation of the three Eastern Slavic peoples of the *Russkii Mir* as the core of the Eurasian Union. In many ways, this strategy reflected traditional Soviet nationalities policy under which the Eastern Slavs had formed the Russian-speaking core of the USSR. It also reflected the more deeply rooted Russian historiography that saw Russians, Belarusians and Ukrainians as *odyn narod* (one people). Putin began referring to Ukrainians and Russians as 'one people' with their joint origins in Kievan Rus that could not be allowed to be broken apart. Russia's chauvinistic rhetoric towards Ukrainians became more visceral and public after Putin's re-election but they were by no means new. Russian views of Ukrainians as not constituting a 'real people' and of Ukraine as a failed and artificial state have deep roots in Russian national identity.

Putin's counter-attack against Western encroachment into what Russia sees as its 'zone of privileged interests' came in the creation of the CIS Customs Union in 2010, which would evolve into the Eurasian Union in 2015. Ukraine would hold its next presidential elections in the same year the CIS Customs Union would transform into the Eurasian Union and Yanukovych's re-election for a second term would be necessary for Ukraine to join Putin's pet project. The Party of Regions launched its 2015 election campaign after the 2012 parliamentary elections, taking its 'anti-fascist' slogans directly from Soviet commissars and Russian political technologists. The Party of Regions adopted the slogan 'To Europe without fascists' (implying that the opposition was fascist) when Yanukovych's ally, Russia was cooperating with and financing European neo-Nazi political forces.[24]

Putin did not initiate a new departure for Russian security policy towards Eurasia but merely drew on a tradition of Russia seeing itself as the dominant centre of Eurasia. Attempts to create CIS structures and unions had taken place throughout Yeltsin's presidency. In 1992, the Tashkent Treaty established CIS collective military forces that became the Collective Security Treaty Organisation a decade later. In 1996, Russia and Belarus outlined plans for a union and they together with Kazakhstan launched the Eurasian Economic Community (which was joined by Kyrgyzstan and Tajikistan in 2000 and Uzbekistan in 2006).

---

[23]   http://www.newsweek.com/leaders-charlottesvilles-alt-right-protest-all-have-ties-russian-fascist-651384

[24]   http://www.bbc.com/news/world-europe-39478066 and https://www.ft.com/content/010eec62-30b5-11e7-9555-23ef563ecf9a For extensive background on this subject see A. Shekhovtsov, *Russia and the Western Far Right*.

In spring and summer 2013, Russian trade boycotts of Ukraine and other forms of pressure compelled Yanukovych to sign a memorandum in May making Ukraine an 'observer' in the CIS Customs Union. The EU, meanwhile, dropped its earlier insistence that Yanukovych release Tymoshenko from prison before an Association Agreement was finalised. By removing an obvious reason why the Association Agreement could not go forward, this concession actually increased pressure on Yanukovych.

Plans Undone: Euromaidan Ukraine, 2013–2014

- Yanukovych's reversal on the EU Association Agreements prompts the Euromaidan Revolution.
- Russian information warfare promotes portrayal of Euromaidan 'fascists'.
- Russian intelligence supports Ukrainian security forces in suppressing protests and training and financing anti-Maidan vigilantes.
- Russian 'political tourists' are transported into Kharkiv, Donetsk, Luhansk and Odesa to swell the crowd numbers.

The Euromaidan and Yanukovych's ouster destroyed Putin's well-cultivated plans for Ukraine to join the Eurasian Union. When Yanukovych 'suspended' discussion of joining the Association Agreement in November-December 2013, Putin believed he had successfully induced Yanukovych to join Russia's regional bloc. Russia followed up by offering to buy $15 billion worth of Ukrainian Eurobonds and by lowering the price of gas from over $400 to $268 per 1,000 cubic metres. The latter price was still higher than that charged to Belarus but similar to what the *Ostchem* gas intermediary owned by gas tycoon Dmytro Firtash had been paying. The preferential price given to Firtash was in return to a portion of his profits being used to purchase strategic sectors of the Ukrainian economy on behalf of the Russian state.[25]

During the Euromaidan, Russia provided advice and equipment to Ukrainian riot police (*Berkut*) and other security forces involved in repressing protestors.[26] Russian intelligence, whether as long-time sleepers or inserted during the Euromaidan crisis, also supported anti-Maidan vigilantes long

---

[25] T. Kuzio, 'Dmytro Firtash Launches New Opaque Gas Intermediary', *Eurasia Daily Monitor*, vol. 10, no.55 (25 March 2013) https://jamestown.org/program/dmytro-firtash-launches-new-opaque-gas-intermediary/ and Stephen Grey, Tom Bergin, Sevgil Musaieva and Roman Anin, 'SPECIAL REPORT-Putin's allies channelled billions to Ukraine oligarch', *Reuters*, 26 November 2014. http://uk.reuters.com/article/russia-capitalism-gas-special-report-pix-idUKL3N0TF4QD20141126

[26] 'Pro-Russian forces in the Yanukovych Presidency' in T. Kuzio, *Putin's War Against Ukraine*, pp.232–238.

before Yanukovych's ouster. Russia's support for paramilitary hybrid warfare on the ground was backed by a barrage of anti-Ukrainian, 'anti-fascist' and anti-Maidan propaganda that inflamed passions and reduced the chances for compromise.

Russian intelligence was not only training and financing anti-Maidan, pro-Russian vigilantes but also organising the transportation of protestors (dubbed 'political tourists') to Donetsk, Luhansk and Kharkiv from Russia and to Odesa from Russian-controlled Trans-Dniestr. Russian nationalists were quickly on the scene and radicalised the crowds who captured state buildings in Donetsk and Luhansk. In Donetsk and Luhansk, the disintegration of the security forces, who had been loyal to the Party of Regions, provided vigilantes with a stockpile of weapons. These developments were supplemented in the second week of April by the arrival of 'muscle' (Russian *spetsnaz*), who expanded the area that protestors controlled and provided training, discipline and military equipment.[27]

Russian intelligence services had penetrated Ukrainian security forces and in particular the SBU during Yanukovych's presidency.[28] The Ukrainian military, Ministry of Interior and SBU in the Crimea were recruited locally, which in hindsight was a mistake. The First Deputy Commander of Ukraine's navy, Sergei Yeliseyev, was born near Moscow, graduated from a Soviet naval school in the Russian city of Kaliningrad and had served with the Russian Pacific fleet. After defecting during the crisis, he was appointed deputy commander of Russia's Baltic fleet. Ukraine's naval commander Denis Berezovsky also defected, along with several of his commanders, and was appointed deputy commander of the Russian Black Sea Fleet. In Crimea, thousands of SBU and military officers, *Militsiya* and prosecutors defected to Russian occupation forces.

The only other Ukrainian region where the security forces defected *en masse* was in the Donbas. Since the end of the gang war between criminal groups in 1996–1997 and Yanukovych's appointment as Donetsk Governor, oligarchs and the Party of Regions political machine had controlled the security forces. *Berkut* riot police and Internal Troops from the local *Militsiya* had been sent to Kiev to quell the Euromaidan protests and returned home angry and bitter at the death and injury of their colleagues and the lack of political will to quell the protests. One hundred thirty protestors and 18 *Militsiya* officers were killed on the Euromaidan. The disintegration of the Party of Regions and flight

---

[27] See the extensive biography in T. Kuzio, *Putin's War Against Ukraine*, pp.362–398.

[28] T. Kuzio, 'Russianization of Ukrainian National Security Policy under Viktor Yanukovych', *Journal of Slavic Military Studies*, vol.25, no.4 (December 2012), pp.558–581 and T. Kuzio, *Putin's War Against Ukraine*, pp.232–238.

of Yanukovych from Kiev after the bloodbath on 18–20 February, led to the loss of command and control over the security forces in the Donbas.

In the majority of regions in Eastern and Southern Ukraine a large proportion of the security forces continued to operate and, assisted by local business-men, Euromaidan activists and self-defence forces, they defeated pro-Russian forces. In Moscow's eyes, the key battleground cities and strategic prizes were Kharkiv and Odesa – not Donetsk and Luhansk. In Kharkiv, Russian political tourists initially stormed the opera and ballet theatre mistakenly believing it was the city hall. Interior Minister Arsen Avakov, who is from Kharkiv, oversaw the defeat of pro-Russian forces in his city by the end of the first week of April. In Odesa, street fighting between pro-Russian and pro-Ukrainian forces ended after a day of violence on 2 May which killed 48 protestors by gunshots and fire. In Donetsk and Luhansk, six factors worked towards the Ukrainian state losing control: the political vacuum after the collapse of the Party of Regions; the passivity and collusion of oligarchs; widespread use of violence by anti-Maidan vigilantes against pro-Ukrainian protestors; covert Russian intelligence operations; the inflow of nationalists and neo-Nazis from Russia who took control of pro-Russian protests; and professional assistance from Russian *spetsnaz* who invaded mainland Ukraine in the second week of April.

Protests, Hybrid War and Annexation, 2014

- EU peace deal falls flat after protestors are killed.
- Yanukovych flees Kiev, eventually to Russia.
- Euromaidan opposition parties take power and remove Yanukovych as president.
- In late-February, Russian 'little green men' invade the Crimea and backed by local nationalists, Cossacks, organised crime and 'self-defence' forces take control of state institutions without Ukrainian government opposition.
- From late-February to late-April, attempts are made to organise pro-Russian uprisings in Eastern and Southern Ukraine but most quickly subside.
- In early-April, Russian 'little green men' invade Ukraine and move to the Donbas to support protestors.
- In mid-April, Ukraine launches an ATO against Russian proxies in the Donbas.
- In May, a nascent pro-Russian uprising in Odesa ends in bloodshed.

Having been prominent in roundtable negotiations during the Orange Revolution, the EU engaged in negotiations over the Euromaidan in February 2014. On 21 February, the EU and opposition party leaders negotiated a deal with

Yanukovych which would return Ukraine to the constitutional arrangement (featuring less extensive presidential powers) that had been in place during Yushchenko's presidency and would hold presidential elections by the end of 2014 (they were scheduled for January 2015).

The negotiated deal was rejected by protest leaders on the Maidan who, in contrast to the Orange Revolution, were driven much more by civil society groups and were much less trustful of opposition party leaders Vitaliy Klitschko (UDAR – Ukrainian Democratic Alliance for Reforms), Arseniy Yatsenyuk (*Batkivshchyna* [Fatherland]) and Oleh Tyahnybok (*Svoboda* [Freedom]). Moreover, anger at the bloodshed that had taken place in the previous three days radicalised the crowds of protestors, who now insisted that Yanukovych had to step down rather than submit to early elections.

The rejection of the negotiated deal, defections from the Party of Regions by deputies in parliament and a breakdown of command and control over the security forces led to a rapid disintegration of Yanukovych's support, as people deserted what increasingly looked like the losing side. Overnight on 21–22 February 2014, Yanukovych and ten of his closest allies packed what loot they could and fled Kiev; at least four others committed suicide.[29] Yanukovych planned to address the 'Ukrainian Front' in Kharkiv, in an attempt to rally Eastern and Southern Ukrainian deputies along the lines of the 2004 Severdonetsk Congress, but many never showed up and pro-Ukrainian protestors, angry at the bloodshed in Kiev, threatened to break-up the meeting. Yanukovych then fled to Donetsk and later to Crimea as it was being seized by Russian forces.

Scholars have debated whether Putin's decision to invade the Crimea was pre-planned or a spur of the moment decision brought on by the victory of the Euromaidan, but the two explanations are not contradictory. With all Russian political forces laying claim to Sevastopol and the Crimea, adoption of numerous resolutions by both houses of the Russian parliament, open interference by Moscow Mayor Luzhkov and extensive Russian intelligence activity in the Crimea by the Black Sea Fleet's naval intelligence and FSB and GRU, it would be highly unusual for Russia not to have prepared a range of plans for militarily intervening in the Crimea. Russia reacted sharply in 2008 after Yushchenko threatened to not allow Black Sea Fleet vessels that had participated in the invasion of Georgia to return to Sevastopol. Before Russia's invasion, Lukashenka claimed to have seen Russian plans for military intervention in the Crimea.[30] The invasion itself showed signs of

---

[29]   https://www.theguardian.com/world/2015/mar/23/ukraine-party-of-regions-members-apparent-suicides-viktor-yanukovych

[30]   Serhiy Leshchenko, *Mezhyhirskyy Syndrom. Diahnoz Vladi: Viktora Yanukovycha*

having been well-prepared, so it seems likely that contingency plans were prepared well in advance, with the decision to implement them made due to the combination of the perceived 'putsch' in Kiev and the opportunity to intervene while chaos reigned.

As mentioned earlier, Russia's intervention in the Crimea was welcomed by many local residents because of their long-standing pro-Russian and pro-Soviet sympathies, as well as by the fear generated by Russia's information war regarding Ukrainian fascists preparing to invade and massacre Russian speakers. Russia's forces consisted of GRU *spetsnaz* without country insignia, Black Sea Fleet marines and intelligence, defectors from the SBU, Ukraine's military and *Militsiya*, Crimean Russian nationalists and organised crime enforcers. The latter two had long been linked and the role of organised crime was reflected in the installation of former organised crime boss and Russian nationalist Aksyonov as Crimean Prime Minister.

Widespread pro-Putin and pro-Russian/Soviet sympathies in the Crimea did not necessarily translate into the ludicrously reported referendum result of 96.7% in favour of joining Russia. That figure would require that the majority of Ukrainians and especially Tatars, who numbered approximately 15% of the population in Crimea, backed union with Russia. According to leaked data, the real turnout was only 30% (not 83%), and of these only half (i.e. 15%) voted in support of union with Russia.[31] Throughout the post-Soviet period, support for separatism (understood as an independent Crimea or union with Russia) had never had majority support in the Crimea.

Elsewhere in Ukraine, between March and May, Russia made numerous attempts to mobilise protestors for uprisings with the purpose of capturing state buildings and declaring the formation of 'people's republics' in what Russian nationalists called the 'Russian Spring'. Russia's hybrid warfare in *Novorossiya*, the name for the Tsarist-era *gubernia* (region) that encompasses Eastern-Southern Ukraine (but not Kharkiv, which had been the centre of the province of *Slobozhanshchyna*), failed. Pro-Putin sentiment and support for separatism proved to be weak in Kharkiv, Dnipropetrovsk (since re-named Dnipro), Zaporizhzhya, Odesa, Mykolayiv and Kherson. Pro-Ukrainian protestors outnumbered pro-Russian protestors in every one of these regions. In the strategically important city of Dnipropetrovsk, oligarch Ihor Kolomoyskyy led the fight against pro-Russian separatists and offered large financial rewards for the capture of Russian soldiers.

(Kyiv: Bright Star Publishing, 2014), p.215.
[31]   https://www.forbes.com/sites/paulroderickgregory/2014/05/05/putins-human-rights-council-accidentally-posts-real-crimean-election-results-only-15-voted-for-annexation/#5060f511f172

Kolomoyskyy funded a number of volunteer battalions. His actions and those of other Ukrainians with Jewish backgrounds belie the notion that Nazism was a major force in Ukraine. Although a Russian speaker, Kolomoyskyy supported the Euromaidan and Ukraine's fight against Russian military intervention. Despite the rhetoric from Russia, anti-Semitism in the Soviet form of 'anti-Zionism' was more prevalent in the DNR and LNR, whose media routinely condemned the alliance of 'Jewish oligarchs', Ukrainian 'fascists' and Western governments. Ukrainian leaders such as Poroshenko, Yatsenyuk and Tymoshenko were mocked for allegedly Ukrainianising their Jewish roots. Russian information operations could not explain why Jews had fled from the DNR and LNR to 'fascist Ukraine'.[32]

Girkin's invasion of mainland Ukraine in the second week of April came too late to assist most of the pro-Russian protests and attempted uprisings in Eastern-Southern Ukraine. Perhaps as a result, Girkin's *spetsnaz* made the strategic decision to concentrate their support in Donetsk, where pro-Russian protestors had made headway. Girkin's forces captured the towns of Slavyansk and Kramatorsk in western Donetsk *oblast* and were able to hold on to them for four months before being forced by Ukrainian forces to flee eastward to Donetsk. Ukrainian forces also re-captured Mariupol in Southern Donetsk *oblast* with relative ease. In Luhansk *oblast's* Northern regions, which historically had been part of *Slobozhanshchyna*, pro-Russian forces had little local support. Overall, the 'Russian Spring' engendered some local support in the Crimea, had limited appeal in the Donbas and barely any in Kharkiv and the remainder of so-called *Novorossiya*. But with Ukrainian security forces largely absent, even a small group, if well-organised and armed, could seize control of key buildings and declare 'independence'.

Ukraine's ATO was launched a few days after Girkin's invasion but only gathered steam the following month. Two decades of neglect, corruption, and asset stripping, combined with Russian penetration of the SBU and military high command, left Ukraine a limited number of reliable military forces. These did include elite parachute (air-mobile) units who took the brunt of the fighting. This was the case especially in Donetsk airport, which had been re-built for the 2012 European football championship, where they became immortalised as 'Cyborgs' after holding off Russian marines and *spetsnaz* and Russian proxies until early 2015.[33] With the Ukrainian armed forces in shambles, volunteers played a key role as fighters in the over 40 battalions that were

---

[32]   See chapter 4 'Anti-Zionism and Anti-Semitism' in T. Kuzio, *Putin's War Against Ukraine*, pp.118–140.

[33]   On Ukraine's defence of Donetsk Airport for 242 days see Iryna Shtohrin, ed., *AD. 242. Istoriya Muzhnosti, Braterstva i Samopozhertvy* (Kharkiv and Kyiv: Klub Simeynoho Dozvillya and Radio Svoboda, 2016).

created. Additionally, large numbers of largely women civilian volunteers[34] collected and transported supplies (uniforms, blankets, boots, telescopic lenses, night vision goggles, medical supplies, food and fresh water) to the front line.[35] Ukraine's military and volunteer battalions were supplemented by a revived National Guard based on Interior Ministry Internal Troops which had existed in the 1990s.

Over time, Ukraine has strengthened its military capacity and volunteer battalions have been integrated into the army and National Guard.[36] In 2017, Ukraine was ranked 30th in the world's armies.[37] A study by Poland's Centre for Eastern Studies found that:

> Despite all these problems, the Ukrainian armed forces of the year 2017 now number 200,000, most of whom have come under fire, and are seasoned in battle. They have a trained reserve ready for mobilisation in the event of a larger conflict; their weapons are not the latest or the most modern, but the vast majority of them now work properly; and they are ready for the defence of the vital interests of the state (even if some of the personnel still care primarily about their own vested interests). They have no chance of winning a potential military clash with Russia, but they have a reason to fight. The Ukrainian armed forces of the year 2014, in a situation where their home territory was occupied by foreign troops, were incapable of mounting an adequate response. The changes since the Donbas war started mean that Ukraine now has the best army it has ever had in its history.[38]

---

[34]   For a survey of the volunteer movement in Ukraine see 'Blahodiynist i volonterstvo-2016' (Kyiv: Democratic Initiatives, 21 February 2017). http://dif.org.ua/article/blagodiynist-i-volonterstvo-2016-rezultati-sotsiologichnogo-doslidzhennya

[35]   Natalya Dzyuba-Prylutska is one of these determined civilian volunteers who has travelled from Kyiv to the frontline delivering supplies to Ukraine's military over one hundred times since 2014. See her interview in *Kray* magazine: https://gazeta.ua/articles/people-and-things-journal/_vijskovi-hochut-zakinchiti-vijnu-gotovi-peremagati-komandi-nemaye-tilki-tim-hto-nazhivayetsya-nevigidne-yiyi-zakinchennya/703066

[36]   Vera Mironova and Ekaterina Sergatskova, 'How Ukraine Reined in Its Militias: The Lessons for Other States', *Foreign Affairs*, 1 August 2017. https://www.foreignaffairs.com/articles/ukraine/2017-08-01/how-ukraine-reined-its-militias

[37]   https://www.globalfirepower.com/countries-listing.asp

[38]   Andrzej Wilk, 'The Best Army Ukraine has Ever Had. Changes in Ukraine's Armed Forces since the Russian Aggression', OSW Studies no.66 (Warsaw: Centre for Eastern Studies, 7 July 2017). https://www.osw.waw.pl/en/publikacje/osw-studies/2017-07-07/best-army-ukraine-has-ever-had-changes-ukraines-armed-forces

Military Invasion, Phoney Peace and Real War, 2014–?

- In July 2014, the war escalates as Russian artillery pounds Ukraine from the Russian side of the border.
- Russia sends sophisticated surface-to-air Buk missiles to counter the Ukrainian Air Force and one of these shoots down Malaysia Airlines Flight 17.
- In August, Russian proxy forces in Luhansk and Donetsk are on the verge of being defeated but are saved by Russian forces invading Ukraine and inflicting a major defeat on Ukrainian forces at Ilovaysk.
- Ukraine signs the Minsk I accord, negotiated by Ukraine, Russia, France and Germany. Despite the agreement, intense fighting continues and leads to the signing of Minsk II in February 2015. Neither accord is implemented.
- Russia transforms proxy militias into a 40,000-strong DNR-LNR army.
- Conflict continues into 2018. Although it is widely assumed Minsk II is dead, there is no Plan B or likelihood of new negotiations leading to Minsk III.

By July 2014, Ukraine's ATO was successful in re-taking control of Western and Southern Donetsk *oblast* and in neutralising Russian proxy activity in Northern Luhansk. At that stage, Putin had to choose whether to abandon his proxies to their fate or to assist them by invading Ukraine. He chose the latter, further damaging Ukrainian-Russian relations and Russia's relations with the West.

Artillery pounded Ukraine from Russian territory making it difficult for Ukrainian forces to maintain control over its border regions. The British Bellingcat investigative network described this as Putin's 'undeclared war'.[39] Ukraine's Air Force had inflicted high numbers of casualties on Russian forces and Russian proxies in May–June and Putin could not respond by sending his own Russian Air Force as this would further undermine the fiction that there were no Russian forces in Eastern Ukraine. Instead, Russia sent surface-to-air missiles, such as the Buk, to shoot down Ukrainian Air Force planes. This sophisticated military equipment could only be manned by trained Russian soldiers – not Russian proxies or Cossacks. In July 2014, a Buk shot down what it thought was a Ukrainian military transport plane but turned out to be a civilian airliner (Malaysia Airlines Flight 17 – MH17), killing all 298 passengers and crew. Despite numerous Russian attempts at

---

[39]   Sean Case, *Putin's Undeclared War: Summer 2014- Russian Artillery Strikes against Ukraine* (Leicester: Bellingcat, 21 December 2016). https://www.bellingcat.com/news/uk-and-europe/2016/12/21/russian-artillery-strikes-against-ukraine/

deception, Russia's involvement was established beyond doubt.[40]

The following month, Russian forces humiliated Ukraine by invading and defeating Ukrainian forces on Ukraine's Independence Day, 24 August. Russia's increased military aggression and the shooting down of MH17 stiffened US and EU responses to the crisis, leading to new sanctions against Russia. Western government policymakers did not believe Putin's claim that Russia was not militarily intervening in Eastern Ukraine. Ukraine's continued use of the term ATO, until a change in legislation in January 2018, was also confusing as it did not designate Russia and Ukraine as being in a state of war.

The US and UK, both signatories to the 1994 Budapest Memorandum that gave Ukraine security assurances in return for denuclearisation, did not participate in the Minsk process. The EU (represented by Germany and France), Ukraine, Russia and the OSCE were parties to the negotiations.

In accepting Russia as a partner in the negotiations, the West was playing its own game of *maskirovka*. While rejecting Putin's claims that Russia was uninvolved in the war in Eastern Ukraine they were at the same time willing to include Russia as a mediator rather than as a participant in the conflict. This led to a situation whereby Ukraine's President Poroshenko sat down to nego-tiate peace with the Russian president whom he accused of conducting hybrid war against and invading Eastern Ukraine while Putin insisted that Russia was not a party to the conflict. The Minsk negotiations did not cover the Crimea.

The Minsk process did not include discussion of Crimea, which for Russia is a closed question. The West has imposed separate sanctions against Russia over Crimea. Some European leaders, echoing populist nationalists, have called for the EU to recognise Russia's sovereignty over the Crimea. During the 2016 US presidential campaign, then-candidate Donald Trump, echoing former US Secretary of State Henry Kissinger, said 'But, you know, the people of Crimea, from what I've heard, would rather be with Russia than where they were', hinting if he were elected he would recognise Russian sovereignty.[41]

After the poor performance of Donbas militias in summer 2014, Russia set

---

[40]   See Bellingcat's research on MH17 at: https://www.bellingcat.com/tag/mh17/ and the Dutch government's investigation at: https://www.government.nl/topics/mh17-incident

[41]   http://www.politico.com/story/2016/08/trump-clarifies-crimea-ukraine-226497 On Kissinger see: http://www.independent.co.uk/news/people/henry-kissinger-russia-trump-crimea-advises-latest-ukraine-a7497646.html

about fashioning them into a 40,000-strong army with Russian command and control and equipped with large supplies of Russian military technology. NATO and Ukraine estimate there are between 5,000–10,000 Russian soldiers in the Donbas with larger numbers stationed just across the border who provide a security guarantee. In transforming proxy militias into standing armies, Putin's policies towards the Donbas were little different to those pursued by Yeltsin in the Trans-Dniestr, South Ossetia and Abkhazia.

The West and Ukraine on one side and Russia on the other have held diametrically different approaches to the implementation of the Minsk accords. Ukraine and the West have insisted on implementing the security provisions first, including the withdrawal of Russian forces, demilitarisation of proxy forces and reestablishment of Ukraine's control over its border with Russia. Putin disagrees, insisting Ukraine should first change its constitution to provide 'special status' for the DNR and LNR and hold local elections. The holding of elections in today's conditions could never be free and fair (Prime Minister Zakharcheko has said Ukrainian parties could not participate) and elections would therefore freeze and legitimise existing control of the DNR and LNR by Russia and its proxies.

That the Minsk accords have failed is not surprising for two reasons. The first is that there is an understandable absence of trust on the Ukrainian side towards any promises made by Putin that security steps in Minsk II would be implemented after Ukraine introduced constitutional changes and held elections. Russia's ability to bargain is undermined by its record of deception; it will be difficult to take Russian assurances seriously when Putin continues to claim there is no Russian military intervention in Eastern Ukraine. A second factor is the potential for further political instability and possibly a third Maidan in Ukraine if President Poroshenko were seen as capitulating to Russian demands. In contrast to Moldova, Georgia and Azerbaijan, Ukraine has not been defeated in the Donbas, so there is less basis upon which to give in to Russian demands. The Ukrainian parliament's attempt to debate the changing of the constitution in August 2015 to provide 'special status' to the DNR and LNR led to nationalist riots and the deaths of three National Guardsmen from a grenade thrown by a veteran of the war. A new factor in Ukrainian electoral politics is the 15% of voters who are veterans and their families.

Charap and Colton point out that Russia's overall goals for Ukraine have not changed since the 21 February 2014 agreement. These include neutrality of Ukraine, adoption of a federal structure in which the DNR and LNR have veto powers over Kiev's domestic and foreign policies, election of governors rather than their appointment by the Ukrainian president, granting Russia the status of a second state language, recognition of the right of the Crimea to 'self-determination' (meaning recognition of Russia's sovereignty over it) and the holding of elections only after adoption of constitutional reforms recognising a 'special status' for the DNR and LNR. Not surprisingly, these demands are a non-starter for all political forces in Kiev other than the former Party of Regions who have re-grouped in the Opposition Bloc.[42]

'Finlandisation' of Ukraine, which some in the West have advocated, is unacceptable to many in Ukraine and might not satisfy Russia. As this book has shown, Ukraine is viewed as one of three key countries in the *Russkii Mir* and central to the success of the Eurasian Union. To the extent that Russia seeks Ukraine's membership of the Eurasian Union – not a neutral successful democracy on its doorstep – 'Finlandisation' will not do.[43] Since 2009, Russia has focused more on Ukraine integrating with Russia, and not just on its staying neutral.

Russian Foreign Minister Sergei Lavrov implied that neutrality might satisfy Russia, saying that 'only a non-aligned Ukraine may escape further territorial disintegration', but it is not clear that this is a firm offer.[44] Moldova and Azerbaijan have never sought NATO membership and yet Russian proxies have occupied the Trans-Dniestr and Nagorno-Karabakh since the early 1990s. Similarly, in 2002, Putin proposed to Lukashenka that Belarus, a country which has never sought NATO or EU membership, unite with Russia in what would amount to a Russian *Anschluss* of Belarus. Lukashenka refused and vowed to defend his country's sovereignty. In Georgia, Russian proxies took control of South Ossetia and Abkhazia more than a decade before Georgia raised the goal of NATO membership. Georgia's interest in NATO was an *ex post facto* justification for invasion, not a cause of it. In the case of Ukraine, Lavrov was being doubly disingenuous as Russia's understanding of returning Ukrainian territorial integrity did not include the Crimea.

Even outside Russia's self-declared 'sphere of interest' in Eurasia, a country with no interest in NATO membership can become a target of Russian hybrid and information warfare, as the case of Sweden shows.[45] The German

---

[42]   S. Charap and T. J. Colton, *Everyone Loses*, pp.131 and 144.

[43]   See chapters 16 and 17, 'Origins of the War in Ukraine' and 'Putin's "Hybrid War" in Ukraine: Five Scenarios' in M. H. Van Herpen, *Putin's Wars*, pp.239–280.

[44]   P. Felgenhauer, 'Minsk Ceasefire Agreements are Dead, but the Russia Offensive is Faltering', *Eurasian Daily Monitor*, vol.12, no.18 (29 January 2015). https://jamestown. org/program/minsk-ceasefire-agreements-are-dead-but-the-russian-offensive-is-faltering/

[45]   Jon Henley, 'Russia waging information war against Sweden, study finds', *The Guardian*, 11 January 2017. https://www.theguardian.com/world/2017/jan/11/russia-waging-information-war-in-sweden-study-finds?CMP=Share_iOSApp_Other and Martin

Marshall Fund reported that Russia has intervened in the internal affairs of 27 European and North American countries since 2004, ranging from cyber attacks to disinformation campaigns.[46]

It is hard to find anyone who believes that the Minsk accords will be implemented. There is no way to bridge Ukraine's insistence on independence and Russia's refusal to accept Ukraine as a fully sovereign country. Russia's plan is for Ukraine to be a fully-fledged member of the Eurasian Union. Russia demands that the West recognises its *droit de regard* over Ukraine and Eurasia and seeks to negotiate a grand bargain with the US over the heads of Ukrainians. Charap and Colton write that 'Russia wanted the deal clinched by the great powers and imposed on Ukraine'.[47]

It is important to recognise a long-term consistency in Russian security policy towards the CIS.[48] Yeltsin, Medvedev and Putin have not differed over Russia's right to dominate Eurasia and its desire to have the US recognise this in a grand bargain. Brezhnev claimed Soviet satellites in Central-Eastern Europe possessed 'limited sovereignty' and Warsaw Pact countries invaded Hungary and Czechoslovakia in 1956 and 1968 to thwart colour-style revolutions. In 1993, only a few years after the disintegration of the USSR, Foreign Minister Andrei Kozyrev outlined Russia's right to protect Russians and Russian speakers in the former USSR. In September 1995, Yeltsin issued a decree claiming the former USSR as Russia's sphere of influence where Russian peacekeepers would 'guarantee peace and stability'.[49] While Russia's capabilities have recovered dramatically since the 1990s, in terms of goals, Putin did not bring anything to the table that had not already been proposed by his Soviet and Russian predecessors.

Conclusion

The conflict in Ukraine is going to be difficult to solve, for several reasons highlighted in this chapter. First, the conflict is not primarily a civil war but an international war. Russia is a party to the conflict, and therefore cannot effectively mediate it. Nor can it permit the West a real role in mediating it.

Kragh & Sebastian Åsberg, 'Russia's strategy for influence through public diplomacy and active measures: the Swedish case', *Journal of Strategic Studies*, vol.40, no.6, (December 2017), pp.773–816.

[46]   http://securingdemocracy.gmfus.org/ and https://www.rferl.org/a/daily-vertical-kremlin-global-campaign-of-chaos-transcript/28723868.html

[47]   S. Charap and T. J. Colton, *Everyone Loses*, p.131.

[48]   The continuity of Putin's policy with that of Yeltsin and Gorbachev is stressed by T. Graham and R. Menon, 'The Putin Problem'.

[49]   M. H. Van Herpen, *Putin's Wars*, pp.57–58, 63–65 and 68–69.

There is no reason to believe that international wars are easier or harder to resolve in general than civil wars, but in this case, Russia's goals are so contradictory to Ukraine's, and to the West's norms, that it will be very difficult to find common ground.

Second, Russia's aggression in Ukraine was many years in the making, even if it took the events of 2014 to provide the opportunity. Because the invasions of Crimea and the Donbas were not responses either to the West's actions or to the specific events in Kiev, resolving those issues will not be sufficient to secure Russian withdrawal. This is particularly true in the case of Crimea, which, through its annexation, Russia has announced its intention to keep permanently. Russia's unwillingness to change its behaviour in the Donbas, never mind in Crimea, have been factored into the July 2017 US sanctions. These call on the Treasury and State Departments, along with intelligence officials, to analyse the 'potential effects of expanding sanctions...to include sovereign debt and the full range of derivative products'[50] which would represent a significant escalation of economic pressure on Russia.

Third, it appears that there is no path toward a negotiated solution; or rather that the existing path is a dead end. Neither side accepts its basic commitments under the Minsk process, but neither Russia nor Ukraine (nor the EU or US) benefits from walking away from the process. As emphasised throughout this book, regaining control over Ukraine is a long-term Russian foreign policy goal. But the invasion of Ukraine has solidified Ukrainian opinion against Russia and in favour of stronger ties with the West. That means that force and subversion will be more necessary than before, not less, to achieve Russia's objectives.

Further Reading

Alexseev, Mikhail, 'Backing the USSR 2.0: Russia's ethnic minorities and expansionist ethnic Russian nationalism' in P. Kolstø and Helge Blakkisrud eds., *The New Russian Nationalism. Imperialism, Ethnicity and Authoritarianism 2000–2015* (Edinburgh: Edinburgh University Press, 2016), pp. 160–191.

D'Anieri, Paul, *Economic Interdependence in Ukrainian-Russian Relations* (Albany: State University of New York Press, 1999).

---

[50] Resource Centre on Ukraine-Russia-/Related Sanctions, U.S. Department of the Treasury. https://www.treasury.gov/resource-center/sanctions/Programs/Pages/ukraine.aspx

Felshtynskyy, Yuriy and Mykhaylo Stanchev, *Tretya Svitova: Bytva za Ukrayinu* (Kiev: Nash Format, 2015).

Ivshchyna, Larysa, ed., *Katastrofa i Triumf: Istorii Ukrayinskykh Heroyiv, Biblioteka Hazety "Den"*, 2 vols. (Kiev: Ukraynska Pres-Hrupa, 2015).

Jensen, N. Donald, *Moscow in the Donbas: Command, Control, Crime and the Minsk Peace Process*, Research Report no.1 (Rome: Research Division, NATO Defence College, 24 March 2017). http://www.ndc.nato.int/news/news. php?icode=1029

Kalinovska, Olha, Oleh Kryshtopa, Yevhen Nazarenko, Valentyn Trokhymchuk and Daryna Fedenko, *Neoholoshena Viyn: Nevidomi Fakty i Khronika ATO* (Kharkiv and Kiev: Klub Simeynoho Dozvillya and Ukraine Media Crisis, 2015).

Kudelia, Serhiy, 'Domestic Sources of the Donbas Insurgency', *PONARS*, 29 September 2014. http://www.ponarseurasia.org/article/new-policy-memo-domestic-sources-donbas-insurgency

Kulchytskyy, Stanislav and Larysa Yakubova, *Trysta Rokiv Samotnosti: Ukrayinskyy Donbas u Poshukakh Smysliv i Batkivshchyny* (Kiev: Klio, 2016).

Kuromiya, Hiroaki, *Freedom and Terror in the Donbas: A Ukrainian-Russian Borderland, 1870s–1990s* (Cambridge: Cambridge University Press, 1998).

Kuzio, T. *The Crimea: Europe's Next Flashpoint?* (Washington DC: The Jamestown Foundation, November 2010).

Kuzio, T. 'Russianization of Ukrainian National Security Policy under Viktor Yanukovych', *Journal of Slavic Military Studies*, vol.25, no.4 (December 2012), pp.558–581.

Kuzio, T., 'Crime, Politics and Business in 1990s Ukraine', *Communist and Post-Communist Politics*, vol.47, no.2 (July 2014), pp.195–210.

Kuzio, T., 'The Rise and Fall of the Party of Regions Political Machine', *Problems of Post-Communism*, vol.62, no.3 (May/June 2015), pp. 174–186.

Laruelle, M. 'The three colors of Novorossiya, or the Russian nationalist mythmaking of the Ukrainian crisis', *Post-Soviet Affairs*, vol.32, no.1 (January 2016), pp.55–74.

Luciuk, Lubomyr Y. ed., *Jews, Ukrainians, and the Euromaidan* (Toronto: Kashtan press, 2014).

Magocsi, R. Paul, *This Blessed Land: Crimea and the Crimean Tatars* (Toronto: University of Toronto Press 2014).

Malyarenko, Tetyana, 'Playing a Give-Away Game? The Undeclared Russian-Ukrainian War in Donbas', *Small Wars Journal*, 23 December 2015. http://smallwarsjournal.com/jrnl/art/playing-a-give-away-game-the-undeclared-russian-ukrainian-war-in-donbas

Mitrokhin, Nikolay, 'Infiltration, Instruction, Invasion: Russia's War in the Donbass', *Journal of Soviet and Post-Soviet Politics and Society*, vol.1, no.1 (2015), pp.219–249.

Orel, Ihor, *Khronika Odnoho Batalyonu* (Kharkiv: Folio, 2016).

Plokhy, Serhiy, 'The City of Glory: Sevastopol in Russian Historical Mythology', *Journal of Contemporary History*, vol.35, no.3 (July 2000), pp.369–384.

Puglisi, Rosaria, *Heroes or Villains? Volunteer Battalions in Post-Maidan Ukraine*, IAI Working Paper no.15 (Rome: Instituto Affari Internazionali, 8 March 2015). http://www.iai.it/sites/default/files/iaiwp1508.pdf

Russian New Generation Warfare Handbook (Fort Meade, MD: Asymmetric Warfare Group December 2016). https://info.publicintelligence.net/AWG-RussianNewWarfareHandbook.pdf

Ryabchiy, Ivan, *Dobrobaty* (Kharkiv: Folio, 2016).

Serhatskova, Ekateryna, Artyem Chapay, and Vladimir Maksakov, *Voyna na try bukvyi* (Kharkiv: Folio, 2016).

Thomas, Timothy, 'Russia's Military Strategy and Ukraine: Indirect, Asymmetric – and Putin-Led', *The Journal of Slavic Military Studies*, vol.28, no.3 (July 2015), pp.445–461.

Tymchuk, Dmytro, Karin, Yuriy, Mashovets, Kostyantyn, and Husarov, Vyacheslav, *Vtorhnennya v Ukrayinu. Khronika rosiyskoii ahresii. Hrupa "Informatsiynyy Sprotyv"* (Kiev: Bright Star Publishing, 2016).

5

International Ramifications of the Crisis: Towards a New Cold War?

Russia's annexation of the Crimea, hybrid war and military interventions in Eastern Ukraine caused a dramatic transformation of the international landscape, especially in Europe, ushering in what some regard as a new cold war. In summer 2017, just after new, tougher sanctions against Russia were adopted by the US, the traditionally liberal *Washington Post* ran an editorial entitled 'We're on the road to a new Cold War' which placed the blame for the deterioration in relations entirely on Russia. The article went on to say that:

> Twenty-five years after the Cold War ended, relations are back in a deep freeze. What happened? The current tension did not come about because the United States suddenly wanted its old adversary back. What happened is a response to bad choices taken by President Putin of Russia. These choices were made deliberately in Moscow, perhaps for Mr. Putin's own reasons of domestic politics and foreign policy. They are the main reason for the tension that now exists.[1]

In Russia, the feeling was mutual: By summer 2017, Russians viewed the US and Ukraine as the two countries with the most unfriendly relations towards Russia.[2] Similarly, 75–80% of Ukrainians held negative views of Putin, the State Duma and the Russian government. This chapter reviews the international ramifications of Russia's annexation of Crimea and hybrid war against Eastern Ukraine. We begin by surveying the dramatic changes in attitudes

---

[1]   Editorial, 'We're on the road to a new Cold War', *The Washington Post*, 31 July 2017.
https://www.washingtonpost.com/opinions/were-on-the-road-to-a-new-cold-war/2017/07/31/213af6be-7617-11e7-8839-ec48ec4cae25_story.html
[2]   http://www.levada.ru/2016/06/02/13400/

prompted by the conflict. We summarise the Minsk I and Minsk II agreements, showing why the Minsk process is needed to manage the conflict, but cannot resolve it. We then examine the politics of sanctions, stressing that the symbolic impact was more important than the economic effects. We then pull back to examine the dynamics of the new cold war, which includes not only this conflict, but the one in Syria and the broader Russian information and cyber war against the West. Ukraine is the central battleground in this new cold war, and the weakness of its government's commitment to reform causes difficult dilemmas for its supporters in the West. Finally, we examine the prospects for settling the conflict, concluding that there is little likelihood of an improvement, because the different sides differ so profoundly in their goals.

Changing Attitudes

On top of its intervention in Ukraine, Russia's interference in European and US elections consolidated the view in the West of Russia as an adversary that could not be trusted and needed to be confronted. For Russia, complaining about Western behaviour was replaced with confronting it, and the ostracism that resulted strengthened old fears about Western hostility and consolidated domestic support for confrontation.

These dire consequences did not result automatically from the annexation of the Crimea and interventions in Eastern Ukraine. While those military actions spurred a rapid hardening in the US, Europe remained much more hesitant. In Germany, for example, many across the political spectrum were sympathetic to Russian claims on Crimea[3]. German-Ukrainian relations in the decade prior to the crisis had been poor, largely due to Germany's prioritisation of ties with Russia, such that in 2009, Ukrainian national security adviser Horbulin told the US ambassador that there are two Russian Embassies in Kiev, one of which speaks German.[4] Even after the annexation of Crimea, many German elites supported a pragmatic policy of accom-modating a great power rather than sacrificing for a small one with little independent history.[5] This drew both upon the legacy of West Germany's *Ostpolitik* during the Cold War and upon

---

[3]   Esther King, 'Christian Lindner, Germany should accept Crimean annexation as 'permanent provisional solution', *Politico*, 6 August 2017. http://www.politico.eu/article/christian-lindner-germany-should-accept-crimean-annexation-as-permanent-provisional-solution/

[4]   'Ukrainian-German Relations on the Rocks', US Embassy Kyiv, 16 March 2009. https://wikileaksua.wordpress.com/2009/03/16/09kyiv465-ukrainian-german-relations-on-the-rocks/

[5]   Susanne Spahn, 'Ukraine in the Russian Mass Media: Germany as an Example of Russian Information Policy' in Timm Beichelt and Susan Worschech eds., *Transnational Ukraine? Networks and Ties that Influenced(d) Contemporary Ukraine* (Stuttgart: Ibidem, 2017), pp.179–202.

an earlier German geopolitical tradition of discounting the smaller countries lying between itself and Russia. Germans had a tendency, Timothy Snyder warned the German Bundestag, 'to overlook a people which was not regarded as a people. All of the language about Ukraine as a failed state, or Ukrainians not as a real nation, or Ukrainians divided by culture – in the German language – that is not innocent. That is an inheritance of an attempt to colonise a people not regarded as a people'.[6]

Putin's dissembling and dishonesty regarding Crimea shifted German elite and public attitudes even among many who had been inclined to compromise. In March 2014, Chancellor Merkel, noted for her pragmatic relationship over many years interacting with Putin, described him as 'in another world' after a phone call discussing the Crimea invasion. Merkel now sees Putin as an existential threat to the European and Trans-Atlantic institutions that have constrained German nationalism and made it one of the strongest European supporters of devolving sovereignty to supra-national institutions.[7]

The downing of Malaysia Airlines Flight MH17 in July 2014 cemented the change in opinion. Because the flight had taken off from Amsterdam, and because many of the passengers were Dutch, the war was brought home for many in Western Europe. The fact that Russia supplied the weapons and the crew that downed the plane made it much harder to ignore Russia's role in Eastern Ukraine. Putin's implausible denial stoked outrage. In Western Europe, it was now much harder for respectable politicians to counsel compromise with Russia. By autumn 2014, Western Europe and the US were more united on Russia than they had been since the days before West Germany's *Ostpolitik* in the late 1960s.

International Mediation: From Normandy to Minsk

In early June 2014, at a celebration of the anniversary of the D-Day invasion in World War II, Russian, Ukrainian and EU leaders agreed to form a Trilateral Group consisting of Russia, Ukraine, and the OSCE to try to negotiate an end to the violence. The group began meeting within days, but not much progress was made until September, when battlefield developments forced everyone's hands. In August, Ukrainian forces nearly succeeded in separating Russia's Donetsk proxies from those in Luhansk and threatened to completely surround and defeat them. Russia responded by invading with regular Russian army units. The Russian army and its proxies routed Ukrainian forces at

---

6   https://www.youtube.com/watch?v=wDjHw_uXeKU

7   'Germany's establishment once believed in conciliation with Russia. No longer', *The Economist*, 23 April 2016. http://www.economist.com/news/europe/21697236-germanys-establishment-once-believed-conciliation-russia-no-longer-fool-me-once

Ilovaysk and pushed toward the Ukrainian port city of Mariupol, seizure of which would be a major step in linking Russia with Crimea. When this attack was blunted, the military basis existed for a ceasefire: Russia was ready to consolidate its gains and Ukraine to cut its losses.

The agreement was based on a plan that President Poroshenko had advanced in June, calling for a ceasefire, a buffer zone from which heavy weaponry would be excluded, and OSCE monitoring. Two political provisions were to cause considerable acrimony in the following months. One committed Ukraine to giving the Donetsk and Luhansk increased self-rule. This would require a change in Ukraine's constitution, which Poroshenko could not unilaterally deliver, even if he wanted to. The second was for new elections in the contested regions, which could not be carried out in conditions of war, and which were certain to provoke conflict over what constituted 'free and fair' (elections organised by DNR and LNR leaders in early November 2014 were recognized by Russia but not by Ukraine or the international community). In the short term, however, the priority was to stop the fighting before it got out of control. In this, the agreement was only partly successful, but the international community breathed a collective sigh of relief that the recent escalation had been stopped.

The agreement was violated frequently in the coming months, particularly as Russia's proxy forces attempted to improve their positions. It broke down completely in December 2014/January 2015, when DNR proxy forces waged a new offensive that seized the Donetsk airport from Ukrainian government forces. The offensive effectively killed the first Minsk agreement, but once the insurgents achieved their goal of seizing the airport, there was again potential for a ceasefire, and the Minsk II agreement was negotiated. The terms were largely similar to those of Minsk I, but the ceasefire would be based on the new territorial reality. The negotiations were challenging in part because Russia claimed no control over the DNR and LNR forces, and therefore said it could not be a party to the agreement (taking instead the position of an external mediator). The fact that Russia has continued to claim the role of mediator rather than party to the conflict continued to hamper efforts to negotiate a solution, but that claim was central to Russia's disinformation campaign and allowed it unusual leverage: when convenient, it could control forces on the ground, and when convenient, it could disown them. This was Soviet-style *maskirovka* in a contemporary setting.

The Minsk II agreement has been in place formally since February 2015, though violations continued to occur on a daily basis, along with a public relations war in which each side tries to draw attention to the other's violations. It is difficult to tell how much effect the Minsk process has had. The fact that Minsk I was jettisoned when one of the actors saw a military advantage indicates that its power to restrain the actors is weak. At the same time, as a way of signalling a willingness to accept the prevailing lines of control, it may have some stabilising effect. Politically, there appear to be costs for being seen as violating the agreement. In particular, Ukraine is constrained from abandoning Minsk, even if it is widely viewed as dead, because doing so would likely trigger a move among some in the EU to remove sanctions on Russia.

In many respects, the West was a peripheral actor, with much of the impetus for ceasefires being driven by the interests of Russia and Ukraine. Prior to both Minsk agreements, Russian proxy forces were making gains at the expense of the Ukrainian government. When those gains had been achieved (saving the DNR in summer 2014 and seizing the Donetsk airport in January 2015), the Russian side was willing to consolidate its gains via a ceasefire. The West's role was to encourage the ceasefire, to help broker the deal, and probably most important, to disabuse the Ukrainian leadership of the hope that significant Western military assistance would be forthcoming.

The OSCE also played an important role, providing the observers who were meant to report on whether heavy weapons had been pulled back in accordance with the agreement and whether the ceasefire was being followed. It is important to recognise that these were observers, not peace-keepers, and they struggled to do their job effectively and safely. Especially in Russian held areas, they repeatedly found themselves denied access and in some cases detained.

Sanctions

The most notable Western response to the conflict has been the sanctions enacted against Russia by the EU and the United States. The diplomacy around the enacting and maintaining of the sanctions has been complicated, and the fact that a relatively far-reaching regime of sanctions was enacted and has been maintained is testament to the breadth and strength of feeling in the West concerning Russia's actions. While the general consensus is that the sanctions have had only a modest effect on the Russian economy, we contend that symbolically the sanctions have been very important. As much as Putin and Russia sometimes seem to relish being cast as outlaws in the West, their reaction to the sanctions shows that they are very sensitive about their perceived international legitimacy.

The sanctions enacted over the Russia-Ukraine conflict were narrowly targeted on specific individuals in the Russian government and on three sectors of the Russian economy: finance, oil and gas, and defence.[8] They identified specific entities in these sectors for whom access to Western capital was limited, and placed travel bans and asset freezes on specific individuals identified with the annexation of Crimea. These sanctions were the result of considerable bargaining within the EU and between the EU and the United States.

Most analysts agree that the effects on Russia's economy have been limited[9], and that the decline in the Russian economy in 2014–15 was driven primarily by decreases in global petroleum prices, not by the sanctions. As Richard Connolly notes, measures aimed at the energy sector were not intended to have a short-term effect, but rather to deprive Russia of the capital and technology it will need to bring new sources of oil and gas on line in the long term.[10] Obviously, the sanctions have not compelled Russia to withdraw from Crimea or from Eastern Ukraine. Whether they have deterred other actions by Russia – such as further intervention in Ukraine, is a matter of speculation.

In some respects, the sanctions may strengthen Putin's grip on Russia. Russia's countersanctions, which focused on food imports, may make Russia more self-sufficient and boost prices for domestic producers at the cost of increased prices for consumers. To the extent that trade decreases, Russian oligarchs will be more dependent on the Russian economy, and therefore on Putin. For particular individuals, the effect might be larger. Those officials no longer allowed to travel to Europe or to buy property will find it much harder to develop a 'Plan B' in case they fall out with Putin, leaving them more dependent on him. Moreover, many have argued that the sanctions have actually helped Putin by providing an excuse for the economic stagnation that has resulted from the absence of reform in the Russian economy. Oddly, both Western governments and the Russian government have incentives to exaggerate the impact of the sanctions. Connolly concludes that the likely long-term effect of the sanctions will be to turn Russia further away from a Western-style (market oriented and open) economy to one that is more closed and statist.[11]

---

[8]   Richard Connolly, 'Western Economic Sanctions and Russia's Place in the Global Economy', in Agnieszka Pikulicka-Wilczewska and Richard Sakwa eds., *Ukraine and Russia: People, Politics, Propaganda and Perspectives* (Bristol: E-International Relations, March 2015), p.213.

[9]   R. Connolly, 'Western Economic Sanctions and Russia's Place in the Global Economy', p.214.

[10]   R. Connolly, 'Western Economic Sanctions and Russia's Place in the Global Economy', pp.216–217.

[11]   R. Connolly, 'Western Economic Sanctions and Russia's Place in the Global Economy', p.219.

This does not mean that the sanctions have not had an important impact. Because they have incurred significant costs for some Western businesses (both directly and as a result of Russian counter-sanctions), they are a 'costly-signal', which is taken more seriously because it has been expensive to send. While simply declaring opposition to Russia's actions is inexpensive ('talk is cheap') the sanctions signal both to Russia and within the West the seriousness with which Russia's actions are regarded, and provide a message that more actions might be taken if the situation worsens. Economic sanctions thus represent a middle point between 'cheap talk' and a military response, which would be a costlier signal. Most importantly, the sanctions demonstrated that the West would come together rather than fragmenting. Whether that unity can be maintained is a question, and for those reasons the symbolic importance of the sanctions will endure.

Finally, it is important to recognize what has been left out of the sanctions. The German government has continued to support the Nordstream-2 gas pipeline project, which is wholly owned by Russia's Gazprom, despite the impact it will have on EU and NATO members Poland and the three Baltic States as well as on Ukraine's energy security. Nordstream-2, when completed, will allow Russia to completely circumvent the Ukrainian pipeline network for its gas deliveries to Germany and much of Western Europe, thus removing the only lever Ukraine has against Russia in general, and making it possible for Russia to shut off gas to Ukraine without harming its customers further west. Nordstream-2 will achieve a strategic goal that Russia has sought since the early 1990s. This project demonstrates the strong interest that Germany and other European states still have in commercial relations with Russia, and the strong incentive they have to sacrifice Ukraine's interests for their own. In one of the earliest and most successful efforts by Putin to gain influence inside Western governments, he established a very close relationship with Merkel's predecessor, Gerhard Schroeder, and then hired him to lead the original Nordstream project. Schroeder's Social Democratic Party, Merkel's coalition partner, has continued its support for Nordstream despite opposition from both Merkel's Christian Democratic Union and the Green Party.[12]

A New Cold War?

There is no agreed definition for a 'cold war', but the application of the label to the current era seems appropriate, despite the differences between the present era and that between 1945 and 1991. The change is in large part one

---

[12]   Markus Wehner and Reinhard Veser, 'Widerstand gegen Putins Pipeline wächst', *Frankfurter Allgemeine Zeitung*, 1 November 2016. http://www.faz.net/aktuell/politik/inland/nord-stream-2-widerstand-gegen-putins-pipeline-waechst-14507991.html

of perceptions: in both the West and Russia, the perception is now widely shared that, at the strategic level, the contest is a zero sum game: what is good for Russia is bad for the West, and vice versa. A report from the UK's Royal Institute of International Affairs (Chatham House) captured a typical Western view:

> Until 2003, it was widely believed that a modernising Russia might be accommodated into the international system as a constructive and benign actor. Variations on this view have given way to the realisation that Russia, on its present course, cannot be a partner or ally, and that differences outweigh any common interests.[13]

Similarly, the Russian analyst Dmitri Trenin states:

> The change that the Ukraine crisis has brought about is not territorial, but rather strategic and mental. Russia has finally quit its policy of trying to integrate into the West and become part of the Euro-Atlantic system. It has returned to its home base in Eurasia and has prioritised links to non-Western countries.[14]

That does not mean that there are not issues on which collaboration will be mutually beneficial, as with the extensive array of arms control and crisis prevention efforts during the first Cold War. It does mean that rather than agreeing on the basic norms and rules of the game, and assuming that at the strategic level the two sides' goals are compatible – the assumption that prevailed prior to 2014 – leaders and citizens on both sides now advance incompatible norms and believe that at the strategic level, the two sides' interests conflict. One wonders whether in the future the period from 1991 to 2013 will be regarded not as a period between two cold wars, but as a temporary lull, analogous to the era of détente in the 1970s, in one long cold war.

The dynamics of the present era resemble those of the first Cold War in other respects as well. The West is widely seen as defending a status quo that, depending on one's view is either beneficial to international security and democracy or represents a US effort to maintain its hegemony at the expense

---

[13] 'Executive Summary and Recommendations', in Keir Giles, Philip Hanson, Roderic Lyne, James Nixey, James Sherr and Andrew Wood, *The Russian Challenge* (London: Chatham House, 2015), p. vi.
[14] Dmitri Trenin, 'Ukraine Crisis Causes Strategic, Mental Shift in Global Order', *Global Times*, 17 May 2015.

of others. Russia once again is seen by many as a revisionist power seeking to overthrow widely accepted norms, and by some as a threatened state trying to defend its security. Again, the conflict has a strongly domestic and normative component, with the West claiming that the conflict is in large part about the battle between democracy and autocracy, while Russia points at various elements of hypocrisy in the West's position.

In another sense, the current era shares a dynamic not only with the post-World War II era, but of the much deeper history of politics in Central and Eastern Europe. At the end of World War II, as at the end of World War I and as during the era of Catherine the Great, the question was where the line between Russia and the West will be drawn. In each of those cases, it was determined by primarily troops on the ground. A Russian commentary published in 2017 took the positive position that 'Russia used a favourable situation to launch an active policy and thereby moved the frontier of its confrontation with the West further away from its border'.[15] Geography offers few natural borders in this region, and bounded by the powerful states of Germany (Prussia) and Russia, the in-between states have struggled for centuries to maintain their independence. Unsurprisingly, each side tends to see as normal or as the status quo the dividing line that best serves its interest today. When Russia invokes distant history, it focuses on the period *after* Russia seized Crimea in the late eighteenth century, not before (and in this context, it is worth noting that from 1815 until World War I, the Russian Empire included Warsaw and much of present day Poland). The West focuses on the status quo post-1991, when Russia was pushed from territory that it had held since the 17th century. From the realist perspective, all the rhetoric about self-determination and history is simply ammunition in a contest for territory.

Several important dynamics of the Cold War have returned, even if the boundary between Russia's 'sphere of influence' and the West has moved eastward several hundred kilometres. First, NATO is once again a very important organisation. Russia complained bitterly about NATO's eastward movement, and some Western authors blame NATO expansion for Russia's military intervention in Ukraine. That remains in dispute, but it is clear that Russia's actions in Ukraine have ensured a renaissance of NATO and the deployment of more NATO forces to regions closer to Russia's borders.[16]

---

[15]   Nikolai Silayev and Andrey Sushentsov, 'Russia's Allies and the Geopolitical Frontier in Eurasia', *Russia in World Affairs*, May 2017. http://eng.globalaffairs.ru/valday/Russias-Allies-and-the-Geopolitical-Frontier-in-Eurasia-18718

[16]   In international relations theory, the paradox in this instance is simply a case of the 'security dilemma', in which the actions that states take to make themselves more secure often spur a reaction by others that leaves the initiating state less secure.

Second, as was the case in the Cold War, Western strategy today is based largely on the assumption that in time, Russian autocracy will be replaced by democracy, and a less aggressive regime will come to power. While there may have been good reason to assume that a post-Soviet regime would be less implacable that the Soviets were, there is less reason to be optimistic that a post-Putin government will be friendlier. The available evidence is that Russia's actions in Ukraine, and especially its annexation of Crimea, are highly popular in Russia, and not merely the project of an unpopular and autocratic government. The majority of Russian opposition leaders and groups, including Alexei Navalny, support the annexation of the Crimea. In a summer 2017 television debate with proxy leader Igor Girkin, Navalny did not criticise Putin's military policies towards Ukraine on principle but only in terms of the cost to the Russian economy.

More broadly, nationalism appears to be genuinely popular in Russia, as it is in many other states. Thus, many have asserted that one reason for Russia to annex the Crimea was that doing so bolstered Putin's popularity in anticipation of the 2018 presidential elections. 'Russia's longer-term interests would best be served by structural reforms at home and mutual accommodation with outside powers, small as well as great. But such policies would threaten the ability of Putin and his circle to hold on to power'.[17] Moreover, with Putin's power relatively well consolidated, he probably has more room to manoeuvre and to make deals with the West than would a successor seeking to build popularity and defend him or herself against nationalist challengers. Overall then, given what has happened in post-Soviet Russia, we may have less reason to believe now than we did during the first Cold War that a change in regime will be sufficient to improve relations between Russia and the West. Putin's view that Ukraine is 'Russian' and is rightfully part of the *Russkii Mir* and Eurasia Union – rather than Europe – reflects a broad consensus among Russians. NATO and the West may therefore need a long-term strategy that does not depend on Russian democracy solving the problem.

The EU Response

The EU was inadvertently at the epicentre of the Ukraine conflict. The EU's offer of an Association Agreement to Ukraine was seen in Brussels as a benign engagement with an important neighbour, but this ignored how Putin

---

[17] K. Giles, et. al. *The Russian Challenge*, p.vi. For a nuanced view that treats domestic politics as one among several drivers of Putin's foreign policy, see D. Trenin, *Russia's Breakout From the Post-Cold War System: The Drivers of Putin's Course* (Moscow: Carnegie Moscow Centre, 22 December 2014). http://carnegie.ru/2014/12/22/russia-s-breakout-from-post-cold-war-system-drivers-of-putin-s-course-pub-57589

had come to view EU enlargement into Eurasia, like NATO expansion, as creating a potentially irreversible loss in the geopolitical contest in Central Europe. It is worth noting that the Eastern Partnership did not envision offering its participants EU membership, and indeed was seen as an alternative to it.[18] The same norms that blinded European diplomats to the danger Russia saw in Ukraine joining an Association Agreement led EU leaders to be outraged that Russia deployed naked force to seize Crimea. '[T]he EU brought a low-politics toolbox to a high-politics construction site'.[19]

The EU was the central arena through which the West discussed economic sanctions and efforts to broker a resolution to the conflict. These two issues were linked in a March 2015 resolution making the implementation of the Minsk II agreement a prerequisite for lifting economic sanctions. While the measure was intended to promote Minsk II, the fact that Minsk II is widely viewed as dead means that the sanctions now look semi-permanent. This is especially the case following the adoption of tougher US sanctions in summer 2017.

Arkadiy Moshes argues that the reason that the EU rejected a Georgia-style response ('complain and then move on') is not because of Ukraine's particulars, but because Russia's behaviour in this case appears to be a much more fundamental challenge to the European order. 'There is currently a much better understanding that the era of Yalta-type partitions of Europe is long gone and that Ukraine is no one's to 'give away', whatever classical *realpolitikers* may say'.[20]

Despite broad agreement on the unacceptability of Russian conduct in Ukraine, Europe is not entirely unified on how to approach Russia and Ukraine going forward, and considerable effort has been expended finding positions that can obtain consensus. In part this is about Russia, because there is considerable opposition in some quarters to entering a long-term conflict with Russia, which so recently seemed like a partner. At the extreme, sympathy for Putin's style of rule among the left and populist nationalists in various countries engenders opposition to sanctions and other measures. Latent anti-Americanism probably contributes to that sentiment. In part,

---

[18]   Nicu Popescu & Andrew Wilson, *The Limits of Enlargement-lite: European and Russian Power in the Troubled Neighbourhood* (London: European Council on Foreign Relations, 2009).
http://ecfr.3cdn.net/befa70d12114c3c2b0_hrm6bv2ek.pdf
[19]   Rilka Dragneva and Kataryna Wolczuk, *Ukraine Between the EU and Russia: The Integration Challenge* (London: Palgrave Macmillan, 2015), p.125.
[20]   A. Moshes, 'The Crisis Over Ukraine – Three Years On: Is a "Grand Bargain" Totally Ruled Out?' (Helsinki: Finnish Institute of International Affairs Comment No, 12, May 2017). https://www.fiia.fi/en/publication/the-crisis-over-ukraine-three-years-on

however, scepticism about a hard line is about Ukraine, for which many Western Europeans are disinclined to sacrifice.

The NATO Response

The annexation of Crimea and hybrid warfare in Eastern Ukraine prompted European leaders to take a fresh look at their militaries, and to think about how to strengthen them. Much of that conversation has naturally focused on NATO. The end of the Cold War and the presumption of a new order in which violence was 'off the table' in Europe allowed European states to focus on the non-military aspects of security, such as migration. That changed rapidly in 2014, in particular for those states directly bordering Russia. In response to the Ukraine conflict, NATO and its members have rededicated themselves to strengthening the organisation and to reinforcing the part of its mission that consists of 'keeping the Russians out'. As NATO itself has acknowledged, while NATO sees its response to the Ukraine crisis as just that – a response, Russia is likely to see it as further proof of a Western plan to expand NATO at Russia's expense.[21]

Russia's use of 'little green men' in Crimea prompted an immediate concern about what could happen in the Baltic States, which had small armies, large Russian-speaking populations, and NATO Article V security guarantee. Were Russia to engineer a rapid invasion in this region, NATO would be hard pressed to defeat it with conventional forces. That reality had led many to oppose membership for those states to begin with, and the fact that they were admitted shows again the extent to which Western leaders believed the rules of the game had fundamentally changed. Now, they had to face the imminent possibility of being unable to resist Russian invasion and hybrid warfare against a NATO member state. Such a scenario was played out in a 2016 BBC drama where NATO forces responded to Russian hybrid warfare in Eastern Latvia.[22] A 60-mile-wide stretch of rural land called the Suwalki Gap between the Russian enclave of Kaliningrad and Russia's ally, Belarus, is NATO's weakest spot. From the Russian perspective, the Russian enclave of Kaliningrad is isolated being surrounded on all sides by NATO members.

The first major NATO response (after the suspension of collaboration via the NATO-Russia Council in April 2014) was the adoption of a series of 'assurance measures' beginning in May 2014 that evolved into a broader 'Readiness Action Plan' adopted at the September 2014 Wales summit. The

---

[21] 'The Ukraine Crisis and NATO-Russia Relations', *NATO Review Magazine*, July 2014. http://www.nato.int/docu/review/2014/Russia-Ukraine-Nato-crisis/Ukraine-crisis-NATO-Russia-relations/EN/index.htm

[22] http://www.bbc.co.uk/mediacentre/proginfo/2016/05/inside-the-war-room

assurance measures were aimed at convincing allies in the East, as well as Russia, that NATO could and would defend all of its members, including the three Baltic States. In the immediate aftermath of the Crimea annexation, there was a particular fear that Russia might not take the Article V commitment to the Baltic States seriously, which could lead to a major war. NATO increased fighter jet patrols, naval patrols, and training exercises in the region. The Readiness Action Plan added a set of 'adaptation measures' intended to materially improve NATO's ability to provide the defence to which it has committed. This envisioned expansion of the NATO Response Force, a rapid-deployment force, from 13,000 to roughly 40,000 troops, and creation of a new 'Very High Readiness Joint Task Force' of roughly 20,000 troops, intended to be capable of deploying a brigade of 5,000 ground troops within a few days.[23] Critics pointed out that the force was small and lightly armed compared to what Russia could rapidly deploy (for example, from Kaliningrad) and that more broadly, the gap between NATO's deterrent posture and its actual military ability to counter a Russian attack was growing, not shrinking.[24]

In the longer term, further actions are being contemplated. Among the proposals has been Germany's 'Framework Nations Project', an idea which predated Russia's military actions but has become much more relevant because of them. The idea is to strengthen the relationships by which the smaller militaries in Europe, many of which have specialised in particular missions, could be operationally integrated into the larger ones, which have a broader range of capabilities but are thin in many specific areas.[25] The centrepiece of this more coordinated army would be Germany's *Bundeswehr*. If these proceed, Russia's military interventions in Ukraine would have undermined a key Soviet and Russian goal in place since 1946, namely to limit the military power of Germany.

While Russia's military interventions in Ukraine have increased a sense of urgency within NATO, they have not solved the long-standing problems that have eroded the alliance's military capabilities. Two essential weaknesses interact. First, many of the member states spend relatively low shares of GDP on defence, an issue that has been raised in visibility by US President Donald Trump. Until the crisis, only five out of 28 NATO members spent two percent

---

[23] 'NATO's Readiness Action Plan: Fact Sheet', July 2016. http://www.nato.int/nato_static_fl2014/assets/pdf/pdf_2016_07/20160627_1607-factsheet-rap-en.pdf

[24] Tom Rogan, 'Obama's Plan to Send New Arms to Europe Isn't Enough', *The National Review*, 23 June 2015. http://www.nationalreview.com/article/420162/obamas-plan-send-new-arms-europe-isnt-enough-tom-rogan

[25] Claudia Major and Christian Mölling, 'The Framework Nations Concept: Germany's Contribution to a Capable European Defence', (Berlin: Stiftung Wissenschaft und Politik [German Institute for International and Security Affairs], 2014). https://www.swpberlin.org/fileadmin/contents/products/comments/2014C52_mjr_mlg.pdf

of GDP on defence. German social democrats are opposed to increasing German military spending to reach the goal of two percent.[26] Second, because NATO consists of over two dozen separate militaries, the whole is less than the sum of the parts. That is a major reason for the Framework Nations Project, but the issue, which has been salient since the 1960s, will not be resolved any time soon.

Russia's Policy

Russia has met the West's outrage over the Ukraine conflict with defiance. It has continued to maintain the legality of the annexation of Crimea, its non-involvement in what it terms a 'civil war' in Eastern Ukraine, and the fault of the West for both conflicts. It has also continued to sustain the conflict in Eastern Ukraine and to increase its capacity to act elsewhere. Moreover, it has upped the stakes by increasing the extent and transparency of its influence campaign in Western capitals and by seeking to interfere in several Western elections. From Russia's perspective, its interference in Western politics is no different than the transnational support for democracy promotion in the post-Soviet region, including the colour revolutions, but this initiative has galvanized resolve in the West and contributed to the further deterioration in relations between Russia and the West.

Russian scholars and leaders focused for years on Joseph Nye's concept of 'soft power', but interpreted it differently than did Nye. Whereas Nye conceived of 'soft power' largely as a resource that increased one's prestige and attractiveness,[27] Russian thinking on the topic tended to focus on it as an instrument, to be deployed to advantage in a conflict. Therefore, rather than increasing Russia's prestige or raising the likelihood that others would choose the policies that Russia wanted without being coerced, Russia's deployment of its version of soft power has had the opposite effect. Russia's and Putin's standing in the international community have been weakened, not augmented by its deployment of 'soft power'.[28]

Two important questions about Russian policy require some speculation, because the policy itself is not transparent. First, what is Russia's envisioned strategy concerning Ukraine? What are its ultimate goals, and how does it

---

[26] 'Germany's SPD rejects NATO 2 percent defence spending target', *Reuters*, 6 August 2017.
https://www.reuters.com/article/us-germany-election-military-spd-idUSKBN1AM001
[27]   Joseph S. Nye Jr., 'The Benefits of Soft Power', *Harvard Business School Working Knowledge*, 2 August 2004, at http://hbswk.hbs.edu/archive/4290.html
[28]   http://www.pewglobal.org/2015/08/05/russia-putin-held-in-low-regard-around-the-world/

believe it will achieve them? Second, to what extent does Russia consider the new status quo – in which Russia has gained a slice of Ukraine but is isolated from and opposed to the West – to be a favourable outcome that it is content to prolong and defend?

One of Russia's central assertions that continues from the Soviet period is that as a great power it expects to have a veto on major international questions. That helps explain its outrage at cases (such as Kosovo and Iraq) where the US and NATO deployed force without UN Security Council approval. In the Ukraine conflict, Russia has the *de facto* veto it seeks. Any solution, or any change from the status quo, must be something that Russia considers an improvement, because Russia has a great deal of ability to maintain the current situation, or to respond to something it cannot control by making things much worse.

On Crimea, there appears to be no room for bargaining. Russia's annexation of the territory and its rhetoric indicate that Russia intends to retain the territory permanently. It is hard to imagine what would convince it to change its mind, or how Crimea's status could change over Russia's objections. If there is to be normalisation at some point, it will almost certainly have to come via a Western and Ukrainian willingness to accept that.[29] Ukraine has tacitly admitted the weakness of its position by not fighting to reclaim the territory.

On Eastern Ukraine, it is much less clear what Russia's preferences are. The status quo, that of a low-level conflict that can be escalated at any time provides Russia much leverage, and prevents Ukraine from tackling many of its domestic issues. The Minsk provision that Ukraine's constitution would be modified to provide for extensive regional autonomy and local elections also appears very good for Russia, as this would keep the most-pro Russian regions of Ukraine, over which Russia could likely retain extensive influence, within Ukraine. The insistence upon autonomy for Ukraine's Eastern regions has been one consistent aspect of Russian policy. Either way, Ukraine would be prevented from doing anything to which Russia strongly objects. But it is not clear whether Russia prefers a (mostly) 'frozen conflict' or a reintegration of the territories into Ukraine with a high degree of autonomy and Russian influence.

Similarly, if the justification for the conflict was the possibility of Ukrainian membership in NATO or the EU, would some formal agreement for Ukraine to remain outside of one or both of those organisations be sufficient? In the

---

[29]   http://www.politico.eu/article/christian-lindner-germany-should-accept-crimean-annexation-as-permanent-provisional-solution/

short term, it does not appear that Ukraine, NATO, or the EU would agree to this, but it may be possible in the future to include such a provision in a deal. Several Western commentators have recommended such a move.

Michael O'Hanlon has proposed the creation of 'permanent neutrality'[30] for countries currently not in NATO stretching from Finland and Sweden through Ukraine to Serbia. While an interesting proposal, it relies on the questionable assumption that Russia views all of its neighbours in a similar manner. While Russia does not contest Finnish or Serbian sovereignty, this is not true of Ukraine, making it highly unlikely that Putin would withdraw from the Crimea and abandon the Donbas. O'Hanlon believes that in return for Ukraine dropping the goal of NATO membership, Russia should acquiesce in it joining the EU. That does not address the problem that joining the DCFTA with the EU would rule out joining the CIS Customs Union. In 2014, Russia intervened in Ukraine when only this EU 'enlargement-light' was on offer. A completely different problem with proposals to make Ukraine neutral is that doing so would rewrite the norms of European politics in a way that the EU has staunchly opposed. Europe would be accepting a return to a world in which 'great powers' imposed rules and territorial revisions on the smaller states.

A third problem is that 'non-bloc' status is economically unviable in a globalised world economy. After 1945, free trade areas were not so important, but in the last two decades, with the EU on one side and Eurasian Union on the other, the countries in the middle would be left in an untenable economic position. Switzerland and Norway are members of the European Free Trade Association (EFTA) while the UK may be seeking to remain in the EU's customs union after it has withdrawn from the EU. All recognise that access to reduced barriers to trade is essential, even if they do not want to participate in the deeper integration of the EU.

A reasonable conjecture is that the Russian leadership has a better sense of its tactics than of its goals. Both in Crimea and in Eastern Ukraine, Russia played a long game, waiting and preparing until the time was right to move. That tactic may continue to be attractive. In this view, even if Russia does not have a specific strategy, it may have a belief that with time, a more favourable settlement will be possible than now. In terms of resolving the Ukrainian conflict, this may mean that Russia sees no need to make concessions. In terms of conflict management, this would be beneficial, because an actor that believes the tide is turning in its favour has less incentive to disrupt the status

---

[30]   Michael E. O'Hanlon, *Beyond NATO: A new security architecture for Eastern Europe* (Washington DC: Brookings Institution, 28 July 2017). https://www.brookings.edu/blog/order-from-chaos/2017/07/28/beyond-nato-a-new-security-architecture-for-eastern-europe/

quo than one who believes that its chances are eroding.

The larger question for Russian strategy is whether another several decades of cold war is in its interest. Is there a viable strategy in building an alliance with others who reject the status quo in international affairs? Do those actors have much in common other than a desire to disrupt what they see as US hegemony in the world? In particular, one wonders whether, as China's power continues to grow, Russia will perceive as much threat from China, with which it shares a very long border, as it does from the US and Europe. Currently, and most likely for the indefinite future, Russia needs China more than China needs Russia.[31]

According to prominent Russian scholars and commentators, Russia indeed has a strategy based on and supported by broad changes underway in international affairs. Andrei Kortunov elaborates a new era in world politics, which he calls 'neo-modern', in which older tenets of international politics, such as nationalism and the focus on the nation-state, are replacing 'global universalism'.[32] A similar conception of the changed world guides the 2016 Foreign Policy Concept of the Russian Federation: 'The world is currently going through fundamental changes related to the emergence of a multipolar international system. The structure of international relations is becoming increasingly complex. Globalisation has led to the formation of new centres of economic and political power. Global power and development potential is becoming decentralised, and is shifting towards the Asia-Pacific Region, eroding the global economic and political dominance of the traditional Western powers. Cultural and civilizational diversity of the world and the existence of multiple development models have been clearer than ever'.[33]

While some of this rhetoric may be aimed at convincing various domestic audiences of the rightness and the likely success of Russian policy, there is no reason to think that many Russians (and many outside Russia as well) do not believe the basic outline of the argument. The notion that the US and the West are declining relative to Asia, and that the liberal agenda of democracy and free markets is on the wane, is not limited to Russian thinkers. As a result, it appears likely that Russia, believing that it holds a hand that is

---

[31]   Fu Ying, 'How China Sees Russia: Beijing and Moscow Are Close, but Not Allies', *Foreign Affairs*, vol.95, no.1 (January/February 2016), pp.96–105.

[32]   Andrei Kortunov, 'From Post-Modernism to Neo-Modernism', *Russia in Global Affairs*, 13 February 2017. http://eng.globalaffairs.ru/number/From-Post-Modernism-to-Neo-Modernism-18578

[33]   Paragraph 4, Foreign Policy Concept of the Russian Federation. http://www.mid.ru/en/foreign_policy/official_documents//asset_publisher/CptICkB6BZ29/content/id/2542248

strong and growing stronger, does not feel much urgency to resolve the Ukraine crisis.

The US and the EU

For much of the post-Soviet era, the United States has been more active in supporting Ukraine than has been the EU. As noted above, however, progress toward an EU-Ukraine Association Agreement and a DCFTA placed the EU in the key spot in the run-up to the crisis. During the Euromaidan itself, the US and EU struggled, generally successfully, to adopt common positions regarding a resolution of the crisis.

Both the EU and the United States sought an outcome to the protests that maintained constitutional and legal processes in Ukraine. The EU, represented by foreign ministers from Germany and Poland, brokered a deal at the height of the crisis on 21 February that appeared to deescalate the crisis, as Yanukovych agreed to restoration of the 2004 constitution and holding of early presidential elections in December 2014. The US supported that deal, but opposition leaders on the Euromaidan (in contrast to the leaders of opposition political parties) rejected it, insisting that after the killings of protestors Yanukovych must leave office. When Yanukovych subsequently fled and was stripped off his office, both the US and EU accepted the act, rather than insisting on obeying the 21 February deal, a decision that Russia saw as evidence of bad faith.

Generally, the US has supported a more strident response than has the EU. This is consistent with the long-term differences in policies and with the fact that the EU had to find a solution amenable to its 28 members. Thus, the US supported further-reaching sanctions than did the EU, although the differences were not insurmountable, and the two sides were able to agree on a common front. Similarly, the US and EU were able to arrive at common positions on economic and financial support for Ukraine.

Following the imposition of sanctions, discussion in the US turned to what kind of military assistance the US should provide Ukraine. Some policymakers and think tank experts supported supplying military equipment to Ukraine, in order to counter the advantage in weaponry that the Russian military was deploying and making available to its proxies in Eastern Ukraine. Lethal weaponry might directly support Ukrainian fighters on the ground, and indirectly raise the costs of Russian intervention, making it less sustainable. Such a policy would echo US support for the Afghan resistance after the 1979 Soviet invasion, leading to high casualties and eventually forcing the USSR to withdraw. While the annexation of Crimea boosted Putin's popularity, the intervention in Donbas is much less popular, and devoting more soldiers and money to the conflict might be unpopular.

Many others in the US opposed providing military assistance to Ukraine. Russia, it was argued, could match any increase in the quality or quantity of weapons being deployed in the conflict, so the only result of providing weaponry would be to increase the number of casualties from the conflict. Many felt that increased US involvement would validate Putin's arguments about US aggression and increase, rather than decrease, Russian resolve. Moreover, opponents argued, Ukraine and the United States had to accept that Ukraine did not have a military path to resolving the conflict, but instead would have to rely on diplomacy. On this question, the US ended up choosing a policy that matched where the EU already was.

For the US, the Ukraine conflict became subsumed in a much larger set of conflicts with Russia, which together constituted the new cold war. Even before 2014, the US and Russia were supporting opposite sides in the Syrian civil war, and that disagreement only worsened. Then, Russia's actions surrounding the 2016 US presidential election toxified the relationship dramatically. Ukraine was increasingly a battleground in a larger conflict, rather than an objective of policy in itself. Most important, perhaps, was the belief that Russia's support for Trump's election made it politically dangerous for his administration to do anything that might be seen as a concession. The US Congress, generally bitterly divided along party lines, nearly unanimously passed a law requiring Congressional approval to lift sanctions. Trump was reportedly inclined to veto the law as an encroachment on executive prerogatives, but feared being seen as soft on Russia. Bipartisan support in the US for a hard line on Russia is stronger than it has been in many years, perhaps since the divisions that emerged in the 1970s over détente.

Ukraine and the West

If the conflict began in part because of Ukraine's pivotal position between the West and Russia, the war has only increased Ukraine's salience. Perhaps the most dramatic impact has been on the EU. For many years, the EU took a back seat to the United States in dealing with Ukraine, but following the Orange Revolution and the launch of the Eastern Partnership in 2009 it took a greater role. In particular, the EU began more seriously applying in Ukraine the same strategy it had applied in the remainder of post-communist Europe; namely, using the attractiveness of a closer relationship with the EU as a means of promoting and consolidating democratic transformation. For the EU, Russia's opposition to the agreement contradicted a dearly held belief, namely that no other country could veto the independent choices of a European state. This notion was crucial to European notions of the post-Cold War order in Europe. Russia's insistence on this point, and its subsequent military intervention, therefore provoked opposition in Europe even among those generally sceptical about Ukraine's European credentials and sup-portive of good relations with Russia. As a result, following Russia's military intervention, the EU became more committed to Ukraine's success than it had been previously.

The US position was compatible to that of the EU, though with different emphasis. The US was less focused on the principle of Ukraine's freedom of choice, and more focused on the broader challenge that Russia's action appeared to present. The result was largely the same: both the US and the EU, along with NATO, have made the success and stability of Ukraine a high priority. 'The critical element in the new geoeconomic competition between the West and Russia is the extent of Western economic support for Ukraine'.[34]

The West's efforts have continued to be undermined by the same patterns of backsliding on corruption and the rule of law that have characterised Ukraine since the early post-Soviet period, led to 'Ukraine fatigue' after the Orange Revolution and could happen again. In short, Western efforts to bolster Ukraine domestically have run into a huge moral hazard problem: because they are so dedicated to combatting Russia's efforts to undermine Ukraine, the West feels compelled to sustain the Ukrainian economy. However, that aid has likely helped the Ukrainian government to persist in power without seriously tackling either the general problems of corruption and the rule of law or the specific commitments it has made to its donors. Under normal circum-stances, donors, represented by the IMF, would stop aid programmes on the grounds of non-compliance. The West has hesitated to do this in the case of Ukraine for fear of the government collapsing.

In 2014, there was some hope that the threat from Russia would change the political game in Ukraine and some promising steps were taken, including the appointment of Mikhail Saakashvili as governor of Odesa *oblast* and the formation of new anti-corruption bodies, such as the National Anti-Corruption Bureau. But Saakashvili did not last and the anti-corruption bodies have been prevented from prosecuting high-level officials. More progress has been made on economic, social, fiscal-monetary and energy reforms. Efforts are underway to transform the Soviet-era *Militsiya* into a European-style *Politsiya* and Interior Ministry Internal Troops into a National Guard. President Poroshenko has presided over the creation of a powerful army. Nevertheless, Ukraine continues to lag in the fight against corruption.

---

[34] K. Giles, et. al. *The Russian Challenge*, p.vi.

A crucial question for the future is whether Ukraine fatigue will resurge to the point where it seems more pragmatic to write off Ukraine than to continue an open-ended commitment to keeping it afloat. A related question is whether a new round of protests might again induce turmoil in Ukrainian politics.

Prospects for Settling the Conflict

The prospects for peace in Ukraine appear to be dim. The minimally acceptable outcomes for the various sides are too far apart to bridge until something significant changes. Moreover, the Ukrainian conflict is now subsumed in the broader cold war between the West and Russia, making it even harder to address. None of the actors can reach a better solution without the acquiescence of other parties who have different preferred outcomes. In such a situation, only the exercise of greater power, and the inflicting of higher costs, might persuade one side or another to change courses.

For Russia, the optimal solution appears to be that the DNR and LNR are rejoined with Ukraine, but with a high degree of autonomy, and with a political leadership controlled by Russia. Russia seeks a kind of 'federalisation' in which the regions would have extensive veto powers over the country's domestic and foreign policies, including the power to block Ukraine joining NATO and the EU. At a minimum, this would provide Russia with a direct and legitimised way to interfere in Ukrainian politics, which Ukraine would see as a threat to its sovereignty. Moreover, any such deal would encounter stiff resistance from Ukrainian public opinion, including veterans of the war and their families and friends, who are growing in number. In August 2015, violent riots broke out outside parliament when it discussed the question of autonomy for the DNR and LNR. Barring Ukrainian capitulation to this regional autonomy plan outcome, Russia appears to be well served by a conflict in which it can ratchet up or down the level of violence as it pleases, without having to take any responsibility for results, claiming the DNR and LNR are breakaway regions of Ukraine over which Russia has no control.

Ukraine's government holds to the implausible position that it is going to retake control of the Donbas and Crimea as well. Both politics and principle prevent Ukraine from dealing with the situation realistically. Politically, the notion of recovering the territory is popular, and leaders cannot admit that the territory is lost. In terms of principle, it seems wrong to acquiesce in what was a clear violation of international law. However, Russia is exceedingly unlikely to give back Crimea, and Ukraine has never shown any inclination to fight for it. The prospects in the Donbas are better, in that Russia has not formally annexed them. But while Ukraine's army is now much stronger than in 2014, Ukrainian officials and think tank experts are concerned that in the event of an outbreak of full hostilities, Russia might annex its two Donbas proxy enclaves – as it did with the Crimea and *de facto* has undertaken in South Ossetia and Abkhazia after its 2008 invasion of Georgia. Two other long-debated scenarios have been that Russian forces might seek to forge a 'land bridge' from Russian territory east of Mariupol to Odesa, which was widely discussed by Western commentators in 2015-2016, or that Russian forces invade Ukraine from Belarus.[35] The latter scenario was widely discussed in Kiev and the West before and during the September 2017 *Zapad* military exercises in Belarus, one of the largest held by Russia since the disintegration of the USSR in 1991.

An increasing number of commentators within and outside Ukraine have recommended that Ukraine adopt what former US Secretary of State Colin Powell, in a different context, called the 'Pottery Barn' policy: 'you break it, you own it'. The idea would be for Ukraine unilaterally to acknowledge the separation of the DNR and LNR from Ukraine, which would allow Ukraine to move forward with a much more cohesive polity and would leave Russia to deal with the mess in the Donbas. This policy has been repeatedly advocated by Alexander J. Motyl.[36] Some steps were taken in this direction in early 2017, when trade between the occupied regions and the rest of Ukraine was significantly diminished, forcing Russia to step in. Similarly, the cutting off of water to Crimea forced Russia to come up with a plan to address the peninsula's water supply. Such a strategy would include changing the legal definition of the war from that of an ATO to recognising the Crimea, DNR and LNR as 'temporarily occupied territory' with the concept of Russia as the 'aggressor' state introduced for the first time. The new approach will permit the Ukrainian authorities to use the army in the ATO outside anti-terrorist legislation. Defining these three regions as 'temporarily occupied territories' provides the legal basis for Kiev to be not held responsible for the political, economic and social situation in the Crimea, DNR and LNR.

From this perspective, for the same reason that Russia would like to see the Donbas reintegrated into Ukraine, Ukraine would be better off without it. In particular, the loss of Crimea and the Donbas dramatically shifts the balance of electoral politics in Ukraine away from Eastern Ukraine and Russia and toward Central Ukraine and Europe. Again, however, both politics and principle make such a strategy implausible. Therefore, Ukraine is in a position of pursuing a strategy of reintegration which cannot possibly succeed and

---

[35] See the special issue on Russian-Ukrainian relations of Natsionalna Bezpeka i Oborona (nos. 8/9, 2015) published by the Razumkov Ukrainian Centre for Economic and Political Studies. http://razumkov.org.ua/uploads/journal/ukr/NSD157-158_2015_ukr.pdf

[36] See his numerous blogs at http://www.worldaffairsjournal.org/blog/100

would weaken Ukraine and its European foreign policy vector if it did.

A variety of other possible settlements have been put forward by commentators in Ukraine and elsewhere in the West. Many include a similar set of pragmatic proposals, such as a cease-fire that freezes the existing lines of control, the delaying of consideration of the permanent status of occupied regions and Crimea into the more distant future, and the neutralisation of Ukraine, in some form.[37] The first of these makes sense, and has been embodied in both Minsk agreements, but has so far been impossible to make stick. The second of these seems inevitable, but on both sides, there are strong feelings that these questions are already answered and are non-negotiable. Russians tend to believe that the annexation of Crimea is an established fact while many in Ukraine and in the West cannot accept the idea of legitimising it. The third suggestion is potentially most interesting because it exposes a profound divide within the West about how to approach the problem and because, oddly, it is an issue on which many in Europe are more intransigent about than many in the US.

Former US Ambassador to Ukraine Steven Pifer has argued that one danger for Ukraine is that Russia will actually implement its side of Minsk II, withdrawing heavy weaponry and returning the border to Ukraine's control. This would obligate Ukraine to fulfil its side of the deal, including revising the constitution to greatly increase regional autonomy. If the Ukrainian government could not deliver on that, Ukraine would be in breach of the agreement while Russia was not. This might tip support in Europe toward normalising relations with Russia. Pifer speculated that Russia has not chosen this gambit because it may get what it wants without any concession, given that US President Trump seemed favourably inclined, that the EU would likely be occupied with Brexit, and that Marine Le Pen was expected to do well in French presidential elections in 2017.[38] With Le Pen having lost to Emmanuel Macron, and Trump constrained from making concessions to Russia, this strategy is unlikely but will depend on how much Russians become dissatisfied with the current level of conflict.

Ukrainian oligarch Viktor Pinchuk suggested that Ukraine commit to not joining the EU or NATO, separate the issue of Crimea from the Donbas

[37]   J. J. Mearsheimer, 'Why the Ukraine Crisis is the West's Fault' and M. E. O'Hanlon and Jeremy Shapiro, 'Crafting a win-win-win for Russia, Ukraine and the West' *Washington Post*, 7 December 2014. http://www.washingtonpost.com/opinions/crafting-a-win-win-win-for-russia-ukraine-and-the-west/2014/12/05/727d6c92-7be1-11e4-9a27-6fdbc612bff8_story.html

[38]   S. Pifer, *The Eagle and the Trident. U.S. – Ukraine Relations in Turbulent Times* (Washington DC: Brookings Institution, 2017).

conflict (acquiesce for the time being in Russian control of Crimea) and allow local elections in the occupied regions, even if they cannot be free or fair.[39] He also suggested that Ukraine support the removal of sanctions on Russia. What is less clear is whether all of those steps, which are not politically viable in Ukraine, would prompt Russia to withdraw and stay withdrawn. A major pitfall of Pinchuk's proposal is that Ukrainian distrust of Russian leaders is at an all-time record high.

A complicating factor for Ukraine is that its position is heavily dependent upon economic and financial support from the West, which may not last forever. The West has a wide range of interactions with Russia, and it is not beyond the realm of possibility that Russia could offer something to the West that it wants more than Ukraine. For example, credible and meaningful help with Iran's latent nuclear programme or North Korea's active programme, or support for ousting Bashar al-Assad in Syria would be tempting to US leaders in particular. Russia has numerous possibilities to foment new problems, which it can then offer its help in solving. So far, the heavy-handed way that Russia has played its cards, especially in interference in Western elections, has made a deal between Russia and the West at Ukraine's expense unlikely, but that could change.

Because it seems inconceivable that Russia will return Crimea to Ukraine, a difficult diplomatic task for the various players in the coming years will be to find a way to accept Russia's ownership of Crimea while not seeming to reward its aggression or undermine the principle that invading one's neighbours and changing borders by force is not acceptable. Put differently, if Russia, Ukraine and the West are ever to move beyond the Crimea annexation, some means must be found to legitimise what seems entirely illegitimate. One alternative would be to follow the policy that the US took relative to the Baltic States during the Cold War. The US never recognised the annexation of the three Baltic States by the USSR, and therefore treated their looming independence differently in the waning months of the Soviet Union. At the same time, the US did not allow the illegality of the Soviet annexation of the Baltic States to block normal relations with the USSR on a wide range of other issues.

Finding a solution of this nature will be much harder on the Donbas question, in large part because Russia, which can veto any arrangement, appears to want neither to annex the territory nor to completely give up control. In other words, Russia's preferred solution is not to have a solution. Trans-Dniestr, the status of which has been in limbo since Russia assisted its proxies to

---

[39]   Viktor Pinchuk, 'Ukraine Must Make Painful Compromises for Peace with Russia', *Wall Street Journal*, 29 December 2016.

separate it from Moldova in 1991–1992, may be a precedent. Similarly, Russia supported the *de facto* independence of Abkhazia and South Ossetia for several years before recognising their independence after it had invaded Georgia in 2008.

Russia's policy of supporting proxy dependencies around its borders is in some respects reminiscent of the Cold War, in which nominally independent governments in Eastern Europe were wholly or largely controlled from Moscow. As that example shows, it is sometimes hard to sustain that control over time. In other respects, Russia's policy represents a throwback to a much earlier period, before the twentieth century, when sovereignty was often incomplete and contingent on deals with great powers, and the borders of states like Poland were revised repeatedly according to the shifting balance of power and the diplomatic needs of more powerful neighbours. It is precisely that system that the EU rejects, and that Russian scholars believe is returning.

Ukraine in the New Cold War

Perhaps the best reminder we can apply from the first Cold War to the second is that it endured for 45 years. The dividing line between East and West was determined largely by the disposition of forces in May 1945. Regardless of whether anyone regarded that line as fair, legitimate or ideal, it endured because no one could change it unilaterally, and the changes that one side would have preferred were unacceptable to the other. A major difference between the Cold War and the new cold war is that there is no 'iron curtain' separating the sides. Information, cyber and to some extent hybrid warfare can be conducted in the 'enemy's' territory much more easily than when the Warsaw Pact faced NATO in Central Europe.

In the absence of some new disruption, the current division of territory could last a very long time, with Ukraine playing a role roughly analogous to that of Berlin. Trans-Dniestr has already persisted for a quarter of a century, and could not be resolved even when Russia and the West were at the height of post-Cold War comity or when Moldova elected a communist president.

However, just as the Hungarian revolution in 1956 and Prague Spring of 1968 threatened to undo the post-World War II status quo, the situation in Ukraine could still be disrupted, perhaps suddenly. Among the possible scenarios are these: A new contest for power in Ukraine could lead to the fragmentation of the Ukrainian state, as in the Euromaidan Revolution. Poor economic performance or disgruntlement at high casualties on the frontlines could trigger a new political crisis, and military veterans and nationalists might seek regime change through another Maidan.

Protests in Russia could give Russian leaders increased incentives to pursue a new adventure in Ukraine to rally domestic unity. Alternatively, the growing popularity of the opposition could lead to declining support for Russian military involvement in Eastern Ukraine. Russian efforts to foster separatism and terrorism in Ukraine beyond the Donbas could be renewed with the aim of pressuring Ukraine to acquiesce to changing the constitution to provide the DNR and LNR with special status and the holding of elections in Russia's two proxy republics. The DNR and/or LNR could unilaterally restart full-scale hostilities, dragging Russia with them. This scenario would be similar to that in Georgia where provocations from South Ossetia led to Georgia's attempt to militarily return South Ossetia to Georgian sovereignty. Georgia's leadership wrongly believed in the likelihood of US military support, failed to appreciate Tbilisi had weak support within the EU and did not foresee that its actions would trigger a Russian invasion.

Western governments (either some or all) could move towards tacitly acknowledging Russian sovereignty over Crimea, as Trump hinted at during the 2016 election campaign. The West could seek to broker a deal whereby Ukraine drops its claim to sovereignty over the Crimea in return for a deal on the Donbas. Having claimed that there are no Russian forces in the Donbas, Putin could quietly withdraw them without being publicly backing down. Putin might be threatened by a nationalist backlash from nationalist groups who already believe that he 'betrayed' *Novorossiya*.

What we should probably not expect is a repeat of 1991, which was a historically unique event. Even if Russia were to have an anti-authoritarian revolution, it does not necessarily follow that a pro-Western government would result, and it is just as likely that Russian nationalists would take power. One major difference between the first Cold War and this one is that in the first Cold War, the conflict appeared to be inexorably linked with communism as an ideology and form of government, so that leaders on both sides could assume that with communism gone, the grounds for conflict were gone. Putin's government is pragmatic rather than ideological; or rather its ideology is that of power politics. There is therefore less reason to hope that a new Russian regime would want to give up territory that Russia has long claimed.

Moreover, we should also remember that Ukraine became independent not because Soviet or Russian leaders acquiesced, but because they could not prevent it. While such weakness in Russia could emerge again, there is no good reason to expect it. Moreover, in contrast to 1991, there is no obvious reason to expect that Crimea or the occupied parts of the Donbas would seek to return to Ukraine, even given the opportunity. The longer they remain outside Kiev's control the more difficult it will be to re-integrate them. A strong, prosperous Ukraine closely connected with Europe might be more attractive, and that provides additional incentive for Russia to stymie progress that could someday emerge in Ukraine's domestic politics.

Further Reading

Allison, Roy, 'Russian 'deniable' intervention in Ukraine: how and why Russia broke the rules', *International Affairs*, vol. 90, no.6 (November 2014), pp. 1255–1297.

Averre, Derek, 'The Ukraine Conflict: Russia's Challenge to European Security Governance', *Europe-Asia Studies*, vol. 68, no. 4 (June 2016), pp. 699–725.

Daalder, Ivo, Michele Flournoy, John Herbst, Jan Lodal, Steve Pifer, James Stavridis, Strobe Talbott and Charles Wald, *Preserving Ukraine's Independence, Resisting Russian Aggression: What the United States and NATO Must Do* (Washington DC: Brookings Institution and Atlantic Council of the US, 2015). http://www.brookings.edu/research/reports/2015/02/ukraine-independence-russian-aggression

Davies, Lance, 'Russia's 'Governance' Approach: Intervention and the Conflict in the Donbas', *Europe-Asia Studies*, vol. 68, no. 4 (June 2016), pp. 726–749.

Delcour, Laure, 'Between the Eastern Partnership and Eurasian Integration: Explaining Post-Soviet Countries' Engagement in (Competing) Region-Building Projects', *Problems of Post-Communism*, vol.62, no.6 (November 2015), pp.316–327.

Einhorn, Robert, 'Ukraine, Security Assurances, and Non-Proliferation', *The Washington Quarterly*, vol.38, no.1 (January 2015), pp.47–72.

Fitzpatrick, Mark, 'The Ukraine Crisis and Nuclear Order', *Survival*, vol. 56, no. 4 (August–September 2014), pp. 81–90.

Freedman, Lawrence, 'Ukraine and the Art of Crisis Management', *Survival*, vol. 56, no. 3, (July 2014), pp.7–42.

Götz, Elias, 'Russia, the West, and the Ukraine crisis: three contending perspectives', *Contemporary Politics*, vol.22, no.3 (July 2016), pp.249–266.

Grant, D. Thomas, *Aggression against Ukraine Territory, Responsibility, and International Law* (London: Palgrave Macmillan, 2015).

Haukkala, Hiski, 'A Perfect Storm; Or What Went Wrong and What Went Right for the EU in Ukraine', *Europe-Asia Studies,* vol. 68, no. 4 (June 2016), pp.653–664.

Kriskovic, Andrej, 'Imperial Nostalgia or Prudent Geopolitics? Russia's Efforts to Reintegrate the Post-Soviet Space in Geopolitical Perspective', *Post-Soviet Affairs*, vol.30, no.6 (November 2014), pp.503–528.

Kundnani, Hans, 'Germany Looks East', *Foreign Affairs,* vol.94, no.1 (January/February 2015), pp. 108–116.

Kuzio, T., 'Ukraine between a Constrained EU and Assertive Russia', *Journal of Common Market Studies*, vol.55, no.1 (January 2017), pp.103–120.

Nitoiu, Cristian and Monika Sus, 'The European Parliament's Diplomacy – a Tool for Projecting EU Power in Times of Crisis? The Case of the Cox-Kwasniewski Mission', *Journal of Common Market Studies*, vol.55, no.1 (January 2017), pp.71–86.

Orlov, Vladimir, 'Security Assurances to Ukraine and the 1994 Budapest Memorandum: from the 1990s to the Crimea Crisis', *Security Index*, vol.20, no.2 (April 2014), pp.133–140.

Ropcke, Julian, 'How Russia Finances the Ukrainian rebel territories', *Bild*, 16 January 2016. http://www.bild.de/politik/ausland/ukraine-konflikt/russia-finances-donbass-44151166.bild.html

Ropcke, J., 'Putin's shadow government for Donbass exposed', *Bild*, 29 March 2016. http://www.bild.de/politik/ausland/ukraine-konflikt/donbass-shadow-government-45102202.bild.html

Rynning, Sten, 'The false promise of continental concert: Russia, the West and the necessary balance of power'. *International Affairs*, vol.91, no.3 (July 2015), pp.539–552.

Siddi, Marco, 'German Foreign Policy towards Russia in the Aftermath of the Ukraine Crisis: A New Ostpolitik?' *Europe-Asia Studies*, vol. 68, no. 4 (June 2016), pp. 665–677.

Wolff, Andrew T., 'The future of NATO enlargement after the Ukraine crisis', *International Affairs*, vol.91, no.5 (September 2015), pp.1103–1121.

6

Conclusion

Disagreement continues over both the causes and potential solutions to the conflict between Ukraine and Russia. We use the word 'solutions' carefully, because there is little prospect for re-establishing the level of confidence or the norms that prevailed prior to 2014. In this brief conclusion, we set out some of the key findings of the book, and pursue their implications for the future.

First, this book has differed from many others in its understanding of the timeline of the conflict. The conflict that emerged in 2014 had its roots at the very outset of the post-Cold War period, because from the very beginning, Russia sought to prevent Ukraine's independence and, when this was unavoidable, sought to limit it both in terms of sovereignty and territory. As Angela Stent astutely points out, 'Every U.S. president since 1992 has come into office believing that, unlike his predecessor, he will be able to forge and sustain a new, improved relationship with Russia.... Yet each reset has ended in disappointment on both sides'.[1] Similarly, structural problems undermine efforts at re-setting Ukrainian-Russian relations; even the most pro-Russian Ukrainian presidents (Kuchma and Yanukovych) struggled to find a stable accommodation with Russia.

In terms of national identity and tactics, the story begins even earlier. As chapter two demonstrated, the approach to information warfare and the use of unconventional tactics ('active measures') has deep roots in the Soviet era, even if the specific tactics of cyber warfare have taken advantage of modern technology. The spread of disinformation, brazen lying, 'whataboutism',[2] and

---

[1]   Angela Stent, 'America and Russia: Same Old, Same Old', *The National Interest*, September-October 2017. http://nationalinterest.org/feature/america-russia-same-old-same-old-21941

[2]   'Whataboutism' is a term coined by western diplomats during the Cold War for the Soviet tactic of countering any discussion of Soviet wrongdoing by pointing to some unrelated flaw in the west. The *Economist* noted an upsurge in the tactic in 2008. See 'Whataboutism', *The Economist*, 31 January 2008. http://www.economist.com/node/10598774

targeted violence were all tactics used by the Soviet Union, particularly in its long-running battle against the Ukrainian inde-pendence movement. As chapter three showed, Russia's conception of its national identity – including the view that Russians and Ukrainians are one people – has sources going back centuries.

This is not to say that military conflict was inevitable, or that the events of 2013–2014 did not provide both added incentive and opportunity for Russia to use force. But it does indicate that the desire to revise the territorial arrangement in Ukraine did not emerge in response to NATO or EU enlargement. While those developments undoubtedly were seen as dangerous to Russian interests, Russian interest in controlling Ukraine predates them.

Looking forward, this interpretation has important implications. While the nature of Putin's regime helps explain the decision to intervene in Ukraine in 2014, the notion that Ukraine is in part or entirely Russian territory is not limited to Putin or to a narrow slice of the Russian elite. To the extent that the Russian creation myth centres on events in Kievan Rus, and to the extent that the territorial expansion under Catherine the Great is seen as the basis for *Novorossiya*, it would appear that Russia's territorial aspirations in Ukraine have not been satisfied. The effort to promote further separatism in *Novorossiya* in 2014 indicated that had the opportunity existed, a much larger slice of Ukrainian territory might have come under the sway of Russian proxies.

This leads us to a second important conclusion, which is that realist analysis, while it contributes much to understanding the dynamics of conflict, does not yield a clear policy recommendation without the help of further assumptions. The most prominent realist analysis of the conflict, that of Mearsheimer, is based on the assumption that Russia was a defensive power, protecting the status quo. To the extent that this assumption is true, the West's acceptance of that status quo might be seen as the basis for a stable peace going forward.

However, the assumption that Russia seeks further revision of the status quo is equally plausible. Territorially, the *Novorossiya* probe, threats against the Baltic States, and continuing pressure on the front lines in the Donbas indicate that Russia might take more territory if it can do so. Just as few expected Russia to seize Crimea in 2014 despite its long record of claiming the territory, we should perhaps take Russia's hints about Kiev and *Novorossiya* seriously. Put differently, having revised slightly the territorial status quo of 1991, will Russia be satisfied that this status quo still leaves the western boundary of its influence far to the East of where it was from 1945 to

1989, and leaves Odesa and Kiev beyond its control? Leaving aside the question of whether Russia is satiated territorially, it clearly seeks revision of the norms that Europe and the US presume have underpinned the security of Europe since 1989, two of which are that states' choices of institutional affiliations cannot be vetoed by third parties and that borders will not be changed by force.[3]

Therefore, depending on whether we believe Russia is or is not satisfied with the status quo, realism points the West to opposite strategies. If Russia is satisfied with Crimea and Eastern Ukraine, then the West can aid its own security by acquiescing to these gains and thus making Russia less agg-ressive. But if Russia is not satisfied, then realism, as it traditionally has done, would counsel that power be met with power. The most basic realist argument is that force is the ultimate determinant of outcomes, so if there is no agreement on the dividing line between Russia's sphere and the West, then it will be determined by the use or threat of force. In this view, the best way to prevent conflict is to deter it with the threat of force.

Clearly, the West erred in believing that Russia could be satisfied with a Ukraine integrated into Western institutions. But, it remains unclear what Russia would be satisfied with. Russian leaders themselves may disagree, and they may not even have a fixed idea. Just as the possibility of Ukraine joining NATO was not on the West's radar screen in 1991, Russia's notion of where its sphere of interest might end could well be determined as much by opportunity as by some pre-determined notion. As hard as it is to assess intentions looking backwards (scholars still disagree on what motivated Soviet policy during the Cold War), it will be even harder to assess them looking into the future. As a result, we should continue to expect that policy recommen-dations toward the Ukraine-Russia conflict reflect the authors' assumptions as much as any analysis that comes from those assumptions.

A third conclusion is that the conflict will not be easy to resolve. Repeated attempts at ceasefires have not lasted more than a day, and a proposal by Ukraine to invite UN peacekeepers into the Donbas has been blocked by Russia.[4] Russia's own proposal for peacekeepers was rejected by Ukraine and the US over the fundamental question of where to station them. Ukraine and the US seek to have peacekeepers on the internationally recognised Russian-Ukrainian border while Russia proposed that they be based on the ceasefire line. Putin's proposal therefore resembled earlier proposals during

---

[3]   See, for example, Sergei Karaganov, 'The Victory of Russia and the New Concert of Nations', *Russia in Global Affairs, March 2017*. http://eng.globalaffairs.ru/pubcol/ Russias-Victory-new-Concert-of-Nations-18641

[4]   http://www.pravda.com.ua/news/2017/08/26/7153204/

Yeltsin's presidency when 'CIS' (read Russian) peacekeepers froze conflicts that Russian proxies had won on the ceasefire line in the Trans-Dniestr, South Ossetia and Abkhazia. Perhaps, rather than thinking of how to resolve the conflict, we should be thinking about how to manage it. It is in this respect that the analogy with the Cold War might be most fruitful. While discussions on both sides about winning the Cold War never ceased, over time increasing attention was paid to managing the conflict to minimize the danger of it spinning out of control.

The conflict is unlikely to be resolved for two reasons. First, the various sides' understandings of the sources of the conflict and the acceptable solutions remain far apart. Even though many in the West recognise that Russia is extremely unlikely to reverse its annexation of Crimea, and are prepared to accept that, recognising it officially and legitimising it will be much more difficult. That is even more true for the government of Ukraine. Assuming the territory is not to return to Ukraine, finding a way to legitimise Russia's annexation will be necessary for a complete resolution of the conflict, and it does not appear that many in the West or in Ukraine are near to finding that acceptable, in part because doing so might set a dangerous precedent. Second, the damage done to various relationships cannot easily be undone, even if there were the desire to do so (and that itself is questionable).

The assumption after 1991 that a harmony of interests had largely replaced conflict of interest in the West's relations with Russia helped smooth over a large number of disagreements. Now, the assumption that the two sides are adversaries again undermines cooperation. Trust is at a minimum and bad faith is widely assumed, undermining the conditions to even search for common interests. Moreover, in the US and Russia (and perhaps in other countries as well), domestic politics rewards an adversarial stance toward the other. Especially after Russia's influence campaign in the 2016 presidential election, it will be very difficult for a US administration to be seen as making deals with Russia. For much of the Cold War, attempting to deal const- ructively with Russia led to accusations of naiveté or 'softness'. Today it is likely to lead to allegations of treason.

This increased level of hostility means that even if a deal were brokered to recognise a new status quo including Russian sovereignty over Crimea and Eastern Ukraine, neither Russia's relations with the West nor Ukraine could return to the antebellum state of confidence, low as that was. Western governments would have to continue to live under the new assumption that military action is now part of relations among these countries.

The fundamental consequence of Russia's intervention in Crimea and Eastern Ukraine is that the 'state of war' now prevails again in Europe, in Hobbes' sense that war is 'on the table' even if not actively underway. Even if those who believed that war had been eliminated from European international relations were naïve, that viewpoint had a powerful effect on the nature of relations between the West and Russia, and hence on Ukraine. That confidence could potentially have become as powerful as that between Germany and France, where the belief that war is impossible helps make it so. Instead, we are seeing the re-militarising of relations between East and West.

This discussion of conclusions belies the reality that at this point we have far more questions than answers about the evolving nature of relations between the West, Russia, and Ukraine. Here we point to two related crucial questions. First, how will the regimes in Russia and Ukraine develop, and second, how will that affect their relationships with each other and the West.

While Russia appears to be in a period of international ascendance, most observers believe that it is fragile domestically. The economy continues to depend heavily on natural resources and to be plagued by corruption and crony capitalism. The political system has become increasingly personalised, leading to the question of whether it can survive beyond Putin himself. We simply do not know. Nor do we know what might replace Putinism.

Ukraine's future is also uncertain. After two ostensibly democratic revolutions, the country's oligarch-driven politics appear remarkably unchanged. The contest among oligarchic groups for power and access to the benefits of corruption and rent-seeking drives the political system. Sustained Western support for reform after the Orange Revolution produced few reforms and no structural change. Following the Euromaidan, economic, fiscal and energy reforms have made headway but Ukraine continues to be characterised by oligarchic influence on the economy and media, limited progress in transforming Ukraine into a rule of law state and the slow fight against high-level corruption. As a result, the country remains susceptible to Russian penetration and influence and reliant on Western financial support. Poroshenko continues in a long line of Ukrainian presidents to support NATO and EU membership. 'The one path we have is a wide Euro-Atlantic autobahn which takes us to membership in the EU and NATO', Poroshenko said on the 26th anniversary of Ukrainian independence, adding that the Association Agreement is 'convincing evidence of our ultimate – *de facto* and *de jure* – break with the empire'.[5]

Nevertheless, both organisations are only offering integration without

---

[5]   http://www.president.gov.ua/news/vistup-prezidenta-pid-chas-urochistogo-zahodu-parad-vijsk-z-42878

membership; the EU has never offered a membership prospect to Ukraine while NATO cooled on this question from 2008. NATO remains cautious because of on-going territorial conflicts with Russia which if Ukraine was invited to join would become NATO's war. The West has additionally been routinely frustrated by Ukraine's inability to meet all of its commitments to reform, particularly in the areas of the rule of law and corruption.

How will these domestic politics influence international politics? Since the Cold War, much policy has been based on the presumed link between democracy and peace, much to the derision of realist scholars. Rather than rehearse that debate, we ask what the future might hold if Russia becomes more democratic; or if Ukraine does not.

Would a more democratic Russia be a more peaceful Russia? That has been the guiding assumption of Western policy not only since 1991, but throughout history. The assumption could never be put to the test until 1991, and the evidence since then is not conclusive. But the electoral success of Russian nationalist parties, and the need of Yeltsin to use his extensive powers to push back against revanchists in the 1990s, provides some evidence against the argument that a democratic Russia would be pro-Western. The majority of Russians, irrespective of their attitudes toward Putin, share a consensus that Russia has the right to control the Crimea and that Ukrainians are not a separate people.

Would a more autocratic Ukraine turn towards Russia? People in both Russia and the West have assumed this, but the evidence is mixed. Yanukovych was autocratic and sought Russian support for his autocracy, but he was not always a willing participant in Russia's efforts at integration. Kuchma, who moved Ukraine toward a competitive authoritarian regime[6] in the late 1990s and early 2000s, and paved the way for Yanukovych to try to steal the 2004 election, also drove a concerted effort to strengthen Ukraine's ties with NATO and to consolidate Ukraine's 'multi-vector'[7] foreign policy. The West supported Kuchma's heavy-handed methods of adopting a constitution with very strong presidential powers because it was seen as needed to overcome leftist conservatives in parliament.

---

[6]   Poroshenko reiterated these views on Ukraine's divorce from Russia even more forcefully in his state of the nation speech to parliament on 7 September 2017. http:// www.president.gov.ua/news/poslannya-prezidenta-ukrayini-do-verhovnoyi-radi-ukrayini-pr-43086
Steven Levitsky and Lucan Way, 'The Rise of Competitive Authoritarianism', *Journal of Democracy*, vol.13, no.2 (April 2002), pp.51–65.

[7]   T. Kuzio, 'Neither East nor West: Ukraine's Security Policy', *Problems of Post-Communism*, vol.52, no.5 (September/October 2005), pp.59–68.

In sum, the relationship between regime type and foreign policy is less clear than many appear to assume. That is a crucial point, because a major contributor to conflict has been the West's desire to spread democracy (assuming that in doing so they are also spreading peace) and Russia's desire to prevent it (assuming that in doing so it is preventing states from aligning against it). Both policies rely on the assumed links between regime type and foreign policy, and both therefore rely on flimsy foundations. Ironically, breaking the presumption of a link between regime type and foreign policy might help ratchet down tensions here and elsewhere.

Note on Indexing

E-IR's publications do not feature indexes due to the prohibitive costs of assembling them. If you are reading this book in paperback and want to find a particular word or phrase you can do so by downloading a free PDF version of this book from the E-IR website.

View the e-book in any standard PDF reader such as Adobe Acrobat Reader (pc) or Preview (mac) and enter your search terms in the search box. You can then navigate through the search results and find what you are looking for. In practice, this method can prove much more targeted and effective than consulting an index.

If you are using apps (or devices) such as iBooks or Kindle to read our e-books, you should also find word search functionality in those.

You can find all of our e-books at: http://www.e-ir.info/publications

CPSIA information can be obtained
at www.ICGtesting.com
Printed in the USA
LVHW052108130422
716121LV00010B/1080